Cock X 68   NOW.

Maintaining the Breed

" That is best wrote which is best adapted for obtaining the end of the writer . . ."

" The words used should be the most expressive that the language affords, provided that they are most generally understood—smooth, clear, and short, for the contrary qualities are displeasing."

BENJAMIN FRANKLIN
1706–1790

The Mark III

*From an original by F. Gordon Crosby, kindly loaned for reproduction
by The MG Car Co., Ltd., Abingdon-on-Thames*

MAINTAINING
THE
BREED

by

JOHN W. THORNLEY

The Saga of

Racing Cars

MOTOR RACING PUBLICATIONS

MOTOR RACING PUBLICATIONS LIMITED
277-279 Gray's Inn Road
London WC1X 8QF

First published . . . 1950

Reprinted 1951

Second Edition . . . 1956

Third Edition . . . 1971

ISBN 0 900549 11 4

This book has been printed in Great Britain by
Cable Printing Services Ltd.
277-279 Gray's Inn Road, London
WC1X 8QF

NOSEPIECE

Most of those who have, at some time in the "tinkering period" of their lives, raised a compression ratio or by other means endeavoured to increase the performance of a machine, have found that speed and reliability do not always go hand in hand. Frequently it is inexpensively simple to reduce the designer's safety margin to zero. Whether, as a result, the engine merely misfires a bit, or the car develops a ravenous appetite for axle-shafts, or worse, is an open question, but it is soon borne in upon the experimenter that the laws of the swings and roundabouts apply here as elsewhere.

It is reasonable to expect, therefore, that in improving the maximum speed of a car from 60 m.p.h. to 180 m.p.h., the designer—and others—are likely to have run their heads into all sorts of bother.

It is the intention, in this book, to trace in outline the development of the MG from its modest beginnings to the period of its all-conquering supremacy in its class, to examine in some degree the effect of racing experience upon the design of the sports car, and to enliven the story as opportunity affords by drawing upon the wealth of anecdote to be found behind the racing scene.

This latter is important. Articles and books a-plenty have been written about motor races, but good though they be, they deal almost exclusively with the drivers and the driving and confine themselves, in the main, to the period between the start and the chequered flag. This is but a moment of time when compared with the years of development and the months of preparation during which that hero of the racing world, the mechanic, has so much to do and so little to say. Designer and driver alike owe him much, and homage has not been overpaid to those whose qualities include, besides devotion to the job and innate mechanical horse-sense, perennial cheerfulness and abundant wit. An effort has been made to capture some small portion of the immense fund of knowledge and humour which these men have to offer.

July, 1950

NOSEPIECE, MOD. I.

When first it became clear that there was to be a new edition of this book, I wanted to call it "Maintaining the Breed, Mark II". But I was advised by the publisher that such a title would obstruct the sale of the book because, believe it or not, booksellers would not know what it meant and would be choosy. So I welcome this preface as an opportunity to make the intention clear.

This is the original *Maintaining the Breed*, modified and brought up to date —Mark II if ever anything was. New chapters cover the life of Goldie Gardner's EX 135 up to his retirement from the active racing scene and the conversion of the car to a museum piece, and the new record car, EX 179, with which George Eyston has returned to quick motoring in MG. Lastly, we describe a new car the evolution of which involves a brief reappearance of the MG marque in Sports Car Racing. If this last chapter, "The Dawn of a New Era", stimulates the imagination and quickens the pulse of the MG addict—be it never so slightly—I shall not have scribbled in vain.

March, 1956.   J. W. T.

NOSEPIECE MOD. 1 was written, I see, fifteen years ago. I find it hard to believe but it must be so. Now, the book is to be reprinted, and I have been asked to write a word or two about the intervening years.

The last chapter of the book heralds the introduction of the MGA. In the ensuing seven years 110,000 of these were made and they found their way into all corners of the world. The logical successor, the MGB, made its first appearance in 1962; has to date, sold nigh on a quarter of a million; and is still being built at the rate of around 1,000 per week.

No sports car—anywhere in the world—has ever sold in anything like such quantity. No marque has ever brought so much "fast safety" to so many. So the policy of providing sports-car motoring at a price which a whole lot of people could afford has paid off handsomely.

Now that I am retired from active participation in the Company I am in no position to talk of future prospects. Indeed, having been "taken-over" three times in the course of my life with the Company, perhaps I may be forgiven if I admit that my crystal ball is a little cloudy.

I have the satisfaction of knowing, however, that I left behind a thriving, profitable operation whose employees contentedly produced desirable sports cars in pleasant surroundings, and at the same time contributed much to the town of Abingdon and its environs.

From this point of vantage I can look back over the years with some satisfaction and, indeed, continue to enjoy the past glories of MG through the medium of the MG Car Club. Anyone who has attended meetings of the Club's Registers will readily understand what I mean by this. Wherever there is a *Concours d'Elegance* there will be found dozens—in some cases hundreds—of MGs of all ages, from current back to 1925, many of them beautifully maintained and spotlessly presented. And, from my own observation, the standard of these presentations goes up each year—eloquent testimony to the continuing and ever-increasing interest and enthusiasm in matters MG.

What more could any man ask?

January, 1971   J. W. T.

PUBLISHER'S FOOTNOTE: Apart from one or two typographical corrections, and the occasional deletion or addition, John Thornley's words are reproduced in their original form in this latest edition. Though hindsight might have encouraged him to amend one or two forecasts or comments, his original manuscript, which embodies all the enthusiasm, hopes and aspirations that motivated the people at Abingdon in the fifties, and which has made *Maintaining the Breed* a classic of MG literature, has benefited rather than suffered through its maturity. To have revised it in the light of subsequent events—not all of which have been for the better—was unthinkable.

CONTENTS

ILLUSTRATIONS

THE PEDIGREE

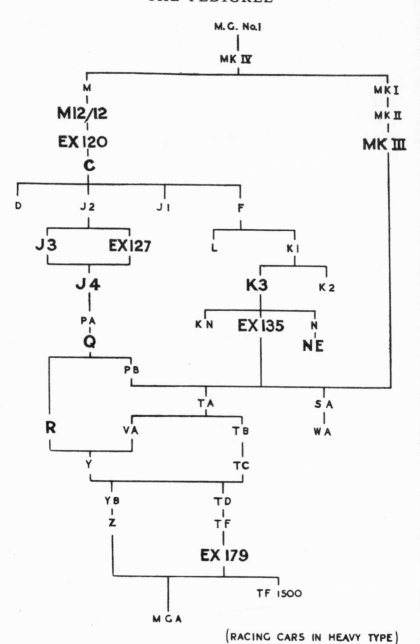

(RACING CARS IN HEAVY TYPE)

CHAPTER I

THE MARKS

GENEALOGISTS, and those of similar proclivities, will say that to delve into one's ancestry is not without its dangers, leaving one to infer that the risk is that time's veil may be torn from a skeleton or, at the very least, that there may be some stages which require explanation. In our present case, no skeletons have been discovered, but there is a question or two to which some attempt at an answer may not go amiss.

The first, often asked and almost as frequently indifferently answered, is simply, why MG? A self-sufficient statement was made on this subject in 1929, thus:

"Out of compliment to Sir William R. Morris, Bt., we named our production the MG Sports, the letters being the initials of his original business undertaking, 'The Morris Garages', from which has sprung the vast group of separate enterprises including the MG Car Company."

The second, which is a matter not quite so fundamental but still a puzzle, seeks a reason why the early model known as the Mark IV preceded the Marks I, II and III. There is no authoritative information on this and it is necessary to fall back on conjecture, but the theory fits all the known facts—which is more than can be said of a good many accepted theories. The 14/40 version of the "MG Super Sports", as they were then called, first saw the light of day in 1927, but it was not until late in 1928 that the idea of borrowing from Army parlance and denoting models by 'Marks' caught on. By that time, three basic chassis designs had already passed into history, so 'Mark IV' as a starting point was logical. Came 1929 and the advent of the 6-cylinder. What was it to be called? Mark V? But not only was this Six something quite new; it was being built in a new works at Abingdon. The company was making a fresh start and, as the names Marks I, II and III had not been previously publicised, they were the natural choice for the new series.

With these little difficulties out of the way we can press on.

There is a record of an MG winning a race in South America in 1927, but in the generally accepted sense, their racing history does not begin until 1930. As, however, this story is to be as much a saga of development as a racing history, there seems to be but one place to begin and that is at the beginning—with MG No. 1 built in 1923.

A

A Morris Oxford chassis of the period was fitted with a Hotchkiss engine with push rod operated overhead valves. The body was the barest minimum of tin-ware, the two bucket seats being staggered echelon fashion to get the overall width down. With extremely brief cycle type wings, no windscreen and—very sporting this—a handbrake lever outside the body, it was a very 'spartan' vehicle. It 'did' over 80 m.p.h., won a Gold Medal in the 1925 Lands End in the hands of Cecil Kimber, and fired the imagination and enthusiasm of all who had anything to do with it.

The succeeding years, up to 1928, saw a succession of models, all in the then 14 horse-power range, culminating in the previously mentioned 14/40 Mark IV. The enthusiastic following which these cars acquired proved the existence of a market for 'a 20 per cent improvement in performance at a 50 per cent increase in price' over the general run of cars of the day. But the market was limited and, if production were to be increased, it was necessary to provide a car with an essentially sporting appeal yet at a price which more could afford.

The motor cyclist, attuned to speed and the rush of wind past his ears, but growing a little older day by day and feeling in wet weather that it would be pleasant not to have to climb into waders and poncho, had no choice between what he regarded as the somewhat sedate and uninteresting 'baby' saloon and the much larger 'sports' car which was probably beyond his means. He knew the meaning of response to his controls, had experienced a surge of power when he opened the taps, had learned the importance of balance and of placing his wheels to a hair's breadth and, in the middle of all this, felt perhaps that to keep the girl-friend on a bracket behind him was a bit of a waste.

Once one accepts that such considerations represent a need, it is not difficult to outline a specification to meet it. The outcome was, in fact, the first of the line of MG Midgets, the M Type, whose importance to our story is such that it shall have a whole chapter to itself. Suffice it here to say that it created the wider demand which was its primary purpose and made possible the astonishing series of events with which we are here mainly concerned.

But that is not quite the end of this beginning. Just as the need for a small car had been perceived, so had the old Mark IV created a demand among those who were neither necessarily young nor impecunious, but who required, first and foremost, performance above the average. There emerged, accordingly, from the new factory at Abingdon, a 6-cylinder 2½-litre chassis embodying all the essentials requisite for safe speed and which was dubbed, as already mentioned, the Mark I. The broad specification, as with all other models to be mentioned, is given in Appendix II, and it will be seen from this that the one feature wide open to criticism in a sports car was that the gearbox had but three ratios. But an effort had been made to keep down weight and the judicious selection of a second gear ratio which gave speeds in excess of 50 m.p.h. provided a very delightful road car. Accommodation was limited, however, by the narrowness of the track and it was not long before re-design introduced a wider track and a four-speed gearbox into the Mark II version.

During the early currency of the 18/80 Mark II, the possibilities of the Midget as a racing car were dawning and concurrently with Midget development, an ambitious project was embarked upon to produce a road-racing version of this Mark II. This car, although its life was brief, is worthy of some detailed study as, not only was it the first car to be built by MG primarily for racing, but also because it had a specification which even to-day makes the sports car enthusiast's mouth water. It is interesting, too, in that it shows the direction of thought of the MG designers right at the beginning of their great racing history—in the latter half of 1929.

The purpose underlying the production of the car established the principle which was to be followed in each subsequent racing design— to provide, at a price within the reach of those who had the will and the opportunity to race, a car fully prepared and ready for the starting line. This was no mean undertaking, but work started on a foundation of first-class engineering skill and boundless imagination and horse-sense. Experience had yet to be bought on road and track, but it is pertinent to mention that the difficulties and triumphs of the Bentleys during the years immediately preceding had not passed unstudied at Abingdon.

The 18/100 h.p. MG Six Mark III Road Racing model, known alternatively and more briefly as the 'Tigress' or B Type, had a 6-cylinder 2½-litre overhead camshaft engine with twin down-draught S.U. carburetters. With inlet ports on the off-side and exhaust ports on the near, and with the valves inclined to give a 'pent-roof' form of combustion space, the charge had a very 'straight-in straight-out' path through the machined ports. Crankshaft and connecting rods were machined all over, and a high degree of dynamic balance, and consequent sweetness was obtained. The drive was transmitted through a four-speed close ratio 'crash' type gearbox with remote control, providing a short vertical lever under the driver's left hand.

Brakes were operated by cables individual to each wheel and coupled to a full width cross-shaft actuated both by the pedals and the hand lever. These were separately adjustable from the driving seat while the car was in motion and with the hand lever was incorporated the now familiar racing type ratchet which flies off at a touch.

The fuel tank had two large fillers—one to put the fuel in and the other to let the air out—and fuel supply lines and pumps were duplicated. Electrical equipment was wired with individual armoured cables laid and clipped in accessible places and the fuse-cum-junction box was, by modern standards, highly comprehensive.

Readers familiar with the *marque* will have recognised that all the design details so far mentioned became consistent features throughout the range of racing cars which were to come from this same drawing board. It is significant, and of the greatest credit to the designer, that, although the racing career of this particular model was extremely brief, its basic features stood the test of six hard fought years on road and track.

The Tigress made its racing debut in the J.C.C. Double Twelve Hour Race at Brooklands in 1930 in the hands of L. G. Callingham and H. D. Parker. While the MG Midgets were already circling the track, having started earlier on the limit of the handicap, Callingham set out on his long journey. Soon he was lapping steadily at 86 m.p.h. and everything seemed grand, but after just 2 hours a shattering noise from the engine house prompted sharp stabs at clutch pedal and gear stick and the car coasted to a standstill. Examination showed that the engine had—as Parker put it—"swallowed its tonsils". The set screws of one carburetter spindle had shaken out and the butterfly had become mixed up in the valve gear. Thus did MG learn their first racing lesson.

The Mark III did not race again. As we shall see, in this same race, the Midget proved itself and positively arrived on the racing scene. Could the development of the two cars proceed side by side? In any case, MG had to make their racing pay its way, and it was apparent that, even at £895, racing the big car was going to be a rich man's hobby. And so, sad though it was, economic considerations dictated that the Tigress drawings should be put away until another day.

CHAPTER II

THE FIRST OF THE MIDGETS

WHEN the MG Midget, Type M was first designed nobody had any idea that it would race—or, if they did they omitted to tell the designer. The engine, at 847 c.c., was a bad size to start with, in a class extending from 751 to 1100. And again, nobody, even in those days, would have deliberately selected, to go racing, a car with its petrol under the bonnet and with fabric disc universal joints in its propeller shaft. But, as a road car, it had a great deal to commend it. Weighing but little more than half a ton and with some twenty horse-power available, acceleration and a good turn of speed were never in doubt. Low built, short, stiffish road springs and large shock absorbers done up fairly tightly ensured good road holding. Little wonder, then, that it was readily accepted by the sporting fraternity as the ideal vehicle in which to compete in the Club events, reliability trials and the like, with which the motoring calendar was liberally bespattered.

One such event was the Junior Car Club's Members' Day at Brooklands, an annual meeting presided over by the all-embracing and efficient Bunny Dyer, at which sportsmen could pit their cars against their friends' in sprint races, hill climbing and so on, on the very track which was the cradle of British motor racing.

One of the most popular events at this meeting was the High Speed Trial in which competitors were required to cover certain minimum distances within the space of one hour in order to qualify for an award. The course varied from year to year, but often consisted of a large part of the track itself, from which a diversion was made on to the service roads leading, sometimes, to a descent of the 1 in 3 test hill. No special glory was intended to attach to fastest times, but, as might be expected, many private battles developed which earned for the event the unofficial title of the 'One Hour Blind'.

With the introduction of the M Type Midget, in April, 1929, it occurred to Cecil Kimber that the High Speed Trial, to take place in June, provided an excellent event in which to prove the new car. Arrangements were therefore made for three of them to be entered and driven by Callingham, Parker and the Earl of March, with Cousins, Jackson and Frank Tayler, of the MG Company, riding as mechanics.

On the morning of the meeting, the cars were at the track with their drivers; the mechanics were in Oxford; and there is an epic story of the journey by which the two were brought together with but minutes to spare, Kimber having delayed his departure until too late—or so it seemed. But the three cars ran faultlessly, and in close company, and secured their awards with time in hand, thus successfully concluding the first appearance of the MG Midget on a racing track. That night there occurred the first of another series—an 'after the race party'— but perhaps it is well that we should tell of that event even more briefly.

Most of the young men at Abingdon owned or had owned motor cycles and they knew the sort of thing which could be done to a bike to make it go faster. Logically, what could be done effectively to one cylinder could equally well be applied to four-in-a-row and so it came about that, shortly after the J.C.C. Meeting, a car was placed at Jackson's disposal to 'play about with'. A rasher off the cylinder head to raise the compression ratio, polished and balanced combustion spaces, carefully aligned and polished ports, followed one another in quick succession and the results were amazing. The quest for reduced friction led to the elimination of the belleville washers by which the rockers were loaded on their shafts and by which the top camshaft bevel gears were kept in mesh. Stronger valve springs raised valve crash from 4500 to 5700 r.p.m. and provided 52 m.p.h. in second gear— but the back end of a rocker shaft broke and necessitated the design of an additional bracket as support.

At about this time, H. N. Charles joined the MG Company as chief designer, and between long stretches at the drawing board evolving the 'Tigress' gave his attention to the tuning of the Midget. He was much impressed by the work which Jackson had done on the car and took it over as his own personal property, christening it 'Shinio' in honour of the large quantities of metal polish which had been expended on the engine's internals. He was astonished to discover that the valve timing, far from having overlap, had a period of about two degrees near the top of the inlet stroke during which both valves stayed shut. Obviously something had to be done about it.

It was at this time, when nothing beyond this rather elementary tinkering had been done, that there occurred an event which, though seemingly unimportant at the time, was to have a profound effect upon the future activities at MG's. Two enthusiasts, Randall and Edmondson, called on Cecil Kimber to say that they intended to run a team of three Midgets in the next J.C.C. Double Twelve Hour Race at Brooklands and wanted his advice on the preparation of the cars. That the odds were heavily against such cars winning the race was evident (that was the job of the 'Tigress', anyway), but Edmondson and his associates who had previous racing experience at Le Mans and elsewhere and who reckoned that they knew a good car when they saw one, had been impressed by the high speed reliability of the cars in the earlier Brooklands event, and felt that the Team Prize might well be attempted. It was therefore agreed, provided that the camshaft brought about the improvement which Charles expected, that the project would go forward. 'Shinio' was accordingly converted to the new valve timing and performed so well that it was at once decided, Double Twelve or not, to adopt the new camshaft as part of the standard specification of the Midget. *Fig.* 1 shows the old and new valve timings, while the relative power curves are at *Fig.* 3.

Beyond careful attention to detail and the incorporation of the modifications which had proved so successful on 'Shinio', no mechanical alteration to the cars was necessary. Considerable changes had to be made to the bodywork, however, in order that it should conform to the regulations for the race, and the exhaust system had to be changed for the same reason. To reduce wind resistance, front wing valances were removed, headlamps were re-positioned '*au pair*' in front of the radiator and an undershield was fitted. Lastly, the cars were equipped with oil and water thermometers and a folding gauze racing windscreen.

The race was to be run on Friday and Saturday, May 9 and 10, 1930, and the cars were at the track, together with the faithful 'Shinio' as a practice car, on the preceding Monday. Engines were tight and in consequence many practice laps were put in at reduced speeds. General reluctance on the part of each driver to put his foot down, for fear of ruining the team's chances in advance, was the cause of an all-pervading depression at the apparent slowness of the cars, which persisted right up to the start. Prior to the race, none of the cars could be compared for behaviour with 'Shinio'. But from the 'off', all went well—so well, in fact, that, so far as these three cars were concerned, it could be said that the race was without incident. Edmondson's pit organisation and timekeeping were superlative so that at any time in the whole twenty-four hours and despite the complexity of the handicap formula, he knew exactly how his cars stood. Of the eight teams which started, only two were running complete at the finish—the MGs and the Austins—the MGs scoring a marginal win over their supercharged rivals. The team cars, and two others driven by H. H. Stisted and Miss Victoria Worsley, finished 14th, 15th, 18th, 19th and 20th in the general classification with average speeds over the whole twenty-four hours varying from 60·23 m.p.h. to 57·7 m.p.h.

It has been said that old MG No. 1 fired the imagination of the men at Abingdon. Certainly, this race showed them that the MG, as a racing car, had definitely arrived. It showed one or two other interesting things as well, besides the obvious one that a small car could be fast and reliable over long and gruelling distances. It was the subject of general comment both during and after the race, that the MGs. were as fast through the corners as any other runners. Furthermore, when it rained—and it fell in sheets and swamped the track on both days—

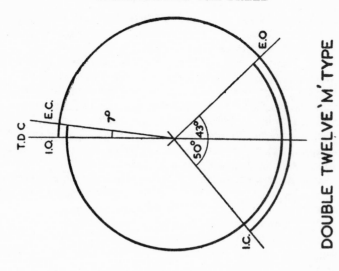

DOUBLE TWELVE 'M' TYPE

VALVE TIMINGS

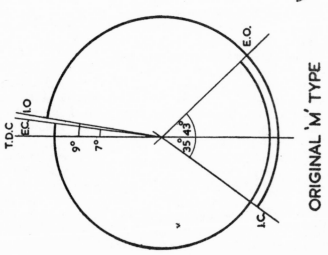

ORIGINAL 'M' TYPE

Fig. 1.

the large cars were slowed, but the Midgets continued without variation in their lap speeds.

As if to rub this lesson well in, another similar car was entered and driven by its owner, F. H. B. Samuelson, with F. R. Kindell as co-driver, in the 24-hour Grand Prix d'Endurance at Le Mans. After some 8 hours of steady running at lap speeds of the order of 55 m.p.h., an oil pipe broke and a 'shortage of white-metal' ensued. Samuelson, convinced of the potentialities of the car, promptly cabled his entry for the Belgian 24-hour race at Spa, due to be run in a fortnight's time, took the engine from its frame and carted it back to Abingdon for overhaul. This done, he and Kindell returned to Le Mans, refitted the engine, and drove the car to Brussels, arriving on the course on the night of the Wednesday before the race. After a little practice on the complicated and hilly course, the car—the only British entry—ran through the race to finish fifth in the 1100-c.c. class at an average speed of over 47 m.p.h.

As a result of these early successes, the '12/12 Midget', incorporating in its standard specification all the chassis and body modifications as used on Edmondson's cars, was put into production in a form ready for racing. Thereby, the policy which had been formulated by the introduction of the Mark III 'Tigress' was continued.

CHAPTER III

EX 120

THE seven months from the time of the Double Twelve Hour Race in May, 1930, to the December of the same year, when George Eyston made his first run in an entirely re-designed car, were so packed with incident and activity that it is not easy to say how work on the new car came to be started. In retrospect, it would appear to have been the logical outcome of numerous concurrent tendencies.

The M Type had proved itself to be fast, controllable and reliable, but competition was keen and it was obvious that, if success were to continue, something better and more suitable for racing was needed. But to J. A. Palmes must go the credit for taking the first practical steps towards converting an MG Midget with which to attack International Class Records. Shortly after the Double-Twelve, he had obtained a special cylinder block with small bores and pistons, which would bring the engine size within the 750-c.c. class and had visions of achieving the magic figures of 100 m.p.h. In this project, he sought the assistance of a man with whom he had shared rooms at Cambridge, Capt. G. E. T. Eyston, who at that time already held several records and had a great deal of experience in this field. Together they went to see Kimber and it was there and then agreed that a car should be developed for the express purpose of attacking records.

During this short time, the MG designers had not been idle and there was already running on the roads of Berkshire the prototype of the Racing Midget for the 1931 Season, known as 'EX 120'. It was obvious that this car should be chosen as the basis of the record-breaker as it could then be proved on the track during the winter which was otherwise the close season for racing.

Apart from the power unit, of which more will be said later, this car incorporated a large number of radical design changes; so many, in fact, that it has been facetiously stated that the only part of the M Type which remained was the track width of 3 ft. 6 in. It is particularly worthy of detailed study because the basic design was retained throughout the whole range of racing cars—and, for that matter, the sports cars, too—which were to follow up to the end of 1934.

The chassis frame was formed from two straight and parallel steel channels, upswept over the front axle and underslung at the rear. Cross tubes passed through the side members and were secured to them by flanges brazed to the tubes in the manner commonly used in the cycle trade. Such a frame, though immensely strong, was built to flex—within limits. Semi-elliptic rear road springs were pinned to the outboard ends of one of these cross tubes and, in place of swinging shackles, the main leaf was ground on its end, and slid, through a slot in the rear cross tube, in bronze half bushes housed inside the tube itself. This method of construction in conjunction with the low build provided by the underslung chassis, gave springs which were parallel to each other and to the direction of motion, substantially flat in the normal laden state, and of immense lateral rigidity. Front springs were similarly 'shackled', in bronze trunnions in boxes fastened to the underside of the frame channel.

A three-point engine mounting was adopted in which the rear of the engine was secured to the frame side-members and the front mounted in a trunnion bush in the front cross-member such that this member could rotate about the engine centre line. The radiator was mounted on an extension of the engine. By this means, the radiator was in one with the engine and troubles with it and with water hoses, by reason of frame distortion, were at an end.

Although braking was not regarded as of very great importance for the purpose of record breaking, the chassis, as a road racing prototype, incorporated a new braking layout. This, too, was to stand the test of years. Cable operation was used for the twofold reason that it was simple to make the brakes independent of axle movement and independent also of most ordinary forms of accidental damage. A cross-shaft was carried amidships between the chassis side-members, having a double grooved pulley on each end enclosed within the side-member channel. Cable ends were secured to these pulleys and ran in the grooves. The cross-shaft was rotated by a push rod from the brake pedal and the handbrake lever stood straight up from the centre of the cross-shaft, its fulcrum being the shaft itself. This latter was fitted with a racing type ratchet—in which the ratchet is normally inoperative until required by the driver—and had the unusual quality of being as powerful in operation as the foot pedal.

Some misgivings as to the advisability of leaving the rear road springs to take care of the torque reaction from the rear axle—in view of the large engine powers expected—caused radius rods to be fitted, but these were later found to be unnecessary and were discontinued. Rudge Whitworth type 'knock-on' wire road wheels first appeared on this model—and came to stay—and one other small but interesting feature was that the front axle was carried *below* the front road springs. This was occasioned by some delay in the production of a new axle beam, which was to be mounted above the springs and which would have lowered the front end of the car by some two inches.

The main difference of the engine from its M Type precursor was in its size. A special crankshaft reduced the stroke from 83 mm. to

81 mm. and the cylinder block was linered down from 57 mm. to 54 mm. This reduced the swept volume from 847 c.c. to 743 c.c. and thus brought the engine within the International Class H. In other respects, differences were in detail only. The M Type engine used clamp screws to secure its wrist pins. It was felt that for this engine it was undesirable to have any form of groove in the wrist pins and that fully-floating pins should be used. To avoid the delay in obtaining new con-rod stampings, standard rods were brought through with the small end machining operations omitted, the set screw bosses were filed away and the small ends bored and bushed. Before many days were to pass, everyone was to be thankful for those bushes.

The Class records to be first attacked—the 50 and 100 kilometres—stood to the credit of S. C. H. Davis on a supercharged Austin at speeds of the order of 84 m.p.h. Eyston's intention was to attempt these without supercharger. It was known, however, that Austins planned to take their records higher and, in fact, aimed at being the first 'baby' car—as these little giants were then known in the popular press—to achieve 100 m.p.h. The science of supercharging of small I.C. engines was then in its infancy, but George Eyston, who was interested in the manufacture of 'blowers', arranged that, although he would run unsupercharged, provision for a blower would be made in the design. This was to be hung between the front dumb irons—a position which was to become traditional—and driven by chain from the front end of the crankshaft. The engineering was felt, at the time, to be somewhat inelegant, but it had the merit that, with the aid of a pocketful of sprockets, the blower drive ratio could be varied as experiment dictated.

Once the car was in running order, the testing of it became a real problem. Brooklands was closed for winter repairs and it seemed a frightful gamble to take the completely new car straight to Montlhery, away from all Works facilities. It was thus decided to chance the long arm of authority, and to try the car early one morning on a stretch of Roman road near Newmarket. The month was November and the night preceding the test was foggy—very. King, with the car in a lorry, started from Oxford and vanished into the gloom at about 6 p.m. Jackson and Phillips left shortly after 10 p.m. and came upon King, fogbound, five miles north of his starting point. There ensued a night-long ordeal to get to Newmarket on time and the cortège finally arrived an hour late, dog tired and bad tempered, to find Eyston, and his engineering consultant in these ventures, E. A. D. Eldridge, who had come from London without encountering as much as a patch of mist, champing to be off. The car was unloaded and Jackson and Phillips set to work on it, feeling rather like a pair of naughty boys and starting at every sound for fear that the police had caught up with them. Jackson's astonishment knew no bounds when Eyston walked up, clad from head to foot in conspicuous white racing overalls, white gloves and goggles—all complete. Such was the thoroughness of the man.

The morning stillness was shattered by the crackle from the open exhaust and George was off. There followed hectic moments, one trying to persuade a yokel to keep his farm cart out of the way and another dashing back to warn Eyston that the level crossing gates had closed across his pull-up distance, but the runs were concluded safely and, generally speaking, successfully. The calculated speed had been 87 m.p.h., which was fast enough, but there had been nothing in hand.

From this point the plot had been to drive straight to the coast en route for Paris, but Eldridge insisted that the car return to Abingdon. Here, the small end bushes were removed and replaced by eccentric ones, which had been machined overnight, so as to raise the pistons in the bores a matter of $\frac{1}{16}$ in., thereby increasing the compression ratio. This done, Jackson, with lorry and car, left for Montlhery on Dec. 26.

It was Dec. 30 before driver, car and weather conspired together to make a run possible, but then, at the first attempt, Eyston took the 50 kilometre, 50 mile and 100 kilometre records at 86·38, 87·11, 87·3 m.p.h. respectively—and then a valve broke. The margin over the existing records—some 3 m.p.h.—was too fine to make any further work with the unsupercharged car worth while, particularly as the next aim was 100 m.p.h., and it was therefore decided that Jackson should take the engine back to Abingdon, have it overhauled and return with it and the blower. Speed was important as it was known that Sir Malcolm Campbell, who was at Daytona, Fa., attempting the World's land-speed record with Blue Bird, had an Austin there, too, with which he aimed to be the first to attain 100 m.p.h., a record which would stand for all time.

As the result of day-to-day telephone contact between Montlhery and Abingdon, preparation and test of the superchargers had been undertaken before Jackson left France. Two had been prepared, one large, one small, and both had done periods of eight hours' continuous running on slave engines by the time the engine overhaul was completed. This part of the job proved to be straightforward, but it was the end of January before Jackson—with Kindell, who had come to assist—arrived back at the track. The weather was now intensely cold and conditions were frequently too bad even for testing, let alone to attempt the record. The car ran well with the small blower, but was not fast enough. With the large blower, and the higher alcohol content of the fuel which it demanded, tuning was very difficult and clean running was hard to obtain. It was a week before the car was judged ready for an attempt and in the middle of it all, news came that Campbell, having collected the World's Land Speed Record at 246 m.p.h., had taken the Austin out and added 7 m.p.h. to the Class H Flying Mile at 94 m.p.h. Four days after this news, Eyston made his run and took the five kilometres, among others, at 97 m.p.h. He was not satisfied. Everyone was convinced that the car was capable of 100, and further modifications and expedients were to be tried. But Jackson and Kindell, having installed engine and supercharger, changed super-chargers, changed drive gears, tuned and tested and tuned again, solidly for seven days, were 'all—in'. It is, in fact, on record that during the seven days immediately following their return from England, Jackson and Kindell had worked one hundred and twenty-six hours. One assumes that they had something to eat now and again during this period, so it is apparent that they slept very little. A call to Abingdon explained the position and Cecil Cousins and Gordon Phillips were despatched post-haste to plug the gap.

The principal difficulty in tuning had been that if sufficient alcohol were used to permit the desired boost pressure, the carburetter—which was hung on the side of the blower out front in the cold—froze as soon as the car got going. Cousins therefore devised a box which completely enclosed the carburetter and which was fed with air through a large duct leading from the back of the radiator. The immediate results were most encouraging, but it was apparent that as the engine was running much cooler than was necessary, further improvement could probably be made by reducing the effective radiator area. A rough and ready cowl was fashioned, with improvised tools, and fitted to the front of the car in the form of what would now be called a 'streamlined' nose and in this form the battered looking machine attacked the records. The track was wet, the tyres were of the smooth racing variety, there was no mean wind blowing, the time-keepers arrived late from Paris, having crashed on the way, so that Eyston's nerves—if he has any— were stretched about as tight as they would go when he took the car away with but half an hour to go to dusk.

The steepness of the banking of the Montlhery track is such that the noise of a car is much reflected and, apart from the effects of wind, one can hear a car quite distinctly all the way round. Even to this day, the watchers on this great occasion would tell you that the little car sang. After two laps or so of warming up, Eyston turned everything full on and, stealing a moment from his pre-occupation in keeping the car on its course, he saw the engine speed indicator reading a steady 7000 r.p.m. and knew that, barring accidents, the record was his. The speeds were: five kilometres, 103·13 m.p.h.; five miles, 102·76; ten kilometres, 102·43; and ten miles, 101·87. The party returned, very happy and satisfied, to England.

This adventure had not secured the flying mile and flying kilometre records. Detailed examination of the power unit disclosed no signs of over-stressing and it was clear that even higher speeds were possible. When Brooklands re-opened, therefore, in the March of 1931, it was decided to take advantage of the warmer weather and have a smack at the short distance records. The car, in the same form in which it had run at Montlhery a month before, was tried out on the evening before the attempt, and found to be running as crisply as ever. Speeds of the order of 107 to 110 were confidently expected and it seemed unnatural, after the experiences at Montlhery, not to be working on the car. Eldridge gave instructions that the carburetter should be cleaned, and Jackson jumped at the opportunity of relief from the tension. He was surprised to find that most of the internals were encrusted with a deposit rather in the nature of verdigris and that this extended also to the jet which normally, to use his own expression, was big enough to crawl through. After consultation with Eldridge, he removed all these deposits, cleaned everything until it shone, and went to bed.

On the following day, the record was attempted and it was apparent from the start that the car was not healthy. Certainly, the records were taken, but at a mere 97 m.p.h.

Thinking this over afterwards, it became clear that part of the steadily improving conditions at Montlhery had been occasioned by a progressively weakening mixture brought about by the gradual constriction of the jet. The moral—to leave well alone—was obvious, but so also was the cure for the car's bad behaviour that day. The next evening, Eyston took the car out for test, and Jackson and Eldridge sat on a gate to watch. As if to atone for recent deficiencies the car cracked round in great form, but, just as the onlookers were heaving their sighs of satisfaction, a cloud of blue smoke enveloped the car, there was a 'terrific bang' and the watchers jumped from their gate and rushed towards the car. On the way, Jackson saw something shooting along the top of the banking, away out ahead of the still fast-moving car, but George's safety being the first consideration, this phenomenon was for the moment forgotten. Eyston was found to be unhurt, but the engine had disintegrated, a connecting rod and the sides of the crankcase having disappeared. The starter motor languished in the bottom of what remained of the sump. A reconnaisance showed that the missile seen earlier on the banking was, in fact, a piston and Jackson still has this in his private museum. It seems that, could the instant have been recorded by the camera, certain of the more recent drawings of Mr. Sammy Davis would have been shown to be far less fanciful than we are inclined to regard them.

The racing season was at hand and EX 120 was wheeled away for the summer. As we shall see, a much faster successor was to arise, in the shape of EX 127, but there was life in the old dog yet. In the late summer of 1931, when the new car went out to raise the short distance records, EX 120 went with it to essay the longer distances. This time, again at Montlhery, the aim was to cover 100 miles in the hour. Apart from the replacement of the improvised tin-ware by properly constructed sheet metal fairings, the car was substantially in the same condition as on its previous appearance. With very little tuning, it completed practice laps at over 106 m.p.h. and Eyston had no trouble in hitting his target at 101 miles in the hour. But of the conclusion of this run, much has already been written and, as the story is certainly among the most dramatic in the whole history of motor racing, it will easily bear telling again.

After some fifty-five to fifty-eight minutes of faultless running, the keen ears of the connoisseurs waiting by the timing box detected a change in the note of the engine. Breath was held, pulse rates increased a little, but the car came round apparently unaffected.

At the conclusion of the hour, Eyston missed the signal and did another lap flat out, then entered upon what he imagined to be his complementary lap but which was, in fact, a completely unnecessary one. The MG boys, realising what had happened, expected him to come sauntering round the track to coast up to them and were, accordingly, looking to the left. A fairly stiff breeze was blowing at the time and it was a second or two before they realised that the engine noise had ceased. As quick as thought Jackson and Marney leaped into the hack car and were off round the track in search of George. Rounding the bend from the brief straight leading from the timing box, they were sickened by the sight of the car, in the inside rim of the track, burning furiously. Now, Eyston is a big man and the car had been built to fit him closely. Both Jackson and Marney had many times assisted to prise him in and out of the cockpit and they knew he could not get out by himself. Ergo, George was in that car, and it was well alight. They rushed at the car, having both, independently, made up their minds to kick the panelling in and pull the driver out sideways. To-gether they fought and it was not until some seconds had elapsed—an eternity, it seemed to them—that they rived the side panel off and dis-covered that Eyston was not there. At this point, it is recalled that Jackson said to Marney, and the fire-fighters who had by then arrived, "Let the — burn. Where the hell's George?" But of George there was no sign. The banking was too steep to climb and, in any case, the safety fence at the top was intact. It was inconceivable that he could have gone over. But search over a wide area of the inside of the track failed to show the slightest sign of him.

Eyston, on his last run past the timing box, had found flames round his feet. The inference has since been drawn that the change of engine note discerned a few minutes earlier had been due to the running of a bearing. Continued full throttle had caused local overheating to the point where the sump oil had ignited. Impelled by the fire, George had somehow extricated himself from the cockpit and, perched on the back of the driving seat, had kept control of the steering. Guiding the slowing car to the inside edge, he chose his opportunity and threw himself off onto the grass verge at a time when he judged the speed to be around

MG No. 1.   The start of it all.

Two slightly differing examples of the MG Mark III 18/100 'Tigress' Road-racing Car.

Top : The drivers (*left to right*) are COUSINS, JACKSON and TAYLER.

Centre : A scene shortly before the start of the Double-12-Hour Race.

Left : MURTON-NEALE'S 12/12 M Type at Le Mans, 1930.

The first MG's to wear racing numbers. The M Types after their return from Brooklands, where they ran in the J.C.C. High Speed Trial, 1929.

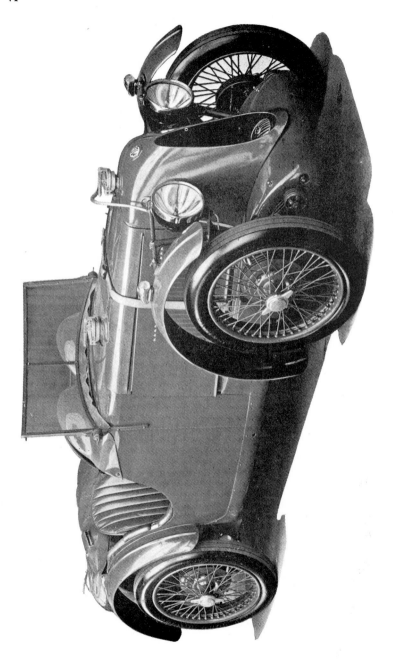

C Type Montlhery Midgets in production trim. Subsequently, the radiator cow s were discarded, super-chargers fitted between the front dumb irons and, in some cases, the back of the body chopped off to accommodate an external 'slab' fuel tank.

The J4 Supercharged Road-racing Midget.

60 m.p.h. Falling in a manner learned in the hunting field, he had avoided serious injury and the car had continued, to bury its nose in a sandbank. It was a feature of the Montlhery track that other users were not debarred from the track while record attempts were in progress, and it was in almost continuous use by test drivers of French car manufacturers. One such, a large serious Frenchman, had come upon Eyston a matter of seconds after the accident. He stopped his large Citroen, picked George up bodily—nobody knows to this day how he managed it—put him in the back and, in less time than it takes to write, bore him off to Montlhery Hospital. Thus when Jackson arrived, the 'body' had disappeared.

It is not hard to imagine the tremendous cavalcade of emotions which flowed through these men in this brief dramatic episode which marked the end of the useful life of EX 120.

CHAPTER IV

THE MONTLHERY MIDGET

BEFORE EX 120 was taken over for conversion for the escapades described in the last chapter, it had been fulfilling its primary purpose as the prototype of the 1931 season's racing car. In the course of extended testing both on the road and at Brooklands, the general chassis and engine details had been proved sufficiently for production of the new models to go ahead. Most of the necessary tooling had been put in hand for the new C Type racing car, and its sports car equivalent the D Type, before the first record breaking attempts, and it was therefore possible to incorporate in these models only detail modifications arising from these experiences.

It would be well to digress here for a moment to examine certain factors which may not be very obvious on first consideration, but which affected the sequence of events in the development and production of MG models.

The *raison d'être* of the MG Car Company was to produce and sell, to a discerning public, sports cars for day-to-day use on the road and which could be used sportingly and competitively in club events. Concurrently with this, it was their avowed intention to produce and sell cars, at a reasonable price, ready for racing. It might be thought, therefore, that the sequence of development would be: prototype—record-breaker, or other high speed sample—racing car—sports car, in that order, the accumulated knowledge of the series being built directly into the sports version. Ideal though that may be, it could not be done, for the dual reason that the small-quantity production had to pay its way and the racing cars had to be reasonable in price. The number of people prepared to buy cars and race them, at any price, is not large and to design, tool and construct a model for a run of about a dozen cars or so would make the price of each prohibitive. It was therefore necessary that new developments, after testing by prototype, should be incorporated in the racing and sports versions simultaneously in order that tooling costs could be spread as widely as possible.

The major difference between EX 120 and the C Type Montlhery Midget was in the bore and stroke. The M Type, it will be remembered, had 57-mm. bore and the stroke 83 mm., giving a swept volume of 847 c.c. These dimensions had been retained in EX 120 in its original role of prototype and were incorporated into the D Type. For record purposes, when it was necessary to reduce the capacity below 750 c.c., EX 120 had its stroke reduced to 81 mm. and bore to 54 mm. This was done in order that existing connecting rods could be used, there being insufficient time to obtain new stampings. In designing the C Type, the original bore size of 57 mm. was retained and the stroke shortened drastically to 73 mm. There were two reasons for this. Firstly, it was thought necessary to increase the crank pin diameters from 1¼ in. to 1⅝ in. and room could be found for the larger big end only by shortening the stroke. Secondly,

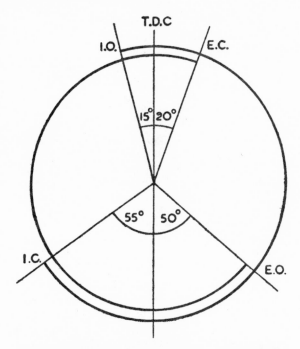

STANDARD MG VALVE TIMING
AS USED ON ALL MODELS 1931-1936
EXCEPT KA AND NE

Fig. 2.

bore diameter was to some extent controlled by the existing cylinder head shape, it being simpler to get maximum possible compression ratio with the larger bore without the piston having to intrude too greatly into the head, with the consequent risk of destroying the shape of the combustion space. This had the additional advantage that the cylinder block, as well as the head, would be common to the 850-c.c. D Type sports car.

A new valve timing was developed, as shown at *Fig*. 2, and it should be mentioned here that this proved so successful that it was used, with two exceptions, for all subsequent cars up till 1935, both supercharged and unsupercharged, racing and sports. The exceptions were the 6-cylinder unsupercharged NE, which won the Ulster T.T. in 1933, and the K.A. Magnette which, because it was fitted with a pre-selector gearbox which rattled rather badly in neutral, had a special timing to smooth out the slow running, even though this entailed a sacrifice of maximum speed and acceleration.

An innovation on the C Type was the use of float-chamber controlled oil feed to the sump from a bulk supply tank mounted on the scuttle. The advantages of this, which proved most reliable in use, despite considerable scepticism at the time, are manifold. In the first place, from the point of view of replenishment at a pit, it was necessary merely to snap open the quick-filler cap of the supply tank and throw in a predetermined quantity of oil. Playing about with dip-sticks, level taps—even opening the bonnet—were obviated. Secondly, the maximum quantity of oil was kept constantly in the sump. This not only had the advantage that the oil was kept as cool as possible at all stages of the race, but reduced the danger of temporary starvation when cornering or braking. It was particularly valuable when the cars were supercharged, as the majority of blowers of the eccentric vane type had quite a considerable oil consumption of their own.

The clutch, and the transmission generally, were designed with an eye on the power outputs which were likely to arise from subsequent supercharging. A special two-plate dry clutch was developed and a somewhat massive 4-speed crash change E.N.V. gearbox was incorporated. The propeller shaft had a critical speed away above the highest likely to be achieved and the final drive gears were in straight-cut form to obviate the reversal of thrust on the pinion when changing from drive to over-run.

The front axle was carried on top of the front springs, brake torque reaction being taken by the road springs themselves, both front and rear. Detailed modifications to the brake gear as described in Chapter 3 were the addition of wing nut adjusters on each of the four brake cam levers, and controls, usable from the driving seat, to take up the main adjustment of either pedal or hand lever.

In standard form, the cars were fitted with two-seater bodies, panelled in aluminium sheet. The pointed tail housed the spare wheel and petrol tank from which a large diameter filler pipe led to a quick-lift cap on the extreme tail of the car. In the front was a radiator cowl which bore an obvious family resemblance to the roughly fashioned thing which had graced the radiator of EX 120 at Montlhery. Notable, too, was the form of the top scuttle panel which rose, on this model for the first time, in two humps in front of driver and passenger, to act as wind deflectors. Finally, electrical equipment was to International Road Racing standards, carried out with meticulous care, and there was, as standard equipment, a gauze windscreen, bonnet strap and external exhaust system, adding the final touches, from the point of view both of utility and appearance, to a thoroughly workmanlike job.

Cars to this specification, wired and split-pinned in every hole, and in all respects prepared and ready for the track, were offered for sale at £295, a price which, in this post-war era, makes one gasp and which was but one hundred pounds in excess of their sports car counterpart. It was small wonder that the racing fraternity, much impressed by the performance of the *marque* in the 1930 races, went for them in a Big Way; so much so that for the Double Twelve-hour race in May 1931, thirteen of them came to the starting line. It is important, too, that there were ten Austins in the race, this not only providing the first of the long series of Austin versus MG scraps, but also swelling the 750-c.c. class entry to a total of twenty-three out of a field of forty-nine cars, testifying to the popularity of 'inexpensive' racing.

Four teams, each of three MGs, had been entered, and there was one 'odd man'. Edmondson and Randall, team winners in 1930, while not themselves driving, had entered cars to be driven by Selby and Hendy, Hebeler and Montgomery, and Gibson and Fell. The Earl of March shared a wheel with C. S. Staniland, the other cars of his team being handled by Parker and Cox, Norman Black and Fiennes. It was on this occasion that the name of Major A. T. Goldie Gardner was first associated with the MG car, an association which was to endure for years and write many pages of motoring history. He was partnered by R. T. Horton, the others of his sextet being Murton Neale and Samuelson, R. R. Jackson and W. E. Humphreys. The fourth team was made from an association of individual entries, the Hon. A. D. and Mrs. Chetwynd, Stisted and Kindell, and—Dan Higgin, the embodiment of the traditional 'wild, red-headed Irishman' who drove, first and last, for the fun of the thing and was a sportsman to his finger tips. Lastly, but far from least, Hugh Hamilton, who planned to drive the whole twenty-four hours single handed.

Although many of these drivers were new to car racing, their names were to live in the game, and, in many instances, particularly in association with MG cars. It is for this reason that they are given in detail.

As has been said, the broad design of the C Type had been decided upon even before EX 120 began its record breaking, but even so, supplies of parts for the new cars were slow in coming through (judged by the standards of those days) and the day of the race was very near before a start could be made on their building. Midnight oil, incessant telephone calls and literally thousands of miles of motoring finally chased the materials in from the suppliers, and fifteen cars were ultimately built during the twelve days preceding the first practice day.

Practice was uneventful, save that, on the last day, Black's engine departed this life in a clatter. There was nothing for it but to fit another, and it is a measure of the keenness—perhaps even the anxiety—with which Kimber regarded the event (for the cars were as yet untried in their new form) that he took this car himself and drove it all night long on the roads of Surrey and Hampshire to run the tightness off the new engine.

The race started in the early morning of a wet, windy and cheerless day and, apart from the admittedly inspiring spectacle of some forty-seven cars tearing off in one howling pack, there was little in the prospect of two days' motoring round and round a very bumpy and uncomfortable two and a half miles of track, to stimulate enthusiasm or excitement either in competitor or beholder. But the race was, clearly, a test of endurance for the machines and could not fail to hold the intense interest and anxiety at least of those associated with the Company whose reputation stood to be made or marred by the result.

Higgin, as expected, drove with gay abandon, set a cracking pace, and came round at the end of the first lap away out ahead of the rest of the 750-c.c. pack. Once the engine was hot, he put in lap after lap at around 70 m.p.h. and, after six hours, was seven miles ahead of the next car in his class, driven by Hamilton. The team cars were driving at a more modest pace, being content to lap at below 65 m.p.h. in the firm belief that Higgin's machine would not stand the racket. This belief was vindicated in the early afternoon when Higgin retired with a broken piston. He was, however, not alone in his trouble, as by the time the maroon sounded to stop the race at the end of the first day, several cars had visited the pits to replace broken valve springs and three were out of the race with broken pistons, a trouble later traced to spring failure.

Overnight Kimber conferred with Reid Railton on this question, the trouble having been so widespread that, in the twelve hours of racing yet to go, it might easily spell disaster. As a result all drivers were warned to restrict their engine speed, it being thought that valve crash, or incipient valve crash, was the cause. The leading cars had built up such a commanding lead over the rest of the field on handicap, that very considerable reductions in speed were permissible. But Cousins, who was managing the Earl of March's team, which was in the lead, doubted the wisdom of such a course. His team had so far been free of trouble and he was of the opinion that it was not high engine speed which was the cause but rather that there was a surge period in the springs which occurred lower down the speed range. He based this assumption on observation of the day's racing wherein, as he saw it, trouble had been confined principally to slower cars, the three cars of his team, plus Gibson's and Hamilton's, lapping steadily at 65 m.p.h. without bother. He therefore held a team conference at the team's headquarters at an inn at Byfleet, and there it was agreed that on the morrow the first day's speeds should continue. It was confidently expected that this would cause Kimber a good deal of anxiety in the course of which he would visit the pit with great frequency to request moderation. To counter this it was arranged to switch the pit signals so that 'slower' meant 'O.K.' and vice versa. After all, what more could a pit manager do than nail the 'slower' sign permanently to the counter? And thus it happened.

The enormous lead built up by the Midgets on the first day presented the larger cars with a serious problem. As was expected, the second day's racing saw great efforts by the Big Boys, who had no little trouble as a result. With the MGs, valve spring failure still persisted, but otherwise little happened to interfere with their steady progress and they finished the race in the first five places, winning, at the same time, the Team Prize and all Class awards. Lord March and Staniland in first place and Gibson and Fell in second place had gone through completely without trouble. Hamilton, having broken and replaced a valve spring on the first day, was dogged by loss of speed for some hours on the afternoon of the second day, later to discover that his entire inlet manifold, with the tall carburetter perched on the top, was loose and flopped over sideways as he came out of the turn, allowing the engine to draw air. Having driven single handed throughout the whole twenty-four hours, he brought his car into third place at a time when he was fast overhauling Gibson.

From this it appeared that, with the exception of the valve springs and some bother with broken front wing stays, the design of the new car was proved. Certainly it had brought off one of the most complete victories in motor racing history, and such was the impression that it created that seven of those who had entered in the Double Twelve requested the MG Company to overhaul and prepare their cars for the Irish Grand Prix, to be run in Phoenix Park, Dublin, just four weeks later. In addition, four new cars were ordered for this race, one of which was for F. S. Barnes, who had driven an Austin in the Double Twelve.

Alterations to the valve springs and wing stays were simple and straightforward, once the race was over and it was possible to take a little time to think about them. Change was also needed because almost all those who had driven at Brooklands had reported that the engines ran too hot. Thus the radiator cowl, born of necessity among the snow and ice of Montlhery a few months earlier and subsequently adapted to the racing cars, died after but one race. With these exceptions, the cars were built for Dublin in exactly the same trim as before, but everyone was well aware that there might yet be much to learn. Twenty-four hours on Brooklands was a severe test not only of the engine, but also of the chassis, suspension and general structure of the car. But it was a 'top gear ride', brakes and gearbox were little used, and there was nothing to load the transmission comparably with what might be expected in a road race. While, therefore, the seizure of Black's gearbox during practice was an occasion for much disappointment and not a little surprise, reason said that, if trouble was to come, the gearbox was one of the places where it might be expected. Even before this outright seizure had occurred, there had been one or two reports of bent selector forks. This, in itself, was not regarded very seriously because the original forks had been made in bronze—part of the price which had to be paid to get the cars to the starting line at Brooklands at all. Steel forks were, however, now available but had not been fitted to all cars. Examination of the seizure disclosed a state of affairs which was much more serious. The third speed mainshaft gear ran on a plain bush, which had seized on the shaft, and it was apparent that either the initial clearance had been too small or that the bush was not up to the job. So far as was known, all gearboxes were alike and it seemed to Cousins, who was the man in charge on the spot, that there was a clear possibility of the other boxes going the same way. Moreover, if they did, the seizure would occur while the car was in some gear other than third and the whole transmission would 'go up solid' as it had in Black's case, which would, to say the least, cause the driver a little excitement. On the other hand, the final diagnosis was made late on the day before the race (another box having been telegraphed for, on spec, in the morning) and it was obviously impossible to re-operate all the boxes before the start. In any case it Might Never Happen. All in all, Cousins invoked St. Christopher and decided to keep quiet about the whole thing.

The Irish Grand Prix was run over a nominal seventy laps of a course some four and a quarter miles in length, on which, at that time, a good surface conduced to high speeds. To encourage large cars to give of their best, the race was run in two parts, cars under one and a half litres racing on one day and larger cars on the next. Handicapping in both races was by means of credit laps, thus providing a massed start on each day, and enabling the large cars to race against the best handicap time established by the small cars. Race arrangements were good and a large board opposite the grand stand gave a clear and continuous picture of the progress of the race.

On this June 5, 1931, at 3 p.m. in pouring rain, ten C Type Montlhery Midgets came to the starting grid to race for the Saorstat Cup. Among the considerable company were also six supercharged Austins and another menace to the MG chances—the Rileys. One of these, driven by Victor Gillow, the race winner of the previous year— also on a Riley—caused consternation in the early stages of the race by the cracking pace which he set, and it is fair to say that had he tempered his skill and dash with a little more discretion, the final result might have been different. As it was, the Midgets chased him and, quite early on, those driven by Horton and Jackson and by Black appeared in the lead of the 750-c.c. class. The pace was furious and, with Gillow out of the running, Kimber saw no good purpose in a dog-fight between two MGs. He accordingly requested their team chiefs to slow them down. But in doing so he lost sight of two things. In the first place, each of these cars was run by a member of a different team and each wanted to win; they were, all said and done, private owners racing for the fun of the thing—not 'Works' entries. Secondly, they were racing not only against one another and the rest of the cars on the track, but also against the clock. It was still possible to put up such a time that the big cars, racing on the following day, would be unable to beat it.

It fell again to Cousins' lot to disregard his chief's wishes. He was then, and at subsequent races, in the difficult position of having divided loyalties, on the one hand to the MG Car Company by whom he had been employed since a boy and on the other to the entrant of the team who had engaged him to manage his *équipe*. Cousins satisfied his conscience with a compromise, assisting with all the cars up to the moment of the 'off' but thereafter giving no thought to any but his own team for the duration of the race. In this particular case he knew Black had more speed if he was called upon to give it. The course was rain-soaked and Black was one of those who prayed for rain on race days. Brought up on motor-cycles, he had spent a large part of his motoring career trying to keep his mind one step ahead of the antics of his front wheel. Cousins accordingly hung out the 'O.K.' signal. Black continued to make up on Horton, passed him, and thereafter went on to build up a substantial lead. Even so, troubles were not quite over. At one point, Black's engine was swamped by another competitor and promptly lost a cylinder. After the best part of a lap on three and just when he was about to come in to the pit, the ignition system dried itself out and the car was away again on its old form. That Black was still in the lead seemed to Cousins to justify his actions. Black won the race, with Horton second and Goldie Gardner, whose team won the Team Prize, third. On the following day, the large cars failed to equal Black's time, and he therefore won the Irish Grand Prix.

Immediately after crossing the finishing line, Black's car was driven into an official garage where it was locked up until it could be scrutineered the next morning. After scrutiny it was driven three miles to the docks, placed on board ship, and sailed to Liverpool. Driven from the ship by Frank Tayler, it was not clear of Liverpool when the third speed seized again. The luck of the game!

With Dublin behind them, the owners of the cars turned their minds to the next event which, for most of them, was the R.A.C. International Tourist Trophy to be run over the 14-mile Newtownards–Comber–Dundonald triangle, outside Belfast, towards the end of

August. Two such decisive wins in two consecutive classic races turned the handicappers' attention somewhat sharply towards the unsupercharged 750-c.c. class and it was no great surprise when the regulations for the T.T. were published, to find that it had been drastically dealt with. In fact, after careful consideration of the figures, it was decided at Abingdon that the cars in their present form had no chance of winning and that supercharging was essential.

The experience of supercharging already gained at Montlhery was limited, EX 120 in blown form having by this time a total of only twelve hours running to its credit during most of which, apart from the isolated historic moments when it was actually taking records, it had, to quote Jackson, 'mis-fired, popped and banged all over the place' and finally blown to pieces. With less than three months to go the necessary knowledge had to be obtained and the equipment designed, installed and tested. Meanwhile Samuelson had taken his car to Le Mans for another twenty-four hours racing, and this provided an opportunity to test the gearbox in which the offending bush had been replaced by a needle roller bearing. This was the only alteration found necessary as a result of the Irish race, all the MGs having run there without trouble. It appeared that a very reliable foundation existed on to which to mount the superchargers. But Samuelson was to have bother in another direction for, after some twenty-three and a half hours running, and while lying third, a connecting rod broke and made a 'bay-window' in the crankcase, Samuelson covering his last lap on three cylinders in a forlorn attempt to qualify. From detailed examination of this failure, it was decided to redesign the connecting rod, particularly having in mind the additional loading which supercharging would impose.

Preliminary work on the blower installation was done on the test bed and within a few weeks the only thing which remained of the original set-up on EX 120 was the position of the supercharger—between the front dumb irons. Sprockets and chains had been discarded and internally cut reduction gears built into a housing integral with the back of the blower—a Number 7 Powerplus—to drive it at 0·68 engine speed. The design of the coupling shaft from the engine presented a nice problem. It was necessary to provide a fully universal action to accommodate the relative movement of engine and blower which was bound to occur with flexure of the chassis frame; movement in a telescopic sense was desirable to relieve the reduction gear of any loading arising from end float on the crankshaft; and, with all, the space was very limited. In its final form, based on a design of G.W.K. where Jackson had been apprenticed, a short splined shaft engaged at each end a spherical member from the periphery of which four half-recessed steel balls protruded into grooves cut in housings fitted to crankshaft and blower drive respectively. It is interesting that, before this drive had been long in use, a slight annular groove was machined on all shafts near their centre, the purpose being to ensure that when the shaft sheared—as they frequently did on account of momentary blower seizures while adjusting the lubrication feed—a substantial length of shaft would be left protruding from the universal by which it could be withdrawn without dismantling. Until this expedient was hit upon, blower seizure was regarded as something of a bore.

The unsupercharged cars had to run on petrol/benzol with compression ratios of 9·5 to 1. As a supercharge of some twelve pounds per square inch was contemplated, the cylinder heads were changed to give a ratio of 6 to 1. Otherwise, the engines remained the same, the carburetter kept its position as on EX 120—on the side of the blower—and a long pipe joined the blower outlet to the induction manifold. At the top end of the pipe a release valve was fitted to relieve the blower of excess pressure caused when the engine fired back into the inlet pipe. Thus equipped, Samuelson's car and the works experimental model, which was to be driven by Hugo Urban-Emmerich, were shipped to Nurburg, Jackson and Kindell in attendance, with spares of all kinds, large boxes of sparking plugs and a big bag of carburetter needles.

On arrival at the track, Jackson set about Emmerich's car—he had had a hand in the original building of it, had several times overhauled it, and knew it backwards. But at once he was in difficulty. The weather was extremely hot and, as soon as he started to flog the car, it boiled and the oil temperature ran dangerously high. Drastic steps were taken to enrich the mixture but the most slender needle available did not have the desired effect. It was at this point that Jackson, sitting on a box in front of the car, taking chunks off a needle with a file, became aware of someone looking over his shoulder, intently studying the carburetter. It was Dr. Porsche, and Jackson seized the opportunity not only to describe the working of the S.U., but also to pour out his troubles. The Doctor was intensely interested and took Jackson along to the Shell representatives and gave them instructions for a special brew of fuel. This completely stopped the overheating and the car thereafter went like a flash. It is an interesting aside that Jackson, in expressing his gratitude, asked the Doctor if he could reciprocate in any way. Dr. Porsche asked him for one of his 'candles'—German equivalent of sparking plug—and Jackson gave him one. This little event had a considerable effect on the course of development of German racing engines during the subsequent year or so, but that is a story which has no place here.

Emmerich, a wealthy Czech manufacturer, middle-aged and courageous, was at the same time a showman. His car was as immaculate in black as his overalls and helmet were spotless white. He drove with great enjoyment, and to some extent 'played to the gallery'. After he had taken over the car for practice, he became the talk of Nurburg. Unfortunately, he could not be persuaded to practise in the rain, race day dawned wet, and he disappeared from the course in spectacular fashion in the opening laps—happily without personal injury.

The adjustments to Samuelson's car had been kept in step with Emmerich's. It was just about as fast, and despite some delay occasioned by a loose fuel feed pipe, came through the race to finish fifth in the 1100-c.c. class. The supercharged version of the C Type car was considered proved.

The preparation of the power units for Ulster followed closely on the lines which had been worked out at Nurburg. Comparison of *Figs*. 3 and 4 will show the direct effect of supercharging which increased the maximum power available by more than 40 per cent. The bodywork of the original cars was designed for endurance with one eye on the Double Twelve-hour race, and was coachbuilt. Such ruggedness, and consequent weight, were unnecessary and undesirable for the shorter races and much lighter bodies were therefore fitted. The possibility of much increased power had been in mind at the time of the original design of the transmission and no changes were necessary here. The only possible cause for doubt was that the brakes might not be equal to the increased speed, but the light bodies helped in this respect. The lap speeds of the Brooklands outer circuit provide an interesting and informative comparison. As built for the Double Twelve-hour race and in touring trim, with wings, lamps and windshield, lap speeds of 74 m.p.h. were returned. With the supercharger, an increase of ten miles per hour was obtained, while, stripped of the touring impedimenta, the speed rose to 96.

Nine of these MGs arrived in Belfast, ready for the T.T. It proved to be a close and very hard-fought race, Black winning on the same car with which he had won at Dublin. With an average speed of 67·90 m.p.h., Black beat Borzacchini, Alfa Romeo, by seventy-two seconds in a race of five and a quarter hours' duration, while Crabtree brought his MG into third place, five seconds later. It is a further measure of the extent by which the MGs beat their handicap speeds that Borzacchini repeatedly broke the lap record and completed the course at a record speed of 79·05, over six miles per hour faster than the previous best. The MG success, when one considers the narrow margin by which it was achieved, was in no small measure contributed to by Frankie Tayler's splendid work in the pit stops. The MG drivers and mechanics had learnt the importance of pit organisation and routine and, as time went on, more and more attention was paid to the perfection of it. This was the first occasion on which it had so obviously paid a dividend, but it was not the last.

Nothing arose from the T.T. to indicate the need for any modification to the MGs. Troubles there were, but they had been random, and it must be remembered that most of the cars had had a pretty strenuous year. Higgin had a recurrence of valve-spring breakage, Hamilton broke a rocker immediately after raising the 750-c.c. class lap record to a shade over 70 m.p.h., and another car sheared a key in its camshaft drive. It was, however, quite clear that the handicappers would be active again, so the quest for more power and more speed had to go on.

The next stages in engine development belong, properly, to the succeeding series, the J Types, but as the new cylinder head which resulted was offered as a conversion set to the owners of C Types in order to prolong the useful racing life of these cars, a description must be given here. This is particularly important as the conversion brought in its train a brand-new set of troubles.

While it was obvious that the limits of supercharge pressures had by no means been reached, further increases were expected to be relatively unprofitable because, for some time, there had been unmistakable signs of irregular burning of the charge in the existing cylinder head. A re-design of the head was, therefore, a first essential, the requirements being increased port area, improved gas flow and more adequate cooling of the valve seats and guides. Over all this hung the consideration of production cost, as the new head was to be used in relatively large scale production in the sports version as well as in the racing cars. This factor, more than any other, dictated the selection from the numerous designs which were sketched and worked out in detail on paper, of a head of similar general shape and dimensions to the existing one but having its exhaust ports in line on the opposite side of the head from the inlets. Single camshaft operation was retained, valves were slightly enlarged and the lift increased, and 14 mm. sparking plugs were provided for. This latter item later caused a good deal of difficulty in that, in the early days of the use of the new head, its demands in the matter of sparking plugs were ahead of development of the then fairly new 14 mm. size. Triple valve springs were introduced at this stage and, further to assist cooling, a water-pump was added, driven from the distributor driving gear at the front end of the crankshaft.

The new head had additional water holes cut in its gasket face which registered with similar holes in the J Type cylinder block, this having been redesigned, in small detail, at the same time as the head. When the new head was fitted to existing C Type cars, the additional water holes had to be cut in the block and this was thereby weakened to such an extent that the gasket joint would not hold. Even with a faced joint, using no gasket at all, it was found that at combustion chamber pressures of 1000 pounds per square inch, the head and block sprung to such an extent that no ordinary joint would remain gas tight.

It is interesting here to read what the chief designer, H. N. Charles, had to say about this moment. In a paper read before the I.A.E. in February, 1935, he said:

"The crisis occasioned by this contretemps left all concerned for a moment helpless in the face of a whirlwind of advice, cries for help

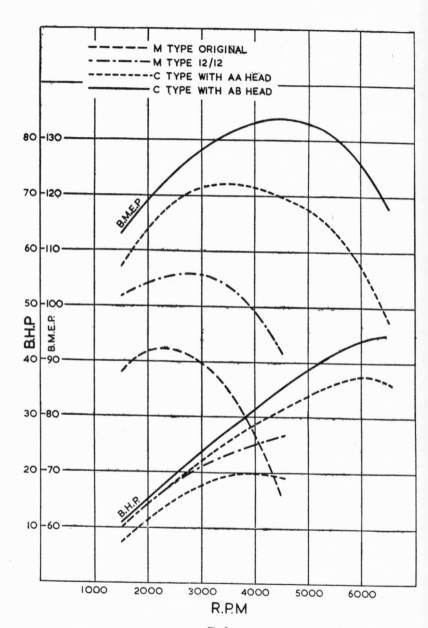

Fig. 3.

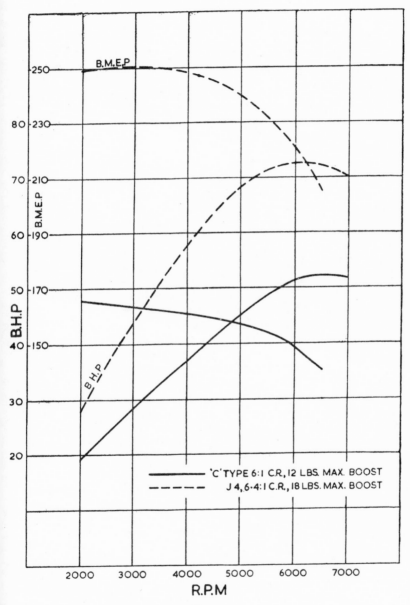

Fig.

*from infuriated racing men, and downright criticism from some of
our strongest supporters, who felt that the new head was foredoomed
to failure with its gasket troubles and its 14 mm. plugs."*

The final answer, as so often happens in such cases, proved to be
extremely simple. Head and block were faced flat and a gasket of a
good grade 20 gauge mild steel sheet was interposed. This gasket was
cut back $\frac{1}{32}$ in. around the combustion spaces, forming a recess in
which burnt oil accumulated and provided a self-caulking joint. Again
to quote Charles: "We have never blown a gasket on a racing engine
since."

The first race in which the new head was used was in the J.C.C.
1000 Miles, in May, 1932, a race which had replaced the Double Twelve-
hour of previous years. The effect of the MG wins at Ulster and in the
500-mile race at Brooklands in the preceding autumn had caused the
handicap to react unfavourably towards supercharging, and the MGs
therefore ran unblown. The gasket trouble was much in evidence at
this time and new ones were fitted to several cars in the course of the
race, the mechanics getting the job down to twenty-one minutes for the
complete operation, in one case. In a race of this duration, on a closed
circuit, pit work can take on a strange, even leisurely aspect. Such is
the impression conveyed by the sight of a driver, leaning nonchalantly
against the pit counter, painting a gasket with jointing compound what
time his mechanic gets the head off. In fact, this race provided a contrast
of extremes in the matter of pit work.

Quite early on the first day, Hamilton's car ran a big-end and a
quick examination showed that the crankshaft oilways were full of
white-metal such that the fitting of a new rod would have been a sheer
waste of time. On this occasion Hamilton was not, as was his habit,
playing a lone hand, but was a member of Goldie Gardner's team and
this failure seemed to put an end to their chances of the team prize.
But as the race leaders had not yet reached the quarter distance, a
decision was taken to substitute the engine from the practice car.
Accordingly, four mechanics—King and Stone on the practice car and
Cousins and Jackson on Hamilton's—deliberately began to change
engines while the race was still in progress. Not the least of the difficulties
was that no lifting tackle was available, but the removal of the old
engine and the replacement of the sound one was accomplished by
means of a rope passed under the engine and round the neck of six foot
four inches of Cecil Cousins who stood astride the frame like a human
crane jib. Hamilton drove the car away three and a quarter hours after
his breakdown and Gardner's team went on to win the team prize.
The contrast was provided by the first visitation of a new trouble which
was to dog the MGs throughout the season—Black's car split its petrol
tank. Charles has since described the petrol tank as the *bête-noire* of the
racing-car designer's existence, but this particular failure deprived Black

of an almost certain win. He first noticed an increased rate of fuel consumption on the afternoon of the first day and came in to refuel early. Examination showed that the tank had a slight split near one of its three mounting bolts, repair in position was impossible but it was decided that Black should continue, keeping a sharp eye on his fuel level. This went on for the rest of the day, refilling every hour or so, but on the second day, when Black lay sixth, he came in for another fifteen gallons after forty-five minutes and again after a further half an hour. By this time, Frank Tayler had perfected his refuelling routine and was getting in fifteen gallons in fifteen seconds. Between stops, Black was lapping at 80 m.p.h. and at this, his race position improved, so that although for the last three hours he stopped every fifteen minutes, he finished in third place. His average speed for the thousand miles was 75·5 m.p.h., ten miles per hour faster than the winning MG's speed in the Double Twelve of the preceding year.

Urban Emmerich's car was converted to the new head, and with superchargers fitted, he and Hamilton ran at Nurburg. Jackson and Kindell, for the second year in succession, went over to help and both cars soon showed great promise. Hamilton was remarkable in that he preferred to prepare his own car and this gave rise to two rather amusing incidents at Nurburg. At the end of one practice day, Emmerich took Jackson to dinner at an hotel adjoining their headquarters. The meal had reached the coffee stage when, in sharp contrast to Emmerich, immaculate as always, and the spotless white of the table linen, the figure of Hamilton appeared in the restaurant, with black hands, an oily streak across one eye, erstwhile white overalls and with a rather sheepish grin on his face. Under one arm he carried an obviously heavy newspaper parcel. He approached the table, excused himself with a formal bow to Emmerich, turned to Jackson and with "what the devil do I do about this, Jacko?", unrolled his disembowelled supercharger on to the tablecloth, to the horror of Emmerich and the consternation of the *maître d'hôtel*. The reduction gears were blue and the engine had obviously run short of oil. A black fuel and oil mixture ran from the open ports on to the table. Neither Jackson nor Hamilton had very much sleep that night, but the car was running again in the morning. Later, at the start, in those few minutes of expectancy and quiet which precede the starting of engines, there was heard, clear and distinct above the murmur of a thousand voices, an emphatic and pungent expletive, essentially British. One of Hammy's great rules of car preparation was 'Do it up tight' and to this end he provided himself with a very comprehensive kit of long-handled spanners. On this occasion, using a T-spanner like a turncock's key, he had sheared off a sparking plug flush with the cylinder head—the only time, Jackson says, he has ever known it happen. The unmistakable nationality of this *cri du cœur* brought an English mechanic quickly to Hammy's side;

Lord Howe's head mechanic Thomas produced an 'Easy-Out'; and Hamilton left the line at the fall of the flag. He ran consistently and very fast to win his class in the German Grand Prix.

The Tourist Trophy in Ulster in 1932 proved many things, among them that Hamilton was developing into one of the finest drivers of the day and another that age was telling on the C Type MGs, now well into their second year of racing. Of nine supercharged MGs which entered, only one, driven by E. R. Hall, finished, but he was in third place. During practice, Hamilton broke the 750-c.c. lap record three times—at 71·2, 74·0 and 75·5 m.p.h., but later crashed, the driver sustaining broken ribs. Of the others, Barnes and Gardner crashed in collisions with other competitors, Hailwood burnt a valve, Paul ran big ends, Crabtree suffered a punctured float, Don Barnes' blower seized and Black had a seized back axle.

To relieve what would otherwise have been a somewhat lugubrious end to the season, Horton drove his C Type into first place in the Five Hundred Miles race at Brooklands at 96·29 m.p.h., a speed which makes one think and hark back a mere ten months to the time when EX 120 was struggling to achieve 100 m.p.h. over five kilometres.

CHAPTER V

EX 127

THE attainment of one hundred miles an hour with EX 120 convinced the world of the potentialities of the small car and infused a great zest for better things into the men who lived and worked under the sign of the Octagon. Up till then, they had concerned themselves with building motor cars which 'went' a bit better than their contemporaries and they knew something of the value of weight reduction and of the need for getting 'more power' out of an engine. They knew too that, from the point of view of selling their cars, attractive lines and 'sporting' shapes were a great advantage. But they had not thought very seriously of engine output in the precise terms of b.h.p. and were undoubtedly vague as to the meaning and effect of frontal area and aerodynamic form. EX 120 changed all that; one hundred miles an hour was an accomplished fact and two miles a minute became much more than a vision.

While the Montlhery Midgets were being built—to the pattern of EX 120—Jackson was busy with the successor, a car to be used entirely for development and record attempts and not intended as a prototype. The intention was to build a car of the smallest possible cross-sectional area consistent with getting George Eyston into it and getting the drive past him from engine to back axle. This resulted in the adoption of an 'angular offset drive' in which the rear axle banjo was off centre and close up against the left-hand rear wheel, and the centre line of the transmission—back axle pinion, propeller shaft, gearbox, crankshaft and supercharger drive—ran forward at an angle of seven degrees to the centre line and direction of travel of the car. The driver sat beside the propeller shaft—his theoretical position also being offset seven degrees—with the bottom of the seat pan but six inches or so off the ground, thus reducing the body height to a minimum. In fact, by means of a 'tailor-made' body, it was intended that, with the exception of the wheels and axles which had of necessity to protrude, the frontal area should not be substantially greater than the fore and aft silhouette of the driver when sitting down with his feet up.

The broad outline of the plan having been determined, Jackson began to build the car under the technical direction of Eldridge. No detailed drawings had been prepared in advance and the various components were fabricated, piecemeal, as the job went along. With the exception of the angularity of the drive, EX 120 was closely followed, wheel-base and track dimensions being retained and C Type brakes, road springs, front axle and steering used. Even the engine was C Type, subject to some external modifications. Where special components had to be made, however, a considerable safety factor was built into them to allow for future increases in engine power. Components which did not lend themselves to fabrication on the spot were sketched—Jackson's sketches, according to him, being "with a piece of chalk on an old sugar bag", the inference being that they looked something like a blue print—drawn, and ordered from specialist manufacturers. One such case caused a furore. The draughtsman responsible for the rear axle banjo drew it in American projection and when the part arrived, the flange to carry the final drive was found to face the rear of the car. But such cases were fortunately infrequent and the work went steadily on.

The shape of the body was a problem all its own. Unknown to anyone, Jackson, having turned it over in his mind for weeks, started to build a quarter-scale model, working at home at nights and weekends. He built a framework in light gauge aluminium angle and then, as he had no facilities for panelling it, brought it for Kimber to see. Kimber was sufficiently pleased with it, on sight, to arrange for it to be panelled and when it was finished, Eyston not only gave it his approval but arranged for Jackson to go with the model to see it tested in Vickers' wind tunnel. The general shape of the model had been prompted by three well-known record breakers of the day, the front section being based on Kaye Don's Silver Bullet, the centre section and cockpit on the then current version of Malcolm Campbell's Blue Bird and the tail was that of the Golden Arrow. So well had Jackson merged the features of these three cars that no alteration was considered necessary as a result of the wind tunnel tests. A full size body was therefore put in hand, scaled to fit Eyston.

The car first went to Montlhery in late September, 1931. Preliminary running there showed that the cooling was inadequate, the radiator being masked by the high built shaft-cum-chain driven supercharger installation. Eldridge had wanted to be able to vary the blower speed in relation to the engine and this had led to the adoption of a rather complicated drive terminating in a pair of motor-cycle type sprockets, and a length of chain. To obtain adequate distance between centres for the sprockets, the blower had been raised higher than on EX 120 and, being mounted on a steel plate, the whole assembly formed a very effective obstruction to the air flow through the radiator. Various expedients were tried to improve cooling, the opening in the front cowl being progressively enlarged with snips and the rear end of the engine cover raised more and more to facilitate the escape of air from behind the radiator. Neither of these courses effected a cure and it was obvious that the wind resistance of the body had been considerably increased by them. Eldridge was finally convinced that to be able to attempt the record, a new radiator was necessary. He went into Paris and arranged for the construction of an aero type surface radiator, to conform in shape to the external contours of the car's engine cover. By this means, the supercharger would now come behind the radiator, its cooling would be reduced to nil and the carburetter made very inaccessible. Moreover, the distance of the radiator from the engine gave rise to some plumbing that was ingenious though inelegant. But everything worked well on test and the car was made ready.

While these preparations were being made, Eyston had made his successful attempt on the one-hour record with EX 120 which had subsequently caught fire and put its driver in hospital. EX 127 stood ready, but the man for whom it had been tailored was unlikely to drive again for some weeks. Eldridge decided to drive. Only those who knew Eldridge, knew his background and knew the circumstances of the moment could judge the courageousness of this decision and the subsequent performance. Many years before, he had sustained a facial injury—also while engaged on record attempts—which had cost him the sight of one eye and he wore spectacles for the other one. Anyone who has at any time had to drive a car with one eye even temporarily out of action will know what a handicap is the loss of a sense of perspective. But more than this: Eldridge had not driven at high speed on a track for years—though it is true to say that he knew Montlhery track as well as anyone. Finally, although he was not as tall as Eyston, he was what is politely called a Big Man, and it was only with difficulty that he was squeezed through the cockpit opening into the car. His only concession to his infirmity—and it is a fair index of his own realisation of the limitations of his vision—was to have a car with headlights on placed at the junction of the piste de vitesse and the piste de routier, facing the direction from which he would come in the course of his record run. This run was to be made in broad daylight and the headlights were to ensure that he did not take the wrong turning at the fork. The car was brought and Eldridge, in a lounge suit with neither overalls nor goggles, was 'inserted' into the cockpit. He was pushed off, covered two or three warming-up laps and then put his foot down, covering the five kilometres at 110·28 m.p.h., thereby beating the previous record by about three seconds. And the radiator burst.

Back at Abingdon, the surface radiator was discarded and Jackson set about redesigning the internal one and installing a new form of blower drive. The new radiator was made entirely by hand by one Whip Howard at the Company's radiator factory. It remained in the car, undisturbed, for two years of strenuous record work. In place of the chains and sprocket of the old drive, a pinion driven by the engine engaged with an internally cut ring gear, thereby making the centre line of the supercharger nearly co-axial with the engine. This gearing, enclosed in a cast aluminium casing, bolted to the back of the blower, had been developed for the Ulster T.T. and had become the standard method of driving Powerplus superchargers on all racing cars. This was true also of the lubrication system which was evolved. A pipe from the reserve oil tank on the scuttle led to a form of tap coupled to the accelerator control and so arranged that it was nearly shut when the throttle was closed and wide open on full bore. From the tap the pipe divided, one branch supplying the oil pump which was built into the front casing of the blower, the other feeding the reduction gear by means of a metering union—known ever since, for some obscure reason, as a 'fuff-fuff valve'.

One of the great difficulties of these early supercharger installations was to secure good idling and a clean pick-up when accelerating from idling speeds. This was partly due to the tendency for the blower to accumulate oil under closed throttle conditions—a matter which the oil tap already mentioned was introduced to overcome. But more particularly was it caused by the low speed of the mixture in the long induction pipe which was needed to couple blower and engine. In this, the fuel was inclined to condense and fall out of suspension in the mixture, accumulating as liquid in the inlet manifold. The remedy was ingenious and effective. Two transfer pipes from blower to engine, one large, one small, were mounted side by side, a butterfly coupled to the accelerator pedal being included in the large one. Thus, only the small pipe was in use at idling and small throttle openings and gas velocity was high. At wider openings, the larger pipe took charge and a smooth take over was effected.

With modifications complete and the engine finally tested, the car, which since its previous run had been christened 'The Magic Midget', was returned to Montlhery in the December for further record attempts by Eyston, now recovered from his burns. There are two ways of going about this record-breaking business, both of which have their virtues. Either one can pile on all available speed, break the existing record by a handsome margin and then sit back and watch the fun of others having a crack at it. Or conversely, one can play cat and mouse with one's competitors in the game, putting the record up a little at a time in the hope that others will beat it and give one something fresh to go for. The drawback to the first way is that nobody will make an attempt to recapture the record unless he is reasonably certain he can do so, and counter attacks are therefore rare. Added to this, times have changed. Some years ago, bonus money paid by the oil companies and accessory manufacturers—even by the firms who made the driver's cigarettes and tooth paste—made record breaking an attractive and lucrative business to the successful, but those days are gone.

Eyston—despite burning his hands and feet and baling out on to the concrete at seventy miles an hour—was having fun at his record-breaking. He had no wish to put any records up too much at a time, particularly as the Austin Company were game and repeatedly came after him. Kimber was, however, on this occasion, impatient for the car to achieve two miles a minute. At the track, Denly drove while Jackson tuned, the former being under strict instructions from George not to give his speed away, in pursuance of which he religiously throttled back after half a lap of full speed. In the middle of it all, Jackson received a cable from Kimber asking how the car was going and he replied giving a very conservative figure in r.p.m. It was not until some while after he had heard again from Kimber telling him to lower the axle ratio that it dawned on him that back at Abingdon they were imagining that the engine was pulling its hardest at the speed he had given. However, he acknowledged the message and took no notice, knowing that he could explain on his return.

Tuning and practice had been delayed by hard weather, but no sooner was the car judged to be on top of its form than the track became ice-bound again. After further waiting and when no break in the frost seemed likely, Eyston decided to make his attempt, ice or no. In any case, it was Dec. 22, and Christmas at a deserted Montlhery was unthinkable. Accordingly the track was swept at the points where the straights joined the banking and Eyston took the car out. The four records from five kilometres to ten miles fell to him in quick succession at over 114 m.p.h. and the party returned to England, arriving on Christmas Eve.

Many of the racing fraternity were very inquisitive as to the fuel and carburetter settings which the car used on these ventures but it was not always expedient for it to be told. The car, on its return from Montlhery, was exhibited at the showrooms of University Motors in London where Hamilton worked, and Jackson was in charge of it when it was transported. On the way he bought a padlock and locked the bonnet. Hamilton confessed to him later that he had found a way in—but the carburetter jet and needle were in Jackson's pocket.

The International regulations covering the flying mile and flying kilometre records required that the distances should be covered in both directions, the mean speed counting for the record. This was a reasonable enough condition as it prevented advantage being taken of gradient or wind. Some closed circuits had received the approval of the A.I.A.C.R. for these records but, at this time, Montlhery was not one of them and Brooklands was closed for winter repairs. Kimber's desire for the car to achieve 120 miles per hour was strong, and immediately after Christmas he persuaded Eyston to go for it. It was decided to run at Pendine on the South Wales coast on a stretch of flat sand which had been used in earlier days notably by Campbell and Parry Thomas for attacks on the World's Land Speed Record.

Although the car was stripped, examined and rebuilt, as was customary after each session at the track, no alterations were made to the engine. It was known that, on the previous occasion, there had been sufficient power in reserve to enable the magic figure to be attained. A preliminary survey of the course had indicated, however, that the ground clearance as used on the concrete was likely to prove inadequate on the sands, particularly when manœuvring or travelling at slow speeds, and the undershield was modified to increase this. Great care was also taken to seal the body shell against the ingress of sand and the radiator opening and carburetter air intake were covered in with gauze. As the run was to be straight, and in order to minimise wheel slip, the differential was removed and a solid axle substituted. Eyston was worried about sand and spray impairing his vision. At best, it was not going to be easy to follow a bee-line between the timing strips on a broad expanse of sand and he felt that the normal type of windshield would rapidly become obscured. Jackson, during his earlier visit to the wind tunnel at Vickers, had learnt of an interesting method of securing direct vision in the face of high wind and this was adapted in the form of a windshield for the car. The principle is illustrated in *Fig. 5.* A rough mock up of this was constructed and it was found that

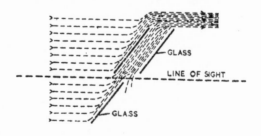

MAGIC MIDGET WINDSHIELD

Fig. 5.

a high pressure hose could be directed straight at it without any water passing through along the line of sight. To confirm these tests, the model was mounted on a car, and while Eyston drove fast along the roads around the MG factory, Jackson, who had been provided with a bag of confetti, sat backwards astride the bonnet and sprinkled the paper in front of the driver's face. Eyston was entirely satisfied and an interchangeable cockpit cover was built, incorporating the new screen.

In the last days of January, the *équipe* moved off and headquarters were established in the Beach Hotel, Pendine, where a large shed housed EX 127 and its equipment. There descended also upon this Welsh seaside hotel—out of season—a very large party of press correspondents, photographers, newsreel cameramen, sound engineers, petrol and oil technicians, and representatives of the accessory manufacturers to a total of some seventy or eighty people, for Kimber was determined to secure the maximum possible publicity for the venture.

For the purposes of very high speed motoring, Pendine Sands have the virtues of being long, wide and level, but that is the limit of what can be said in their favour. The direction of the wind, and the sea that happens to be running on the ebb, determine between them whether the sands are left smooth, rippled, or downright rough. Moreover, they are so flat that the tide does not come up *over* them so much as *through* them and they are, in their waterlogged state, 'quick'. Doyen of the district, in these matters, was Wilfred Morgan, owner of the village shop and of the barn which housed the car, who, having been born and bred in these parts, had an intimate knowledge of the foreshore. One of his favourite pastimes was to survey the strand with an eagle eye for motorists in difficulty with their cars in the quicksands and then to pull them out with remarkable speed and efficiency with the aid of a length of rope and a very ancient and bedraggled model T. Ford. Not only was he able to advise on the best location for the course, but could predict with some accuracy the state in which it would be left by the next tide. Consistent unsuitability caused a day-to-day postponement of the attempt, but during this time trial runs were made, the car was proved, and the assembled company in the hotel got to know one another better and better.

A room had been set aside as a mess for the mechanics, while Kimber, Eyston and the host of visitors had their meals in the dining room upstairs. It soon became the habit for these latter to drift downstairs after dinner, in ones and twos, to the mechanics' room which rapidly became over-crowded, hilarious, and the centre of unparalleled bonhomie. Among the 'visitors' were Jimmy and Johnny, two very likeable News-Reel types, endowed with an immense capacity for beer and extremely winning ways. It was not long before they had Eyston and his company eating out of their hands. One of the resulting exploits was that Jimmy dug a hole in the sand wherein to insert a clockwork camera. He lay beside the hole while Eyston drove the car straight at it at 70 m.p.h., Jimmy tripping the camera and rolling out of the way at the last minute. Undoubtedly George was much more frightened than Jimmy, but a very remarkable shot was obtained.

A member of another news-reel team was Paul Wyan, since risen to great heights in his profession. His interest in the car and its task was intense and he had first-hand knowledge of the game, having previously been mechanic to Parry Thomas, who lost his life in a record attempt on these same sands. It was he who suggested to Jackson that all the bolt heads and other projections on the car should be 'streamlined' with plasticine. It had been noticed that the irregularities in the surface of the car collected a paste of sand and water on its journey over the course and it was obviously of advantage to minimise their effects. The job was thoroughly done even to the extent of building a trailing edge on to the front axle beam, steering arms and rear chassis cross tube, and though no figures are available, the total improvement must have been considerable. This led, later, to a re-design of the method of attachment of the undershield, whereby all the fixing bolts were blind and a perfectly smooth exterior obtained.

On the Saturday, on the advice of Wilfred Morgan it was decided to make the record attempt on Monday, Feb. 8. The timekeepers were summoned by telephone, the car given a final pat of approval and the company relaxed preparatory to the great day. The most noteworthy item of the week-end's activity was a golf match, played over the adjoining course, between MG's and the Press. There is no record of the result—if, indeed, one was obtained. Suffice it to say that the match was played with two balls, one set of golf clubs, and fifteen players a side, went on nearly all day and was, from all accounts, excruciatingly funny. Faces straightened considerably, however, when news came through that the R.A.C. timing officials on their way down from London had crashed in their car. For the moment it appeared as if further delays were inevitable. But in due course they arrived, unhurt and with their apparatus undamaged, and it was learned that they had been involved in collision with one of the MG mechanics who was on his way to Abingdon a little bit out of temper at not being allowed to remain to see the attempt.

Came the dawn, and preparation of the course began. The timing strips were laid out, start and finish banners erected and the entire length of the course, from the beginning of the run-in to the end of the pull-up distance in each direction, was scoured on foot for obstructions, chief among which were pieces of razor-like sea shells. In due time, Eyston made his trial run. On each occasion he was followed by a fire tender and by Jackson in the service van. This latter could hardly drag itself along on the soft sand and it seemed to remain a mystery to Eyston why he should have to wait so long for Jackson at the end of each run. Certainly, Jackson on arrival had no time to spend putting his van on boards and his drill was to tie the steering on full lock with a handkerchief, put the van in first gear, get out and let it go, to wander round and round in a circle until he should want it again.

The official runs were to be made just after the bottom turn of the tide, when the sand was expected to be in its best condition, but with the test runs completed, news came that the timing apparatus had broken down. The ensuing period of waiting—two hours in all—was most exasperating to all concerned, particularly Eyston. There was nothing to do but keep the car warm and watch the tide turn and come creeping up towards the course. In addition, the weather turned cold and cheerless and rain threatened. Ultimately, Kimber took a C Type over the course to test the timing apparatus and everything was declared to be in order. Eyston was pushed off. By engine speed, he was touching 126 m.p.h. in the middle of the distance and by hand timing his speed was 122 over the mile. But in the official timing gear, the ink had run dry! Previous experimenting had used all but the last drop and this was used up before the end of the run.

By the time all was ready again, patches of water had appeared on the course and conditions were deteriorating rapidly. Eyston made his runs in a flurry of spray and with a distinct 'bow-wave' over much of the distance. Jackson, following in the van on the seaward side of the course, was at times in six inches of water and could see the car check as it hit the wetter patches. No-one was surprised, therefore, when the official timing showed that 120 had not been achieved and it is an indication of the rapid deterioration of the course that the forward run gave a speed of 119·48 while the return, made less than five minutes later, was at 117·30. The mean speed, 118·39 m.p.h., broke the existing record and was, up to that date, the fastest officially recognised speed for a car in the 750-c.c. class, but the goal of two miles a minute had not been achieved. Regretfully it was decided not to persist in the attempt at Pendine.

The car was returned to Abingdon for its customary overhaul, but with the advent of the racing season, apart from a brief but glorious appearance at Brooklands at Whitsun when it recaptured the Class H lap record at 112·93, it remained unseen until the following September. Then Eyston and Palmes made the surprising decision to enter it for the Junior Car Club's 500-mile race at Brooklands. The car had been built primarily to attack short distance records up to a maximum of ten miles. It seemed to be mainly as a gesture of confidence in its mechanical reliability that Eyston was to run it in what was at that time the fastest long distance race in the world. It may be mentioned here that, although this was not to be the only occasion on which the Magic Midget should run in a race, it never achieved any success. More than once, however, it was responsible for breaking up the opposition by the cracking pace that it invariably set in the early stages. This 500 miles race, on Sept. 24, 1932, was a case in point.

No important alterations had been made during the summer and the car came to the starting line in much the same trim as at Pendine. Forty cars had been entered, among them a number of Montlhery Midgets—some supercharged, some not—and four supercharged Austins, three of which were the works team entered by Sir Herbert.

One of the other supercharged MGs was another single-seater entered and driven by R. T. Horton. On his car, which had a standard C Type Montlhery chassis, the single-seater effect had been obtained by off-setting the body and radiator, a method which gave the car a distinctly odd appearance. The handicap speed for these blown 750's was 95·78 m.p.h. and for the scratch car, Capt. Wolff Barnarto's eight litre Bentley, 120·01. Great was the consternation in the pits of the larger cars when it became apparent that both Eyston and Horton were beating their set speeds. With the race two and a half hours run, Eyston had averaged over 102 m.p.h. and was leading. Even so, Dunfee brought the Bentley up to fourth place at this stage, at the amazing average of 124·35. The pace was terrific. It could not last. And about one hour later, the front wheel of the Bentley went over the rim of the banking, Clive Dunfee fought to get it back again but the car crashed into the trees, killing its driver.

This accident happened right in front of Denly, who was co-driving with Eyston and four laps later he brought the car into the pits with a broken piston. When the engine was later dismantled for examination, Eyston advanced the theory, which was generally accepted, that Denly, confronted by the lurching Bentley, did what in ordinary circumstances he would never have done—took his foot off the throttle suddenly.

It is an interesting comment on the sportsmanship of the racing game in general, and of George Eyston in particular, that, no sooner had he notified the retirement of his car, than he set about helping Horton. Horton prepared his own car for races and, on this occasion, the sole occupant of his pit was his one faithful mechanic. Not even a superman can spot, keep a lap chart, work the stop watches and give pit signals, let alone minister to the other requirements of driver and car. In short, Horton was off on his own. If the car kept going, he would be likely to be somewhere in the money at the finish, but beyond that, he had little information about what was going on around him. Eyston saw from his chart that Horton was lying fourth and immediately gave instructions for his own pit to be closed and for the entire personnel and equipment to move into Horton's. After a few minutes' intensive work with the watches, Eyston was to be seen holding out Horton's 'Faster' signal and the entire pit cheered and waved each time the odd-looking car came by. Gradually Horton improved his position, finally to win the race at an average speed of 96 m.p.h. for the 500 miles.

With the race over and with it the end of the racing season, attention turned again to the question of attaining 120 m.p.h. That this was not a matter of great difficulty everyone knew, but the problem was complicated by Eyston's intention of using the car for an attack on all the class records up to twelve hours. It was essential that the car should not have to be stressed too near its limit for the mile and the kilometre. During the summer, the new AB Type cylinder head had been developed and tested on the C Types and production plans were well advanced for the new J Series of sports and racing cars on which it was to be a standard fitting. Up to the time of Pendine, EX 127 had retained the old original AA head as Eldridge had fitted this with his own design of valve gear and was loath to part with it. But now the change was made, the only indication being that the familiar three exhaust pipe stubs on the left side of the bonnet were replaced by four. To improve the shape, the cockpit was re-designed so as completely to enclose the driver, and Eyston planned, should he be troubled with fumes, to wear a face mask and breathing pipe. His appearance, clad in asbestos suit—which he had worn ever since the fire on EX 120—and adorned with gas mask, climbing into the tiny car called to mind some of the mechanical extravaganzas of H. G. Wells.

The plan for his next visit to Montlhery was bold and comprehensive. In fact the intention was to attack every Class H record from the flying kilometre to the 24 hours, and to achieve, into the bargain, 120 m.p.h. It had been decided to use EX 127 for the records up to 12 hours, and for one of the new J3 supercharged sports cars to carry on from there up to 24 hours. If the venture were successful, MG would hold every Class H record, E. R. Hall having two months previously captured the standing start mile and kilometre records with a blown C Type. With T. H. Wisdom to share the driving of the J3, Eyston, Denly, Jackson and Marney and the two cars set out for Montlhery at the end of the first week in December.

On arrival, they found the track ice-bound and waited for a break in the frost, but when this came, rain fell and, after a further period of waiting, it was decided to make a start on the wet track. After test, Eyston complained that the 'shut in' feeling given by the new cowl was most unpleasant and that, although there was little in the way of fumes, the atmosphere was oppressive. So the cowling was partially cut away, the ventilation improved and, after a change to smaller wheels, the car was pushed off. It fled round the track, took the one kilometre and one mile at 120·56 and went on to take the records up to ten kilometres.

There followed a long period of waiting for the weather, fog having come down, and it was five days before they could continue. Then, at three o'clock in the afternoon, Eyston took the J3 away on the first three-hour spell of the twenty-four hours. This run, too, was uneventful except for the fracture of a fuel line as the result of which Wisdom, who was driving at the time, had to push the car for the best part of half a lap to bring it into the pit area. But apart from this it ran steadily on through the night and the following day, to raise the 2000-kilometre and 24-hour records by some five miles per hour at over 70.

Immediately this was over, Eyston declared his intention of taking advantage of the fine weather and starting on the 12-hour record with EX 127 the next morning. To make use of every minute of daylight he would start before dawn, the car being equipped, for the first three-hour spell, with batteries and four headlamps on a bar across the front. Further to assist, hurricane lanterns were to be placed at intervals round the track. All was in readiness by 6.30 in the morning and in the eerie light of a lowering sky, which added the finishing touch to a fantastic scene, George took the car away. For the first three hours he averaged 94·59, and then brought the car in for the headlamps and batteries to be removed and for Denly to continue. At six hours the speed was 92·79 and Eyston took over again. Denly, in the pit, began to worry about his last spell, knowing that he would have to finish in the dark. The headlamps were to be refitted at nine hours, but they—somewhat naturally—did not illuminate the car's instruments. In Denly's estimation, Eyston, having settled his speed by the tachometer and then attuned himself to the engine note, would go sailing merrily round. Denly, on the other hand, liked to have a look at his oil pressure and his thermometers from time to time. They told him much even if they did sometimes tend to instil a little anxiety. So, before nine hours were up, a pocket flash lamp had been procured and lashed to Denly's chest with string. He could, periodically, switch it on and momentarily view the dials. How important this was to be nobody then knew.

During Eyston's second spell the weather deteriorated, wind increased in violence, and bits broke off the surrounding trees and blew about the track. Denly took over at nine hours and for his first lap or two could be heard cutting his engine as he fought for control, the car being repeatedly blown off its course. As soon as he had become accustomed to its tricks, he settled down to a steady speed and Eyston, having despatched all available hands to collect debris from the track, turned in for some sleep. Darkness fell and the waiting mechanics and drivers, watching the fleeting car, could see now and again a faint yellow glow from the cockpit as Bert used his lamp. Suddenly and literally at the proverbial eleventh hour, the watchers heard the engine splutter and cut. Eyston heard it too and came sprinting, blear-eyed, across the track. Simultaneously Denly came coasting in with the cockpit cover raised and yelling 'oil pressure'. Examination showed the reserve tank empty and about one quart of oil in the engine. This was rapidly replenished with the spare oil which was kept constantly hot on a spirit stove, and Denly was away again, cracking off with laps of 95. But in a very short time he returned, needing more oil and with the cockpit full of smoke so that it was thought at first that the car was on fire. To keep the cockpit clear, the cover was discarded and Denly, from then on, wore goggles. Now a yet more serious situation arose. It was clear that the stock of oil in the pit would not last the distance; such a voracious appetite for oil, from any cause, had not been foreseen. Immediate action was imperative, and Eyston was equal to the occasion. Shouting to Jackson to follow, he rushed across the track, scaled the inner wall, and ran to the Wakefield store, only to find that it was shut up for the night. With improvised implements, George and Jackson stove in the door, seized a five-gallon drum of 'Castrol R' apiece, and set off back, Eyston, with a full drum in his arms, running all the way. (This is a feat which is recommended to those who from time to time cast anxious glances at their waistlines.) Denly, still fighting wind and rain, continued to call every few laps for replenishment, but kept going until the twelve hours were completed, the car averaging 86·67 m.p.h. for the whole distance and taking eight other records on the way. Denly was plastered from head to foot in oil and was found to be sitting in a large pool of it, subsequent investigation showing that the back half of the rear main bearing had broken away, letting oil straight into the clutch and thence into the cockpit. How the clutch held, nobody could say. But MG, at this point, held every Class H record.

While the old C Types were showing signs of their age, during the summer of 1932, the design of their successors, the new J Series, was reaching finality. One particular feature of the C Type, in the latter stages of the development of its engine, was that it had become too fast for its brakes. The road racing version of the J Type, the Series J4, was therefore equipped with brakes twelve inches in diameter, as distinct from the eight-inch drums of its predecessor. These were adapted to the Magic Midget for the J.C.C. International Trophy race, in which stopping power was to be of great importance, but the test was prematurely curtailed by the loss of a rear road wheel after only a few laps. The inquest on this showed that one of the discs with which the rear wheels were fitted had become nipped at the hub and, although the wheel nut appeared to be quite tight, in fact it was not, and the heavy braking to which the car was subjected undid the nut and the wheel fell off. Thus, for the second time, this car failed in a race.

In August of 1933, Hamilton's new J4 put up an astonishing performance in the Ulster T.T., as will be recounted later. It was with the engine from this car that the Magic Midget was equipped when next it appeared at Montlhery. And in the meantime, the car had been re-bodied.

It had been apparent for some while that the original body was a good deal larger than it need be and it was decided to reduce it. Unfortunately, the limiting factor was George Eyston who already fitted it quite closely. An attempt was made to narrow the front and tail leaving the cockpit at roughly the same size as before, but the result looked all wrong—the widest part of it was behind the centre point of the car and there was a fairly sharp change of section just in front of the driver. Something had to be done about it, but time was running short. The body builders worked day and night to finish it and when they had done so—Eyston could not get in. There was only one thing to be done—Denly had to drive.

The next visit to Montlhery, in October, was particularly interesting because of the presence at the track, in addition to the Midget, of a Riley, prepared by the brothers McClure, with which Eyston was attacking Class G records, and of Murray Jamieson, who was tuning the blown Austin for attempts on the Midget's records. A close camaraderie grew up between the crews, as a result of which they assisted in the work on one another's engines—a most unusual occurrence between rival camps. Jamieson took a particularly keen interest in the MG just as Jackson and Denly did in the Austin, but afterwards Jamieson confessed that he was completely misled by the seemingly happy-go-lucky methods of the other two. Denly, on the other hand, was under no illusions as to what the Austin was doing. The workshops at Montlhery were under the track, the latter forming the roof. Above the MG stall was a joint in the concrete and it was necessary only to stand underneath with thumb poised on stop watch trigger to get a fairly accurate timing of the Austin, the crash of its passage over the joint at one hundred and seventeen miles per hour or so being sufficient to cause involuntary operation of the watch.

When the MG was ready and on a favourable evening, the car was wheeled out, and Jamieson came over to witness the trial. Denly was pushed off, handling the car so expertly—and with such fox-like guile—that nobody who did not already know realised that there were no intermediate gears in the gearbox. These had been removed to save weight, spinners being fitted to the mainshaft to lift oil to the bearings, and Denly slipped the clutch—the top gear ratio was over four to one—so as to simulate acceleration through the gears.

With all their experience of Montlhery, the MG crew had no need to take complete lap times to assess the behaviour of the car. They had long since devised a system on the basis that, if after passing point A at 4000 r.p.m. the car had achieved, say, 5700 at point B, it was good enough. On this occasion the car ran sweet and crisp and went as it had never gone before. Denly brought the car in and said, simply, "We'll just about scrape it", but Jackson caught half a glance and knew from Denly's demeanour that he was excited. The car was locked up for the night, and the boys went off into Paris for a party.

On the following day the attempt was made. Work on the other cars stopped and everybody came to watch. The car was brought from its lock-up and the mechanics proceeded to change the rear wheels and fit those having 19 × 4·75 in. tyres. These, propped against the car alongside the 19 × 4's that had been used for the test the night before, looked, as somebody said at the time, like 'the wheels off a bus'. Even at this stage Jamieson thought that an elaborate 'gag' was being perpetrated by the crazy MG crew as he did not believe that it was possible for the car to pull a gear ratio five per cent higher than had been used the night before. But Denly had not been excited without

A good view of a typical early MG supercharger installation—in this case, the J3 with No. 6A Powerplus.

X

The Q Type Track-racing Midget. The engine in standard racing tune gave the equivalent of 150 b.h.p. per litre and provided 175 h.p. per ton. The car sold, in 1934, for £550.

The Zoller-MG Supercharger installation on the Q Type.

Top: EX 127 at its depot at Montlhery, 1933, BERT DENLY, begoggled, has just

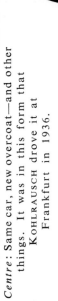

Centre: Same car, new overcoat—and other things. It was in this form that KOHLRAUSCH drove it at Frankfurt in 1936.

Below: GEORGE EYSTON with the tap turned on at Montlhery.

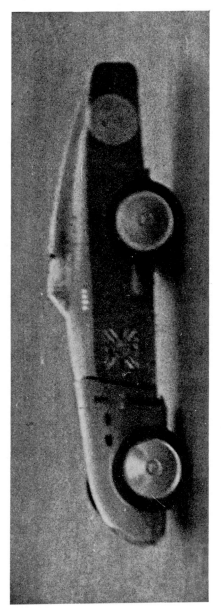

For many years I ran it in FX 420. In thi... when the car is running on an M.Type front axle beam and the whole of the front...

This is the first MG record-breaker. Clearly there was a lot to learn about 'streamlining'.

Coppa Acerbo, Pescara, Italy, 1935. The R Type begins to show signs of its characteristic outward lean.

DENIS EVANS, R Type, having lost his crash-hat on the previous lap, goes on to break the Brooklands Class H Mountain Lap Record.

reason and had a pretty shrewd idea what the car would do. He was driving under Eyston's instructions 'to keep a little in hand for the next time', but he had set his heart on earning a Montlhery 200-kilo badge with a 750-c.c. car. This was a badge presented to drivers who lapped the Piste de Vitesse at a speed of over 200 kilometres an hour and whereas many were worn by those who had driven cars of two litres or so of engine size, nobody had so far earned one with a Class H car.

The banking of the two semi-circular ends of the track is very high and steep, joined by two short, almost flat, straights. Denly, once he had got the car going well, skimmed round the turns high up, diving down on to the straights and then climbing away up the other side. It was a most inspiring sight, but Denly's only comment was that the steering wheel, which had been reduced to a mere ten inches in diameter, 'kept him busy'. After a lap or two, the figures '206' appeared in the window of the timekeepers' box and three of the watchers, each holding a board five feet square, stood on the edge of the track so that Bert might read his speed next time round. He covered the mile and kilometre at 128·62 and went on up to ten miles at over 125, reporting on completion that he had sufficient power in hand to do 135 when required. The performance bewildered Jamieson, who frankly admitted that he knew he could not equal it during that year. It was a very crestfallen crew which packed up the Austin and its gear and set off back to England.

Eyston, Denly and Jackson stayed on, the former performing further 'deeds of dash and daring' with the Riley while Jackson prepared EX 127 for a further attempt to improve the one-hour record and any others which might be encountered on the way. This involved, primarily, the provision of cooling for the oil sump which, for the short records, had been blanked off by the undershield. In addition, Denly asked for the front Hartford shock absorbers to be removed. In the original design, the damping of front axle movement had been shared between hydraulic and friction type shock absorbers, both of these being adjusted to a fairly light setting. But the latter type, which were of scissor action, came outside the front fairing and hung in the slip stream. It was decided to run without them in the interest of reduced weight and wind resistance.

The decision proved to be a mistake, for, after some forty minutes of faultless running, observers near the timing box—opposite which was the only serious inequality in the surface of the Montlhery track— noticed that the right-hand front wheel was leaving the ground. As time went on, the condition grew worse and each time round the wheel seemed to rise higher and higher until it was obvious that Denly was having a most uncomfortable ride. Only the top of his head was visible through the cowl, but this was sufficient to show the grimace which he

D

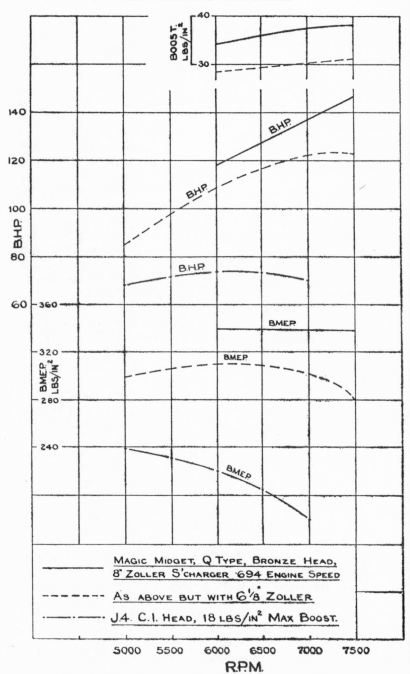

Fig. 6.

pulled in anticipation of each bump. The effect of this upon the car is clearly reflected in the speeds at which the records were taken, fifty miles being covered at 114·47 and one hundred miles at 111·17. In one hour, the car covered 110·87 miles, breaking the previous record by a handsome margin.

This proved to be the last appearance of EX 127 in the hands of the Eyston-Palmes scuderia, although there were yet to be several occasions on which it was to shock the motoring world. By change of ownership, it ceased to be an instrument of trial and development under the direct eye of the MG Company, though they were yet to learn much from it.

The new owner was Bobby Kohlrausch, a German racing driver who had achieved considerable prominence at the wheel of Opels, Austins and MGs. He took the car as it stood, but with the addition of the front brakes it had worn for the International Trophy, and entered it in road races. Bobby was small in stature and sat so low in the car that his feet were inches higher than his seat. He found that, in road racing, the blood drained from his legs and cramp ensued. It was not long before he had removed the body and returned the chassis to Abingdon for a new one to be fitted. By this time, the new Q Type car had been built and the opportunity was taken to re-engine the car with the latest type in which a three bearing crankshaft was used. The new body was a single-seat, light-alloy-panelled affair in which the driver sat much higher and obtained a commanding view all around him—a feature notably absent from the original body. Finished in white—the German racing colour—the tail was embellished, on Kohlrausch's instructions, with his racing emblem, a four-leafed clover on one side and a Union Jack on the other. It is significant that, on his first subsequent appearance in Germany, the Nazis made him remove the latter!

In May, 1935, Kohlrausch took the car to Gyon, in Hungary, and despite the unsuitable nature of the body for records, attacked the flying mile and kilo and the standing start records over the same distances. The former were taken at a shade over 130 m.p.h. Difficulties with fuel and carburation had delayed the attempt until late in the day and there was no time to change the rear axle ratio, as had been intended, before attempting the standing start records. Despite this Kohlrausch raised the kilometre record by four miles an hour to 81·79 and pushed the mile record from 85·5 to 93·4 m.p.h., thereby not only proving the car, but setting a seal upon his own ability as a front rank driver. It is a forceful comment on the rate of development of the 750-c.c. car that this speed for the standing start mile eclipsed the record for the flying mile of but five years previously.

A string of successes in road races and hill climbs followed, in the course of which Bobby made and fitted a bronze cylinder head. Then he decided to have another crack at the flying mile and kilometre, having been convinced on the previous occasion that, given more time, much higher speeds could be achieved. The engine was removed and, accompanied by Artur Baldt, Kohlrausch's mechanic, it was returned to Abingdon. After overhaul, tests were run with two sizes of Zoller supercharger and with two sets of blower gearing, the idea being that Kohlrausch could subsequently pick the combination to suit the particular event for which he was entering. Attention was concentrated, however, on the large blower with the higher gearing.

It was on one Sunday morning that the final tests were to be run and it was with elation and no little surprise that Jackson, Enever and Baldt saw the indicator on the test bed brake run up to 145 b.h.p. when the 'taps were turned on'. This indication was only momentary as 'everything then lit up' and the motor banged and spat and had to be shut down. But the power was there—they had all three seen it and Baldt, particularly, would be satisfied with nothing less. It remained to find out how to sustain it. With the head off, a detailed examination of valves and plugs was made and Enever came to the conclusion that the cooling of the exhaust valves had to be improved. The only simple way to do this was to extend the bronze valve guides to embrace the stem right up to the valve head, but it was Sunday, no bronze bar was available, and Baldt was due to return to Germany next day. The method adopted was crude but effective; the bronze guides were pressed out of the head, sawn in two, and short lengths of cast iron guide were interposed as packing pieces. Next time up, the engine recorded, and held 146 brake horse power; the engine speed was 7,500 r.p.m. and the blower pressure 39 lb.! The noise set all Abingdon by the ears.

Back in Germany, the engine was installed, the original single-seater body was fitted and on the Frankfurt Autobahn, Kohlrausch covered the flying mile at 140·6 m.p.h. This was almost the end of the story of this astonishing vehicle, but in the years immediately preceding the war, Bobby parted with it to Mercedes-Benz. Whether this was done voluntarily or under Nazi duress we shall never know, but one smiles wryly when one pictures the mystification of the German designers when they stripped the engine and the valve guides pressed out in three separate little bits!

CHAPTER VI

THE J's

WHAT'S in a name? Maybe that is a mere cliché, but it is still the essence of a very important problem to anyone who has anything to make and sell. Boards of management, in every industry, spend hours deliberating upon the label to be applied to their products, and motor manufacturers have given examples in the names of their vehicles of every possible approach, it seems, from Model T, 30/98, Mark IV, to 6/80, Typhoon, 4 CLT, and so on *ad lib.*—or *ad nauseam*, according to what you feel about it.

An attempt was made in an earlier chapter to show how MGs came to be known by Marks, but this system soon died, partly because the large 6-cylinder car was discontinued and partly because, when Mark III was reached, Mark IV had been used already. That, too, has been explained. Someone in the Records Office, seeing this difficulty coming, started to use the alphabet, so that the Mark II was known alternatively as the A and the Mark III as the B Type. Thus, when the Montlhery Midget came along, C was ready waiting for it, and so on with subsequent types. It was a minor snag to this system that M was already bespoke, as it were, though how the original Midget came to have that letter nobody quite knows. The alliterative association undoubtedly had something to do with it, but it is now another case of the chicken and the egg.

Shortly after the alphabetical system was established, it became apparent that if a new letter were taken up for each model having a shade of difference from its precursor, the alphabet would very soon be used up. To avoid this it was decided to couple cars which were basically similar under one letter and differentiate them by suffix numerals. Thus in this chapter, we are concerned with the J1, the J2, the J3 and the J4, all of the same general design but differing in some more or less major particular. The J1 chassis carried four-seat open and closed bodies, the J2 was the open sports two-seat version, the J3 similar but supercharged, and the J4 the racing car.

In order to get the whole pattern of the evolution of these models quite clear it is as well to 'recap', as they say. The M Type Midget started it all and from this grew the C Type Montlhery, the first racing model. We have seen that each racing car, in order that it should pay its way and yet be moderate in price, had its sports counterpart and, in this case, the sports chassis was the D Type, to which four-seat open and salonette bodies were fitted. All three of these—the M, the C and the D—were being produced concurrently, and between them formed a complete range of Midgets. There arose, however, simultaneously with the D Type, the first of a new series of small 6-cylinder cars, the F Type Magna. This, although it formed an integral part of the range, might be regarded as a composite car in that, with the exception of its engine and the fact that the chassis had been lengthened by eight inches, it was built almost entirely of components used in the C and D Types. D Type axles, brake gear and bodies, C Type gearbox and an engine which was virtually M Type with two cylinders added, combined to form a car of which it was facetiously said that it had length but no breadth, but which was, nevertheless, much sought after in its day. Its importance at this stage of our story is, however, that it provides a first-class illustration of the use of interchangeability of major components between models.

As the end of the allotted span of the D and M Types came in sight, their successors, the J1 and J2, began to take shape. It will be remembered that a limit was set to the performance of the C Type by the AA cylinder head, in which inlet and exhaust ports were all on one side, and that the AB head, with inlets on one side and exhausts on the other, was developed to overcome this. This AB head was designed primarily for the J Series, and on the unsupercharged sports versions twin carburetters were used—a feature which was to remain invariable for years. The original racing four-speed gearbox was unnecessarily massive for the sports car and a new lightweight close-ratio box came into being, this too, remaining constantly in production on a succession of models up to the end of 1936. In all other respects the J1 and J2 chassis followed well-tried C Type practice very closely.

But the J2 model broke new ground in the design of its super-structure, and it was here that the rather spartan two-door body, with severely cut-away sides, first appeared in production form, perpetuating the improvised modification made to some of the C Types during the previous year. Whereas the M and C bodies had carried tapering tails, the J2 was square and short, providing a flat surface on to which a large deep petrol tank could conveniently be bolted, and permitting the spare wheel to be carried accessibly and unobtrusively on a bracket behind the tank. This general form of body construction, first employed on the J2 MG Midget in the middle of 1932, established a line which was followed almost unchanged down to 1955 through a succession of some seven distinct Midget models.

The racing member of the J family, the J4, did not appear until the spring of 1933, some nine months after its sports counterpart, and it is instructive to examine the reason. Supercharging on the C Type had produced a car which was a little too fast for its brakes, and there was every intention of making the J4 go a good deal faster. All the small cars so far produced, from M to J2 and including the F Magna, had used the same eight-inch brake gear, and it was therefore necessary to develop new gear for the new racing car. Again the grisly problem of cost reared its head—the price per car of, say, a dozen and a half sets of special brake gear would have been prohibitive—and it was necessary to incorporate this brake gear in a standard sports model which would be produced in some quantity. Such an opportunity was afforded by the successor to the F Magna, the new 6-cylinder car, Type L. Of this model we shall say more anon, but it was destined to be very fast, and good brakes were imperative.

The J4 therefore consisted of the J2 chassis frame and axles, L Type twelve-inch diameter brakes, the C gearbox, and a doorless racing body in light alloy in the new shape with a large slab petrol tank behind. The cylinder block was redesigned in detail, partly to permit an increase in the diameter of the head studs from $\frac{5}{16}$ in. to $\frac{3}{8}$ in., and partly to provide water holes to coincide with those of the new AB head. The crankshaft was fully counterbalanced and machined from the solid, being similar to that used in the later C Types. No. 7 and No. 8 Power-plus superchargers, giving twelve and fourteen pounds maximum boost respectively, were available as standard equipment, but before the car had been long in use, the boost pressure was raised to eighteen pounds. The induction system was re-designed, the double diameter pipe being dispensed with, and, by turning the blower upside down so that the carburetter came on the left-hand side, a reasonably short inlet pipe from blower to manifold was achieved.

The J4 first saw the daylight in the spring of 1933, in the same month as the 1087 K3 Magnette. This latter car was to prove to be as big a surprise to the handicappers—and others—as the C Type Midget had been two years earlier, and it tended to steal the J4's thunder. The new Midget, however, had a great exponent in Hugh Hamilton, who drove it with conspicuous success in road-races and hill climbs all over the continent of Europe, as well as taking it into second place behind Nuvolari on the Magnette in a very hard-fought Ulster T.T. Hamilton took delivery of the first J4 to be built, put it on a train to Nurburg, and won his class and broke the lap record in the Eifelrennen. Later in the year in July he found himself in Germany again, whither he had come to race in the German Grand Prix, but this event was with little notice postponed until October. He therefore cast around for an opportunity to use his well-prepared car and entered it—standard axle ratio and all— in an event which, at the time, was certainly not his cup of tea, the German Grand Prix Hill Climb at Freiburg. He found the hill to be over seven miles long and to have, reputedly, one hundred and seventy bends amid very beautiful but very terrifying mountains. Nothing daunted, Hammy turned the wicks well up and not only won his class and broke the class record, but made the fastest time of all cars up to two litres.

All this time, Hamilton was learning and, ere his untimely death in the Swiss Grand Prix of 1934, he was to prove himself to be in the top flight of racing drivers. He acquired his skill not only by competing in every event that presented itself, but by the most critical observation of other drivers. Indicative of this was a remark he made on his return from one of the many excursions overseas that, in sharp contrast to the heavy and almost brutal manipulation of the gear stick by the average British driver of his acquaintance, the Continental driver "handled his gear lever knob as if it were a precious stone". Only those who had the good fortune to know Hammy will realise that this was a strangely romantic phrase to be used by one so hard-headed and down-to-earth, and that he must have felt very strongly about it. It is open to question, however, whether he ever translated this particular lesson into his own practice, as most of us will remember him driving with dash and precision but conveying, by the hunching of his shoulders over the wheel and despite flickering smiles of sheer enjoyment, an impression of fierceness which boded ill for any mechanical contrivance which did not immediately go exactly where he wanted it.

Whether it was this tendency or whether his enthusiasm outran his discretion, there was one occasion on which he blotted his copy-book pretty badly with the boys at Abingdon who had prepared his car. It had been made ready for an attempt on the Mountain Lap Record at Brooklands and was fitted, therefore, with a very much lower axle ratio than normal. It was loaded on its lorry and sent off to the track on the Thursday preceding the meeting, and all who had been working on it sighed with relief to see it go in such good time.

Cousins was summoned, on the Saturday night, to meet Mr. Kimber at the factory on Sunday morning. This was not altogether an unusual occurrence during the racing season, but on this occasion Cousins felt it was a bit queer, as he had no prior intimation of what it might be about. He arrived at the factory somewhat ahead of schedule, and there found Hammy's car looking as if a hand grenade had been lobbed into it. A quick examination showed that beyond doubt the propeller shaft had parted in the middle, and that the car had not been sauntering at the critical time. Kimber arrived and proceeded, straight away, to dress Cousins down in no uncertain terms for permitting the car to leave in such a dangerous condition.

Now, the racing department at Abingdon had had some of this sort of thing already and had grown a little tired of straightening out over-revved engines. Only a few weeks before this particular incident they had begun to fit, to the tachometer dials, a very small non-return-able finger which stayed at the maximum reading obtained. Cousins had noticed that, on Hamilton's car, this pointed to 8,200 r.p.m.!

What is more, he knew that Hammy, even in his wildest moments, could be relied upon not to exceed the permitted maximum engine speed by more than ten per cent or so on the indirects, but that, in top, the sky was the limit. Foot flat on the floor and do all the rest on the steering wheel—that was Hamilton.

When Kimber paused for breath, Cousins was able to begin to point this out, explaining the while that, with this particular axle ratio, 8·2 in top represented 120 m.p.h.; that it was clear that Mr. Hamilton had taken the car round the outer circuit; and if that was the sort of thing he was going to do with cars that the chaps burned their midnight oil on, then Mr. Hamilton so far as he, Cousins, was concerned could — — — mend his own propshafts. Or words to that effect. Later, Hamilton confessed that he had been so carried away by the behaviour of the car that he had done just as Cousins had divined. Moreover, he explained that it was the bump over the Water Bridge, where the back wheels came off the ground for longer than usual, that put the finishing touch to things. On the credit side of all this, Hammy never did it again.

It is almost inevitable that a story of the achievements of the J4 should become, for a short spell, a motor-racing biography of Hugh Hamilton, though this does not mean that the type did not distinguish itself in other hands. Mansell's car stayed the course in the astonishing Mannin Beg race in the Isle of Man in 1933 when all but three cars 'blew up'—as we shall see when we come to tell of the K3 Magnette. Ford and Baumer took another J4 into third place in the same race, having been placed sixth in the general classification at Le Mans earlier in the year. And Tommy Simister won the Southport 100 miles with a similar car. But nothing could eclipse the 1933 T.T. In this race, Nuvolari on the K3 and Hamilton on the J4 had an absolute dog-fight for over three hours, each repeatedly breaking his lap record, until Hamilton, having stopped for petrol on his last lap, finished forty seconds behind Nuvolari, who crossed the line with a dry tank. Hamilton's speed for the race, 73·46 m.p.h., exceeded the *lap* record speed of the previous year. A week later, he captured the Brooklands mountain lap record at 69·28 m.p.h., and a week later still, the 1100 c.c. class lap record in the Masaryk Grand Prix in Czecho Slovakia, after which he crashed and spent some weeks in hospital.

We cannot leave this subject of the Js without specific reference to the J3. Strictly this was not intended as a racing car, but was a super-charged sports car in series production. Basically it was a J2, with the engine modified to bring it within the 750-c.c. International Class H and with a No. 6A Powerplus supercharger fitted in the normal position between the dumb-irons. The engine alteration was achieved merely by shortening the stroke to 71 mm., a forged crankshaft, referred to colloquially as of the 'bent wire' variety, being used in place of the fully machined and counterbalanced crank of the racing engines.

One such car, in the hands of W. E. Belgrave, secured a Coupe des Glaciers in the International Alpine trial of 1933, and another won the Reineck Mountain Race in Liechtenstein in the same year. But the model's greatest single contribution to our story was its record-breaking run at Montlhery in December, 1932, when, as already recounted, it took all the 750-c.c. records from twelve to twenty-four hours, and helped to secure for MG the signal distinction of holding every International Class H Record.

CHAPTER VII

K 3

WHEN one is making a successful 4-cylinder car, it is a very attractive proposition to add two cylinders to the engine, insert the requisite corresponding inches in the length of the chassis frame and call it a day. This reduces design and tools to a minimum, practically everything being already in existence, even down to the majority of the engine details. That the higher engine power necessitates stronger transmission and more powerful brakes, and that the whole machine may possibly exhibit marked signs of instability because of the departure from an ideal wheelbase to track ratio, tend to become secondary considerations. This was certainly the case with the F Type Magna already mentioned, and the position might have been serious had it not been for the fact that the power output of the engine was, fortunately perhaps, not as clever as it should have been. Those who hotted up their engines found that the margin of safety, particularly in the transmission, was pretty low.

Thus it was that when the successors to the F Type were being considered, an adequate margin of safety was left to take care of future development, while practical use could be made of the enormous fund of knowledge and experience which had derived from EX 120 and EX 127.

The shaping of the 1933 programme, which was taking place during most of the previous year, was complicated. The Midget sports cars, J1 and J2, were straightforward and were in production by the middle of the year. The 750-c.c. racing car, the J4, was settled and merely awaited its brake gear. The direct successor to the F Type Magna was to be the Magna L Type, but in addition to these models, a somewhat larger chassis, suitable to carry full four-seat open and closed bodies, was decided upon.

Thus began the series of K Types, with the most potent of which we are primarily concerned in this chapter. It should here be recalled that, although building of the 18/80 Mark II Saloons had terminated during the latter part of 1931, such cars were still selling from stock well into 1932, and a car was needed to maintain this particular market. And behind the planning of these various types lay the important consideration that, the Class H board having been swept pretty clean and the handicappers being now wise to the potentialities of the Midget, the next racing car would have to be in the 1100-c.c. Class G.

The C, D and F Types appeared during 1931; the J, K and L Types in 1932. So it is clear that design and development shops became attuned to high pressure work during this period. But this was nothing to the fever which was created by the decision, taken late in 1932, to enter a team of three supercharged K3 Magnettes in the Italian Mille Miglia, to be run on April 8 and 9, 1933. With less than six months to go, the initial design was not complete, building of even the prototype had not begun and the engine—a completely new design for use in both the new L and K Type cars—had not turned one revolution in supercharged form. Yet in those six months the prototype was to be completed, it was to spend five weeks away from the factory on a trip to Italy for test on the Mille Miglia course, certain bits of the design then revised, three cars built, shipped to Italy, tested 'on site' and then driven to victory in their class, breaking the existing class records by a handsome margin and winning the Team Prize. This object lesson in getting things done reads, in these days, it is to be regretted, rather like a fairy story.

The track width of the K3 was 4 ft., greater than the Midgets' by 6 in.; the wheelbase 7 ft. $10\frac{3}{16}$ in., an odd measurement which had no particular significance—it just worked out that way.

The chassis frame followed existing MG practice very closely, and, leaving aside engine and gearbox for the moment, it can be said that the car as a whole was a scaled-up version of the J4 Midget. Specific mention must, however, be made of the steering and brakes.

Orthodox steering layouts on the majority of small cars of the period incorporated a transverse push-pull rod, or drag-link, coupling the steering box to the left-hand front wheel, which in turn coupled to the right-hand wheel by a track rod. There were two main disadvantages of this system. In the first place, the road movement of the left-hand front wheel was normally vertical, whereas the end of the drag-link was constrained to move in an arc about its steering box end. Road shocks, therefore, produced either an unwanted directional variation of the front road wheels or a kick of the steering wheel, or both. In the second place, it was customary for the ball joints at each end of the drag-link and at each end of the track rod to be spring-loaded. Admittedly, the spring movement was very small, but it sufficed, often enough, to give the steering a spongy and indefinite 'feel'. An attempt to eliminate, or at least alleviate, these disadvantages was made in the design of the K Type steering. A secondary steering arm was introduced, hinged near the centre of the front axle beam at a point where the movement of the beam relative to the chassis, taking the average of all forms of road-shock, would be a minimum. The free end of this arm was coupled to the steering box and also, by two short 'half track rods', to each wheel. The spring-loading of the joints of these track rods was so arranged that the steering of the inner wheel, which, on either lock, turned through the greater arc due to the Ackerman principle, was solid, i.e. the springs were on the unloaded side of the balls.

Brakes followed the normal MG lay-out, with cables actuated from a central cross-shaft, but, on the K Types, the diameter was increased to twelve inches. A determined effort was made to keep weight within reasonable bounds by the use of Elektron for back-plates, shoes and drums, with cast iron liners in the latter.

The engine, while following the general form of previous types, was subjected to re-design in practically every detail, whereas the counterbalanced cranks of the C and J4 Types had been carried in two bearings, one of which was a ball race, the new engine had, per-force, to have four. The two intermediate bearings were carried in circular housings which exceeded in diameter the overall dimensions of the crankshaft and these, after being fitted to the shaft, were threaded endwise into the block. This system had already been employed in the F Magna engine but, whereas the F Type had detachable, bronze backed bearing shells held in an aluminium alloy housing, the new engine used forged steel housings with the bearing metal applied direct. This arrangement, taken in conjunction with cylindrical sleeve bearings at front and rear, had very high inherent rigidity.

Two additional cylinders of the same dimensions as the J4 would have brought the engine over the 1100-c.c. limit. The stroke was there-fore shortened by two millimetres to give six cylinders measuring 57 by 71 reducing the swept volume to 1086 c.c., a convenient capacity to permit moderate re-boring without exceeding the Class G limitations.

The by now standard valve timing was retained, but the camshaft was of larger diameter to increase rigidity. Size and disposition of valves and combustion chamber space remained as on J4, but the valves were made of KE 965. Straight cut bevel gears replaced the helical bevels in the camshaft drive, as gear noise was of little con-sequence in a racing car. A water pump was added, mounted on the left side of the front bearing housing, the drive being taken from the same skew gear as drove the oil pump and distributor shaft. The distributor itself was replaced by an angle drive box feeding a magneto mounted on the right side of the engine. In front of the engine, a No. 9 Powerplus supercharger was mounted, driven through a built-in reduction gear at approximately three-quarters engine speed. Ki-gass starting equipment sprayed into the induction pipe, close to the inlet ports.

It was aft the engine that the revolutionary feature of the car was to be found—the preselector epicyclic self-changing gear box, which was to contribute so much to the car's success, and on one occasion, at least, bring about its downfall. The use of such a box on a racing car was not new, but this was the first time it had appeared as part of the standard equipment of such a machine. The method of control had an air of novelty about it, too, the preselector lever being mounted in a fore-and-aft quadrant on an extension of the gearbox top, in a position similar to that occupied by the normal MG gear stick. For the rest, as has already been said, the car followed previous MG practice very closely.

The building of the prototype in this from was pushed ahead as fast as possible; the first power unit was tested on the bed and exceeded one hundred horse power on a quick run up to maximum speed; and at the end of the first week in January, Jackson left Abingdon with the car, en route for Milan where the members of the team, Earl Howe, Sir Henry Birkin, Captain Eyston, Bernard Rubin and Count Johnny Lurani, were to test the car over the actual Mille Miglia course. The sixth member of the team was to be Hugh Hamilton, but his job of work tied him to London at this time. Lord Howe travelled with the car from Newhaven, and a visit was paid to the Bugatti works at Molsheim en route. M. Ettore Bugatti himself displayed great interest in the car and examined it in detail. Notably on seeing the front axle, he waved a deprecatory hand and stated categorically that it was not strong enough.

Northern Italy in January is likely to be a very different place from Northern Italy in spring and this particular year exhibited the variation very strongly. Some of the mountainous parts of the course through the Apennines were impassable because of snow, and a large part of the rest of the route was ice-bound. Despite this, the car was given a very thorough test and, although full of promise, a long list of modifications was yielded. As far as possible, these were notified to Abingdon as they arose, so that their embodiment into the final design of the three team cars could begin, but there was inevitably much that could not be dealt with until the prototype returned to England. A few examples will indicate the sort of troubles which were thrown up by the test, and serve to underline the fantastic task which confronted the technicians at Abingdon in the short time available. To start with the great Ettore had disliked the look of the front axle beam and he was not likely to say such a thing for fun. Jackson therefore telephoned the bare bones of this information to Abingdon; the stress-men had another go at their calculations; and conference decided that the safety factor was, perhaps, not what it might be. The decision to bring through a new beam was taken less than seven weeks before the completed cars finally left for Italy! Second gear was found to be too low for the mountains. Furthermore, this particular gearbox used a pint of oil in 700 miles. Although this latter was ultimately found to be due to a defective oil seal, it was agreed, as a safety measure, to build the new boxes with a chicken-feed oil reservoir. This, together with the new gear ratio, meant a substantial re-design of the box. Road wheels broke up. The only answer to this was to increase the spoke base which in turn meant re-designing and lengthening all hubs. All these things, and a host of lesser ones, followed one another over the telegraph wires from Italy.

The prototype was back in Abingdon in the third week in February, with the race six weeks off. Apart from the preparation of the cars, there was much to be done in Italy before the race began: drivers had to familiarise themselves with their own machines and fuel consumption tests had to be conducted in order that replenishment depots could be sited. Moreover, the cars had to be transported. All in all, the cars had to leave England three weeks before the race, which left just twenty days for the building of the race cars and the re-building of the prototype, which was to continue as the practice car. Somehow the job was done despite such setbacks as, for instance, the first two power units being twenty-five per cent down on horsepower on first test, and it is on record that Nobby Marney, for one, worked straight through the last seventy-two hours preceding the shipment of the cars.

Even now technical troubles—and miracles—were not at an end. During the first day's practice, each car was reported by its drivers to have spongy brakes and erratic steering. Examination showed all cars to have split brake drums, despite the fact that the brake gear was identical to that on the practice car. The reason was, of course, that the ice-bound condition of the mountain roads earlier in the year had prevented full application of the brakes, and the drums were now splitting at their junction with the liners. Practice continued on the defective drums while communication with the Factory produced new ones, modified to overcome the trouble, not only in time for the race but in time for a limited amount of practice as well. The erratic steering was overcome by altering the lay of the front axle torque reaction cables. These had been fitted, to restrict front axle movement under heavy braking conditions, from the chassis frame to the top of the swivel pins. It appeared that, when cornering, they constrained the axle in an oblique direction, which was undesirable. Brackets were made so that the cables lay parallel to the chassis frame and steering was pronounced satisfactory.

All through practice, and in the race itself, the cars were to be dogged by sparking-plug trouble. It seemed to be impossible to find a plug which would withstand both the heat of the supercharged engine when driven hard and the tendency to oil on the down-grades in the mountains or on the relatively slow transits of the bigger towns along the route. But Lord Howe's car oiled up one plug more than usually persistently and this was traced, in time for rectification before the race, to a loose valve guide. Another car seized its water-pump, and at the last moment it was found that the regulations—written in Italian, of course—required all cars to be fitted with silencers, whereas the MGs had straight-through pipes. These troubles, too, were overcome

—with the notable exception of the oiling of the plugs—and the cars moved up to the start at Brescia in battle order amid scenes of tremendous enthusiasm from the Italian populace, who appreciated this foreign challenge on their home ground.

During the days preceding the start much time and thought had been given to the 'ground organisation' for the team. Petrol consumption tests had shown that 250 miles between refuelling stops was well within the tank capacity and that, therefore, only three depots were needed. These were to be set up at Siena, Perugia and Bologna. The team's manager, Hugh McConnell—an ideal person for the job, not only for his knowledge of the racing game, but also for his fluent Italian—would be at Bologna and an elaborate system of reporting was laid on whereby observers on the course would telegraph news to Mac who would sort out the information and relay instructions to the depot next ahead of the cars.

The setting up of these depots, the sorting of the equipment and getting it to the right place at the right time was an art in itself and involved a great deal of motoring across Italy and back again. There is an amusing anecdote connected with one such journey when Kesterton, of the S.U. Company, together with other members of the *équipe*, were on a jaunt across the Apennines. Late at night, Kes. pulled off the road—he knew not quite where in the darkness—and he and the others made themselves comfortable in the van and went to sleep. Greeting the coming daylight with a good stretch, they observed that they were at the top of a not inconsiderable defile and that some few hundred feet below them was a lorry quite obviously on fire. They piled into the van and tore off down the hill, dismounting their liberal supply of fire extinguishers en route. Arriving at the lorry—thick black smoke pouring from under the bonnet—they took charge of the proceedings, brushed the excited little Italian driver to one side, and put out the fire in no uncertain manner. It was only then that the Italian was able to explain that to wrap an oil-soaked rag round his induction pipe and set light to it was his normal method of cold starting.

In the Mille Miglia, the small cars start first—which, from many points of view, seems to be the wrong way round. But the three Magnettes were to be the first away of the 1100-c.c. class, the yet smaller cars having left an hour earlier at 7 a.m. The form for the team was for Birkin and Rubin to go as fast as possible in the early stages in an attempt to break up the Maserati opposition. Eyston and Lurani, Howe and Hamilton, would follow at a slightly more modest pace. This part of the plan succeeded, Birkin breaking the class record to the first control, 220 miles distant, by 25 minutes, there to retire with a burnt exhaust valve and to learn, shortly afterwards, that Tufanelli, on the leading Maserati, was out with gearbox trouble and that its sister car was in bad health.

HUGH HAMILTON takes to the pavement in the 1933 Mannin Beg—the K3's Waterloo.

Despite complete re-design, the **R** Type, even in rear view, is unmistakably MG Midget.

Designed for a purpose. The R Type MG Midget had everything—except the opportunity to be thoroughly developed.

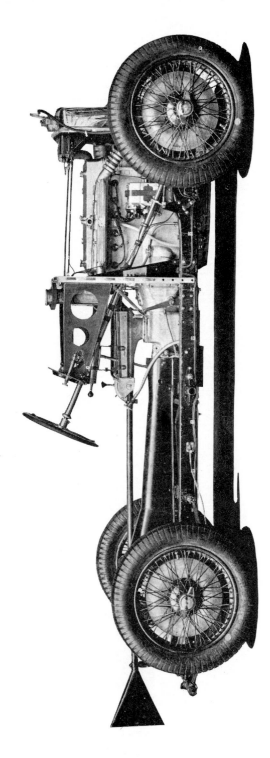

Built for Battle:—This photograph of the K3 chassis and the one on the opposite page leave no doubt that it was designed to go fast, keep right way up, and keep on going.

NUVOLARI doesn't miss the masonry by much, either. HOUNSLOW seems to be quite at ease. The car: the winning K3 Magnette. The occasion: R.A.C. T.T. Ulster, 1933.

XXIII

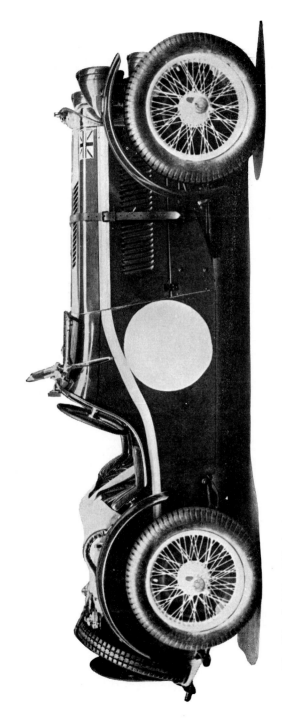

The K3 of 1933. This is the actual car which Earl Howe and Hamilton drove in the Mille Miglia of that year.

Birkin averaged 87·95 m.p.h. for the 130 miles from Brescia to Bologna, and in places all three cars had exceeded 110 m.p.h. This, let us remind ourselves—this was 1933; the race was one of 1000 miles; the engines were less than 1·1 litres in size; and the cars were what, today, would be categorised as sports cars, for they were running with wings, windscreen, lamps—lots of them—crews of two, spare wheels and what-have-you. Perhaps the science of 'automobilism' has not progressed so very far in the intervening years.

With Birkin out, Eyston and Lurani took the class lead and continued the headlong dash through the rest of the day and most of the following night, with Howe and Hamilton in second place. As, by shortly after half distance, both cars had overtaken all the runners in the smaller classes, the two MGs were the first cars on the course, and were, in fact, the first cars to reach Brescia again and the finish. This they did after eighteen hours of the hardest possible driving, with but ninety seconds between them, having averaged 56·9 and 56·82 m.p.h. respectively.

But on both cars, plug oiling trouble had been chronic, and the speeds recorded would have been much higher had it not been for constant stops to change plugs. For instance, Eyston and Lurani fitted one hundred and fifty-seven new sparking plugs in the course of the thousand miles. Assuming the best condition, under which this number would have been accounted for by the whole set of six being changed each time, then the car would have had to stop every forty miles throughout the entire race. It would not be altogether fair to pin the responsibility for this trouble on to the plug manufacturers. Sufficient oil had to be fed to the supercharger to keep it happy under high-speed full-throttle conditions, and this proved excessive on over-run. It was a major problem, but clearly neither fundamental nor insurmountable.

Although the team did not finish complete, neither did any other team, and the MGs received the team prize in accordance with the provision in the regulations that, in such an eventuality, the prize would go to the team putting up the most meritorious performance.

Thus was the MG Magnette K3 proved in all its main essentials— or so it seemed. Certainly it is impossible to imagine any other way in which the design could have been brought to completion so quickly or tested so thoroughly. Yet even so, there remained an undetected weakness which was to be uncovered with dramatic completeness within the ensuing three months.

By the time the Italian dust had settled, series production of the K3 was under way and drivers were taking delivery of their new mounts. In May, four were entered for the J.C.C. International Trophy, a race in which artificial barriers interrupted Brooklands track and forced upon the cars a degree of braking, cornering and acceleration. The new cars took second, third and fourth places in this race at speeds, for the

260 miles, in excess of 80 miles per hour, giving a complete demonstration of reliability, an excess of zeal having impaled the fourth car on a sand-filled barrel. Two months later, this over-zealous driver put himself right with the world by taking third place in the British Empire Trophy race, at the same track, at 106·88 m.p.h. At the same meeting, R. T. Horton who had built for his car an off-set single-seater body, similar in general form to one with which he had taken records on a supercharged Midget, broke the Brooklands outer circuit 1100-c.c. Class lap record at 115·55 m.p.h. It seemed that the new car was invincible in its class.

The disenchantment was produced by the Mannin Beg race in the Isle of Man, less than a fortnight after the Brooklands meeting. Six Magnettes were in the field of fourteen cars. One crashed, one retired with valve trouble, one suffered breakage of the camshaft drive, and three went out with rear axle failure. And so there were none. A fourth rear axle failure had occurred in practice. It now became clear that the previous races, despite their length, variety and apparent severity, had not, by a long way, stressed the transmission to its limit. The Mannin Beg was a 'round the houses' race, 230 miles on a circuit 4·6 miles long, in and around the streets of Douglas. Constant fierce acceleration and equally fierce braking, assisted by the self-changing gearbox, had proved too much for the differential. Fortunately, it was a simple matter to replace the two-star wheels with a four-star arrangement, and from that moment, until the close of the 1933 racing season, the K3 carried most things before it, though it continued to be a good deal too temperamental in the matter of sparking plugs.

In August, Whitney Straight, a lone British entry, scored a dramatic win over a flock of single-seat Maseratis in the Coppa Acerbo at Pescara in Italy; a fortnight later, Nuvolari won the R.A.C. Ulster T.T.; a fortnight later still, E. R. Hall came first in the B.R.D.C. 500 miles race at Brooklands; and in the following month, Whitney Straight captured the Brooklands Mountain Lap record. Divers lessons were learned from these events—which we will briefly examine—but in connection with the last-named it is worth mentioning that, at this stage, MGs held the Brooklands Outer Circuit lap records and Mountain Lap records in both the 750-c.c. and 1100-c.c. classes.

Renewed mention of records, particularly in connection with the Brooklands Outer Circuit, prompts a digression on the subject of Mr. R. T. Horton. Here was one of those men who loved quick motoring for its own sake, his job—the brewing of beer—having nothing to do with the motor trade. He, moreover, bought his cars from the factory and then pursued his own line in the matter of making them go faster and faster—and succeeded admirably. So far as MGs are concerned, he started with a Midget C Type, performed his own particular mystic rites over the engine in collaboration with Robin Jackson, mounted a strangely off-set single-seat body, won the 1932 500-mile race at Brooklands and, at least once, broke the outer circuit lap record of the same track. Early in 1933 he did much the same thing with a K3 and with at least equal success. It must be said that, in plan view, these single-seat bodies looked distinctly queer and, according to theory, ought not to have worked too well. The radiator, and therefore the front of the bodywork, remained central in the frame, the bonnet and cowling then sweeping back obliquely across the frame—and the direction of travel—to envelop the driver in his normal seating position on the right-hand side of the transmission. Undoubtedly, such a configuration must have produced a measure of weathercock effect at speed, but this is nowhere recorded and, in any case, did not prevent the car going very fast. As already mentioned, Horton broke a long-standing Class G Brooklands lap record at 115·55 m.p.h. almost first time out. He raced fairly consistently for the rest of the season, and in March of the following year essayed the one-hour class record, also at Brooklands, taking it to 117·03 miles in the hour and capturing five other records on the way. Then in July, to demonstrate his—and the car's—versatility, he took the Standing Start Mile Record at 83·2 m.p.h.

Such were the high-lights. In later years, the car was to pass into the hands of Lt. Col. A. T. Goldie Gardner, who took it to Germany and raised the Flying Mile to over 148 m.p.h., the engine finally being transferred to a rebuilt version of EX 135. But we anticipate.

With regard to the Ulster T.T., it has been refreshingly instructive, after the passage of the years, to discuss with Alec Hounslow his recollections of his ride as travelling mechanic to Nuvolari, for obviously only the salient impressions will have remained in the memory. Such fright as he experienced was, it appears, confined entirely to the first practice lap, during which Nuvolari had not got the hang of the self-changing box, selecting third but not kicking the pedal, and in consequence arriving a good deal too fast at most of the hazards. The score on the very first lap was three complete gyrations in the Square at Newtownards, a rearward visit to within inches of the famous butcher's shop in Comber, and an excursion up the escape road in the direction of Belfast at the Dundonald hairpin. Otherwise, the lap passed off without untoward incident, ending with a visit to the pit where McConnell explained that the left-hand pedal did rather more than perform its conventional function of disconnecting the drive. Thereafter Alec had no qualms, but before reassurance came spent some time in wondering what he had let himself in for.

Most drivers on an unfamiliar course, it is to be assumed, start off their practice modestly and work up to somewhere near their limit. As an indication that Nuvolari worked the other way round, the first eight laps of practice completely wore out a set of tyres, whereas in the race itself each set lasted over twice this distance. Even so, tyres, not fuel, were regarded as the limiting factor in terms of distance, and the arrangements were that Hounslow would signal to the driver when the breaker-strip on the tyres first showed and he, in turn, would signal to the pit his intention to come in next time round. As it so happened, the tyres lasted to exactly half-distance and only one stop was made throughout the race.

Hounslow cannot recall, from the period of the race itself, any perceptible application of the brakes. Even towards the end of the run, when 'the little man' was turning things full on, his braking did not amount to much more than steadying the car, and the fast cornering was achieved by positioning and timing. All corners were cut extremely fine—Nuvolari had suggested that Hounslow might care to put a coin down in the road, and that he would wager to put his front wheels over it on every lap—and on one occasion a rear hub chipped a splinter out of a roadside telegraph pole. Alec is of the opinion that the cornering technique was an early example of that now generally seen in Grand Prix racing, where the car is put into a four-wheel drift in the approach to the corner and arrives there pointing in the right direction for a straight run forward as soon as the slide stops. The car seemed to float round the bends rather than that there should be any perceptible use of the steering. One such drift did not finish as early as desirable, and the car came precariously near to the curb on the outside of the bend. Nuvolari glanced at Hounslow, and shook his head in an expressive gesture of self-admonishment.

On form, the Magnettes were outsiders, their handicap speed being 77·93 m.p.h., over one mile per hour in excess of the class *lap* record. The MG camp were hanging their hats on the Midgets, which were relatively in a better position. Largely on this account, Nuvolari and Hounslow had done virtually no pit practice together, though individually they were not exactly novices with churns, knock-on wheels and such. By virtue of long experience, and, in the case of the driver, in contradiction of the reputation of the Italian temperament, both were extemely calm and methodical in their one pit stop. The driver attended to fuel and oil; Alec changed all the wheels and topped up the radiator. When all was finished in something under two minutes, Nuvolari grabbed the wheel hammer, ran quickly round the car and tried all the wheel nuts. There is a moral there somewhere.

In contradistinction, Hamilton, the race leader in Midget No. 25, had an Irishman as mechanic. At the risk of precipitating an International incident, it must be recorded that, early on in their pit stop, a slight error was made in their routine, temperament got the upper hand, and thereafter everything went wrong. Result—a pit stop of over seven minutes, which let Nuvolari through into the lead.

From this point on, Hamilton drove as one inspired, improving his speed on each successive lap, breaking and re-breaking the lap record time and again. This did not pass unnoticed in Nuvolari's pit, which called—not in vain—for a reply. No. 17, in its turn, started to break lap records, but the margin was insufficient and Hamilton again took the lead on handicap. At this, Nuvolari waved to Hounslow to make himself scarce in the bottom of the car, and then gave his all. With three laps to go, No. 17 lapped in 10 minutes 4 seconds—81·42 m.p.h., and 27 seconds less than his handicap time. Hamilton's lap was in 10 minutes 37 seconds—77·2 m.p.h., and 36 seconds less than his handicap. Hamilton was picking up nine seconds per lap and, on form, he could not lose. On the penultimate lap, moreover, with Hamilton but seventeen seconds in front of him Nuvolari's engine cut dead. Hounslow recalls that after he had instinctively switched on the reserve fuel pump, and in the second or two before the engine cut in again, Nuvolari took both hands from the wheel and raised them above his head in a typically Latin gesture of despair. But at the end of this same lap, Hamilton had to take on fuel, a stop which cost him the race by forty seconds. As already recorded, Nuvolari needed petrol to complete his complementary lap.

The Magnette's average speed for the race was 78·65 m.p.h., well over four miles an hour faster than the best car in the same class the previous year. It had exceeded its handicap speed by ·72 m.p.h., a feat which, before the race, nobody had thought possible, But, as Hounslow now says, if Hammy's pit stop had been at all reasonable, Nuvolari would 'never have seen him'.

E. R. Hall's win in the B.R.D.C. 500 miles race at Brooklands was another instance of a faultless run. The race normally marked the end of the racing season and, with all winter to mend the machinery and no obstacles on the track, speeds were usually terrific. It was known as the fastest long distance race in the world—and, in fact, in 1931 had been won by a 6½-litre Bentley, starting from scratch, at over 118 m.p.h. This year, 1933, the handicap speed for the scratch man was close on 123 m.p.h., and that for even the smallest class, which included the MG Midgets, was as high as 104·85 m.p.h.

Hall had run fifth with his car at Belfast a fortnight before. Moreover, he had been involved, in the course of the race, in a *divertissement* with Nuvolari, as a result of which he had crumped the bank pretty soundly and bent his back axle casing. The car had, however, been rebuilt meanwhile, and had been fitted with a single-seat body and a pair of high ratio final drive gears. Its maximum lap speed of the Brooklands Outer Circuit was estimated to be somewhere in the region of 115 to 118 m.p.h. In the race, his pit organisation and control was, as always, superlative and, in accordance with a predetermined plan, he lapped steadily from the start at 110 m.p.h. By half distance, much of the opposition had been forced out of the race by mechanical failure of one kind and another, and Hall lay second to Dixon's Riley. He stopped, refuelled, changed wheels and took on oil and water and went away again, back on his old speed, driving to maintain his race position in the hope—or expectation—that the pace would tell and that Dixon would blow up. And sure enough, Dixon blew a head gasket and, though he set to and fitted a new one, he was unable to get going again. As soon as Dixon stopped, Hall's pit control instructed him to ease his speed and, despite several laps in the closing stages at a lap speed of the order of 102 m.p.h., he finally ran through to win at an overall average speed for the five hundred miles of 106·53 m.p.h.

With the close of the racing season, sporting interest moved to Montlhery with the Magic Midget, as already recounted, while at Abingdon design and development continued at even greater pressure. At this period, an entirely new series of sports cars was under way: the P Type Midget; its 6-cylinder counterpart, the N Type; the KN Saloon; and, lurking not far in the background, a new racing Midget, the Q Type. In the midst of this hurly-burly, the technicians found time to apply themselves to a re-design of the K 3 in readiness for the 1934 season. 1933 had seen the potentialities of the supercharged 1100-c.c. car convincingly demonstrated, but it would be necessary for the cars to perform a good deal more consistently in the ensuing year if they were to maintain their ascendancy.

Attention focused, first of all, on brakes. Increasing speeds had, in accordance with the inescapable laws of physics, made disproportionate demands on stopping power, the energy to be dissipated in the brakes—in the form of heat—when steadying the car from 100 down to 90 m.p.h. being as much as that used in bringing a car from forty miles an hour to a standstill. The conflicting requirements of light weight and rapid heat dissipation had already led to the use of Elektron alloy for drums, shoes and backplates, but the two last-named had both exhibited signs, during the season, of lack of rigidity. Shoes were therefore re-designed from rolled T section mild steel and an entirely new method of brake cam operation was designed in order to relieve the backplate of the bending loads applied by the cable. In place of the single brake cam lever—which had been pulled by the inner cable, while the outer casing terminated in a positive stop—two levers were arranged, scissor fashion, one operating each shoe, so that one was pulled by the cable and the other pushed by the outer casing, thereby halving the cable load. The two levers rolled back-to-back and the shoes were inter-connected by a linkage which ensured that any tendency of the leading shoe to grab was balanced by an increasing pressure on the trailing shoe. The fulcrum of this linkage was not positively fixed in its location on the backplate, but was very stiff to move, so that the first heavy application of the brakes shifted its position and brought the whole assembly into concentricity with the brake drum. Finally, steel liners replaced cast iron in the brake drums. The total result was highly satisfactory, temperature rise being kept within such bounds that fading was very small, wear being so reduced that some of the cars ran through the entire racing season on one set of brake linings.

At about this period, the tendency in British racing was for events to become more and more open to the racing car, as such, and—with the exception of the R.A.C. Ulster T.T.—less and less favourable to the sports car. An attempt was therefore made to produce a body for the K3 which, while still conforming dimensionally with the requirements of the International Sports Car regulations, more closely approached the ideal racing-car shape, with its small frontal area and attenuated lines. Wings, lamps and electrical equipment were made available for the cars, but these items were easily and cleanly removable, and were not supplied with the vehicle unless specifically ordered. As in the previous year, the instrument panel was built up on fixtures integral with the chassis, but now the efforts to keep all functional components clear of the bodywork were intensified, such that the chassis could be built and tested as a complete entity and the body, a mere shell, clipped on afterwards. This had great advantages from the point of view of accessibility.

Petrol tanks received close study. It was desirable, for the sake of long-distance events, to increase capacity both to provide a greater margin of safety—*vide* the T.T.—and to allow for the heavier consumption rates which would follow any increase in power output which might be obtained. Moreover, in the absence of the square back of the coachbuilt body to which the tank could be bolted, careful mounting would be required to avoid the ill effects of the buffeting which would come from the chassis frame. After much experiment, a twenty-seven and a half gallon tank was devised, built up in cellular form to provide rigidity and freedom from surge, and having a shape which conformed to the general line of the car, the outside of the tank itself forming part of the outer skin of the body. This tank was mounted, by steel cables passing round grooves formed in its outer surface, on a bed of sponge rubber in a sub-frame which was, in turn, attached to the chassis, at three points, by rubber bushes. Insulated thus from road shocks and the effects of chassis distortion, the tank proved to be entirely reliable.

Normally, fuel feed was by two S.U. electric pumps through duplicated fuel lines so arranged that only one pump would deliver the last three gallons, thus providing a measure of reserve. In view, however, of the arrangement whereby it was possible to jettison the electrical equipment, air-pressure fuel feed was provided as an alternative, a hand-pump being fitted close to the gear lever and an air-pressure gauge being incorporated among the standard instruments. In these circumstances, too, plug contacts were fitted to the side of the chassis for the attachment of slave starter batteries.

As for the engine, a new cylinder head was now available, which had been designed for the N Type sports cars and which had considerably improved porting. No great attempt was to be made to increase the power output of the standard unit as this was already of the order of one hundred horse-power per litre and the cars had given good accounts of themselves in terms of speed, though dogged to a greater or lesser degree by plug trouble. It was felt that, if only the cars could be made dead reliable, their performance would be adequate for the forthcoming season, particularly in view of the general reduction in weight which the new body afforded. In order finally to put paid to the plug trouble, the Powerplus supercharger was abandoned in favour of the Marshall No. 85, a Roots pattern blower which, though still providing almost as much boost when driven at engine speed, had far less exacting lubrication requirements.

The combustion space of the new head was larger than on the old, and the opportunity was taken to provide a sufficiently low compression ratio—5·4 to 1—for the car to be driven comfortably on a petrol/benzol mixture. This head, being interchangeable with its predecessor, was applied as a conversion to some of the earlier cars, whose owners then used them for fast touring. For racing, however, the head thickness was reduced and, in addition, the gasket was dispensed with, the head being faced direct to the cylinder block, so that the resulting ratio was within a point or two of the previous year's engine. Power curves of typical K3 engines are shown at *Fig.* 7, from which it will be noted that, for the new season, some power was sacrificed in the interest of reliability.

Cars to the new specification were not ready in time for the Mille Miglia, but previous year's cars were used with the new type brake gear and Marshall blowers. The pace was very fast, set by Taruffi driving the latest thing in Maseratis. Before half distance, the leading MG was out with a blown head gasket and shortly afterwards Earl Howe crashed with the second car. Though this latter occurrence originally appeared to be a major disaster, it did in fact produce an amusing incident. Howe was driving with his head mechanic, Thomas, as co-driver. Patchy mist was encountered in the mountains and the car emerged from one such patch at far too great a speed to negotiate the next corner. It slid into the rocky bank, demolishing the supercharger, Lord Howe receiving a blow on the head from which he lost consciousness. Recovering shortly afterwards and recognising Thomas before he was fully conscious, his first irascible comment was 'Thomas ! What are we waiting for? Get on with it.' Lurani and Penn-Hughes in the back-marking car ran on faultlessly to the end, but could not catch Taruffi. Their speed for the race, however, improved on the previous year's winning speed by nearly two miles per hour.

The first excursion of the completely new-series cars was in the Junior Car Club's International Trophy race at Brooklands at the end

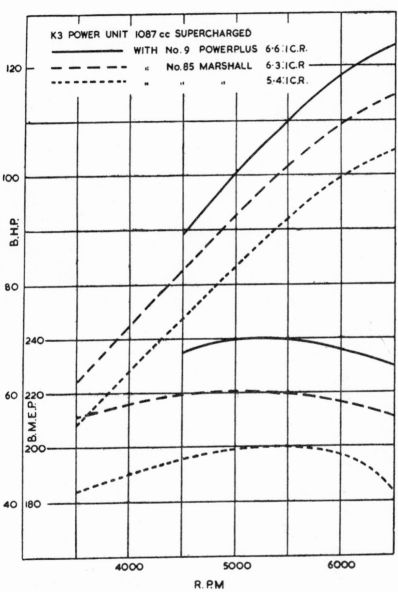

K3 POWER UNIT 1087 cc SUPERCHARGED

WITH No. 9 POWERPLUS 6·6 : I.C.R.

" No. 85 MARSHALL 6·3 : I.C.R.

" " " 5·4 : I.C.R.

B.H.P.

B.M.E.P.

R.P.M

Fig. 7.

of April. Here, a handicap based on the previous year's performances re-acted to their disadvantage and they were not fast enough to better 8th, 9th, and 10th places in the general classification, though it appeared that they were now completely reliable even when driven near the limit of their capabilities. Their final justification came in the Mannin Beg race in the Isle of Man at the end of May, the race in which, in the previous year, they had met their Waterloo. Magnettes filled the first five places, but the success of the race was completely overshadowed, at Abingdon, by the death of Frank Tayler in an accident during practice. Motor racing, even at its best, is a chancy business and it is perhaps to be wondered at that in the closely packed drama of the three or four preceding years no tragedy had occurred which had struck quite so near home. But Frankie was one of the few original employees who had formed the nucleus of the Company in its earliest days and who had been in the Competition Department from its very beginning, working for the fun of the thing, regardless of time, risk or reward, almost always good-humoured, but doubly amusing it seemed in his odd spells of bad temper. At this distance in time, one is perhaps better able to see his true worth and certainly better able to assess the reaction of his fellows when the sad news came through. Time invariably softens the recollection of personal grief, but one does not easily forget the sight of grown men in tears.

But the game went on. George Eyston had a special built—EX 135—the history of which has a later chapter to itself. With it he won the British Empire Trophy at over 80 m.p.h. Hamilton and Seaman took their K3s all over Europe where, in company with one Cecchini, they made a big impression, their first excursion being to take the first three places in the Coppa Acerbo. The 1100-c.c. record for the Klausen Hill Climb was captured and Cecchini won his class at Modena. The hand of Fate fell again towards the end of August when, while Seaman was busy winning the 1½-litre class in the Swiss Grand Prix, Hamilton's brilliant career came to an untimely end at the wheel of a Maserati in the same race. Unquestionably he was, at that time, recognised as a front-rank racing driver, not only by his own countrymen, but by most Continental racing men as well. Had he lived, he would soon have had his place among the regular Grand Prix teams of the period.

Over the two years, some thirty K3s were built in all. Most of them in their subsequent lives were much modified by their owners, particularly as to their bodywork, so that an original two-seat sports K3 became a bit of a rarity. But here was a vintage car if ever there was one: impressive in appearance, practical in lay-out, sturdy to a degree and, withal, fast, safe and dead reliable. Taking the world as a whole, it is doubtful if even now the K3 has won its last race.

CHAPTER VIII

REVERSIONS TO THE UNBLOWN

THE main object of entering a race is to win. Some there are who will race for the fun of it, regardless of the fact that, in their own estimation, their chances—if they bother to consider them at all— are virtually nil, but they are in the minority. If a game is worth playing at all, it is worth serious consideration, and when the game is as expensive as motor racing, most entrants will wish to have some chance of a return on their outlay, in the form either of prize money, or publicity, or an increase in knowledge, before they accept the risk. Thus it is that race regulations are carefully studied and the entrant decides whether his car is suitable for the event or, if he is more favourably placed, selects the car which he considers has best chance of success.

It was not until about 1932 that the supercharger became either sufficiently potent or sufficiently reliable to be regarded as a serious factor in motor racing. But as soon as it established itself on the motoring scene, controversy began to rage not only over the extent of its value, but also over the very ethics of its use. As a result, the handicap penalties imposed upon the supercharged car varied in severity, and in some races these devices were banned altogether.

The Midget had graduated from the unblown to the blown, and the Class G challenger, the K3, was built as a supercharged vehicle from the outset. It was, moreover, rugged and therefore somewhat heavy, and very definitely unsuited to run *sans compresseur*. The appearance in the 1933 racing calendar of events favouring unblown 1100-c.c. cars would be likely to leave the MG addict helpless for the want of a suitable machine. It was this which turned attention seriously in the direction of the L Magna, the car which, it will be remembered, was the 1933 successor to the Type F.

The L chassis used J Midget axles, fitted with the twelve-inch brake gear as used on the J4 racing car. The wheelbase had been increased by eight inches relative to the Midget, in order to accommodate the extra length of the 6-cylinder engine, which itself was basically that of the K3, but with an atmospheric induction system and coil ignition. The J2 gearbox was used, but a special two-plate clutch had been designed to take care of the increased torque. In standard form the chassis carried two-seat and four-seat open bodies, a small four-seat salonette, and a fixed-head coupé known as the 'Continental'. But it was, of course, upon the open two-seater version that attention focused for the purpose of trials as a near-racing car.

It was decided to try the cars in the Light Car Club's Relay Race to be held at Brooklands in the July. Not only did this afford a reasonably early opportunity for test, but in this race each car—and therefore each team—was handicapped individually on a basis of known or estimated performance. The three cars were entered, as an MG Car Club team, by the then Honorary Secretary of the Club, Alan Hess, and were to be driven by him, by C. E. C. Martin and by G. W. J. H. Wright. A modest increase in engine power was secured by raising the compression ratio to 6·8 to 1 and Martlett pistons were fitted similar to those which had been used consistently in the C Type Midgets. Beyond this, preparation was confined to the customary meticulous attention to detail, wings, windscreen, spare wheel and carrier were jettisoned in the pursuit of weight and frontal area reduction, and an exhaust system was installed which conformed to the Brooklands regulations. The cars came to the race weighing 14½ hundredweight, and with engines delivering 50 h.p. at 6,000 r.p.m. as shown at Curve B of *Fig.* 8.

The venture proved to be entirely successful as, not only did the team win the race—at 88·62 m.p.h.—but the cars gave a remarkable demonstration of consistency, all completing their allotted thirty laps and each returning a fastest lap of 93 m.p.h.

The self-same cars, with their engines returned to standard tune, and with wings and other touring equipment replaced, next assaulted the mountains in the International Alpine Trial. Driven by W. E. C. Watkinson and H. A. F. Ward-Jackson, the brothers L. A. and D. F. Welch and by Mr. and Mrs. T. H. Wisdom, they won their class and secured the Manufacturers' Team Prize, the Coupe des Alpes. On the journey to the start, however, there occurred one of those mechanical mysteries which befall the motorist from time to time, and which is worth mention here purely for its 'curiosity value'. At one particular rendezvous, Watkinson was late and eventually came limping in with the engine very definitely firing on no more than five cylinders. All external methods of repair had been tried, but compression was conspicuously lacking on number two, so the head had to come off. And there, reposing on the crown of the piston, in the midst of all the evidence of its struggles to escape, lay a five-sixteenths nut. Both valves were bent, the piston top was deeply pitted and even the bore had not escaped. But where the nut had come from, nobody had any idea. It could not have been in the cylinder for long and must therefore have entered by the inlet valve—'the proper way' as someone said at the time. Sabotage? Who can say? Suffice it that the car was running again in time for the start.

The high speed of the L Type and its undoubted stamina—as demonstrated by these two signal successes—confirmed its suitability for wider use. It will be remembered that, by the end of 1932, MG held all the International Class H Records, and that steps were being taken to enter Class G, a move which led to the introduction of the K series cars, with which the L engine was associated. Further attempts were to be made during the winter of 1932/33 to raise the Class H records to yet higher speeds, and it was felt that perhaps the L Type Magna would be capable of beating certain existing long-distance Class G records. By way of dress rehearsal for this, one of the Relay Race cars was prepared for the B.R.D.C. 500 miles Race—the race which, as already recorded, was won by E. R. Hall's K3. This car, driven by C. E. C. Martin and L. A. Welch, ran into second place behind Hall at an average speed of 92·24 m.p.h. and thus confirmed the opinion that it was capable of covering long distances at near its maximum speed.

A second car had been prepared specifically for the record attempts and, since the Relay Race, a good deal of experiment had been made with induction systems. In fact, induction pipes became something of a mania, and interest in them spread through the Abingdon factory like a disease until everyone who knew anything about carburation—and some who only thought they did—had a smack at designing and making pipes. Some of the results were astonishing things to look at, resembling the inner intricacies of a pipe organ, if not an anatomist's model of human entrails. But, as so often happens, the final result was simple and straightforward and consisted partly in re-positioning the carburetters and partly in the introduction of a slight taper into the existing pipe. The improvement in engine power derived from this change was quite appreciable, as is shown by the curves of *Fig.* 8.

The adaptation of a large petrol tank and the fitting of a 'straight-through' exhaust system completed the preparation of the car which was then driven by Marney from the factory to Montlhery, there being little to differentiate it from a standard model except the ear-splitting noise which arose from injudicious use of the loud pedal. On arrival at the track the car was subjected to a routine check, and tests were run to determine the correct carburetter settings for the prevailing weather conditions—wet, windy but warm—it was October. The MG camp was busy with the preparation of the Magic Midget, but while this was going on, the L Type came out to attack the Class G records from twelve to twenty-four hours. It was to be driven in three-hour shifts by George Eyston, Denly, Wisdom and Yallop, and shorn of its front wings and step-boards, and equipped with four spot-lamps in a row mounted low down on the front, it started in the late afternoon of 7th October. The intention was to take the records at a shade over 80 m.p.h., and the lap speed through the night was controlled accordingly.

It was found, however, that with the track tyres—which had smooth, longitudinally ribbed treads—the car skated on the wet track to a disconcerting degree. The effect was undoubtedly enhanced by the long beam of the driving lights, and what is more, the directional stability of the model, even under the best conditions, was not entirely above suspicion. All things considered, it was decided, before morning, to call the car in and change to road-treaded tyres, a change which was accomplished in but thirty-seven seconds. Shortly after dawn, the car completed its twelve hours and captured its first record at 81·23 m.p.h. From then on the monotonous round continued, past the 1000 miles, the 2000 kilos, 3000 kilos, until twenty-four hours had elapsed, at which time the average speed was 80·56 m.p.h. At this point, everything was going so smoothly and satisfactorily that a snap decision was taken to keep the car running for another fifty minutes and collect the record for 2000 miles, which was accordingly achieved at 80·49 m.p.h.

Thus the first of the reversions to the use of an unsupercharged MG for official racing and record purposes was satisfactorily concluded. A model which had been designed and produced as a sports car for day-to-day use on the road had, with little alteration, demonstrated its ability to compete, on the track, with the fastest racing cars of its time. And those who care to dally with statistical calculations can start on the basis that the engine turned over some seven million times in the course of the twenty-four hours at Montlhery.

The following year, 1934, was to pose a much tougher problem. MG had won the R.A.C. Tourist Trophy race in 1931 with the supercharged C Type Midget, and in 1933 with the supercharged K3. The regulations for the 1934 race, due to be run on Sept. 1, were published in April, and *superchargers were banned*. Moreover, the speeds expected of the unsupercharged cars appeared to be very much on the high side. The whole situation took MGs by surprise, and if they were to have a chance of winning again, something had got to be done— quickly. The L Magna was out of production by this time, its place having been taken by the new N Magnette, a somewhat larger car, and the first of a series of models using a track of 3 ft. 9 in. Its engine had a swept volume of 1271 c.c., having six cylinders of 57 mm. bore and 83 mm. stroke, measurements which were used on the original M Midget and had re-appeared on many models since. As the T.T. race regulations provided separate handicap speeds for cars with engines up to 1200 and 1300 c.c., as well as up to 1500 c.c., it was decided to see what could be done with this Type N. And as, judged by present-day standards, the regulations were fairly loose in the matter of what could be done to the car, extensive alterations were contemplated.

The adventures with the L Type had taught a good deal about induction pipes and cleared the ground in readiness for a straightforward approach to this part of the problem. Valve timing came under review, as it had been realised for some time that better filling, and therefore more power, could be obtained provided valve gear noise could be disregarded and no undue attention need be given to an even slow-running. The timing finally decided upon is shown at *Fig.* 9, in which the standard timing is repeated for the sake of comparison. Triple valve springs were introduced having a seat pressure of fifty pounds compared with the standard forty, and with a rate fifty per cent higher. It was intended that the engine should operate up to 7000 r.p.m. if need be, and these higher speeds, as much as the anticipated increase in operating temperatures, dictated a change of valve material. Fuel was limited by regulation to petrol/benzol mixture, and the highest usable compression ratio was reckoned to be of the order of 9·8 to 1. To achieve this, high-crown pistons with sloping tops were incorporated and, to take care of the increased bearing loads, a racing white-metal was used together with an oil pressure twenty-five per cent above normal. The induction pipe finally selected was similar in general design to that of the special L Type, and had two horizontal SU. carburetters, 1⅜ in. diameter, disposed midway between each of the end pairs of cylinders. On test, the new engine delivered just over 74 h.p. at 6500 r.p.m. compared with the 57 h.p. at 5700 r.p.m. of the standard engine. Comparative power curves are shown at *Fig.* 10.

To transmit the increased power, the two-plate Roper and Wreaks clutch was used, as on the L Type. First and second gear ratios were raised, and the propeller shaft was balanced to 7000 r.p.m. The final drive was by a straight-toothed crown and bevel of which the normal ratio was 8/39; 8/36 and 8/33 gears being available as alternatives. Other chassis alterations were the incorporation of the reserve oil tank with float-chamber feed to the sump, as used on previous racing types; an increase in steering ratio; and the use of hydraulic shock absorbers on the front axle in addition to the standard duplex friction types.

Race regulations decreed that bodies should conform to A.I.A.C.R. dimensions. The standard two-seater body was fairly wide of the mark, and there was nothing for it but to build a special one. This took the form of a narrow sheet alloy shell, in which the two seats were staggered echelon-fashion, an eighteen-gallon fuel tank being blended into the tail. The complete car weighed 16¼ cwt. ready for the track and was named the NE Type.

Again, the Light Car Club's Relay Race was chosen as the occasion for full-dress rehearsal and trial, but there was, at first, an intention to keep the works interest in the background in the hope of 'foxing the opposition'. The management of the team was therefore entrusted to Mr. Graham Evans, and it was agreed that those members of the MG staff who were regular attendants at race meetings should, on this occasion, keep away from the track. The plot failed miserably and

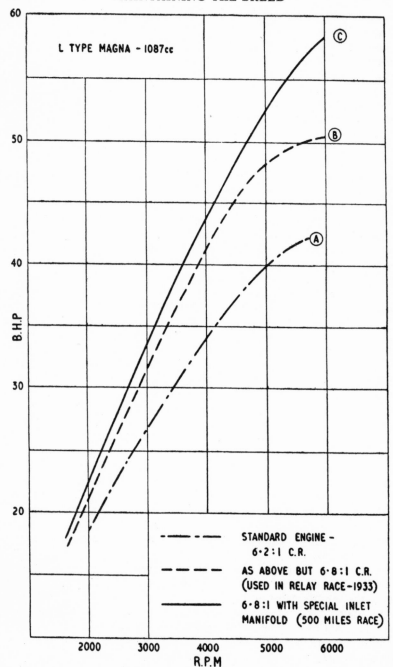

Fig. 8.

everybody knew the cars were the T.T. aspirants long before practice was over—and sat up and took notice accordingly.

Since the previous year, a trophy had been presented to the L.C.C. to be competed for in the Relay Race, and to be won by the first all-women team to finish. With this in view, the team entrant was Miss I. Schwedler, who was also to drive, the other cars being driven by Miss Margaret Allen and Miss Doreen Evans. The cars, designed and built in less than three months, ran consistently and without trouble, taking third place in the race at 87·85 m.p.h.

This, together with the subsequent examination of the cars, cleared the ground for the T.T., for which six of the new NE cars were entered, three as a team to be driven by George Eyston, Wal Handley and C. J. P. Dodson, and three lone entries, Bill Everitt, Norman Black and A. P. Hamilton. It is significant that Handley, Black and Dodson were all ex-racing motor cyclists, and this was Dodson's first year on four wheels. The team plan was for Handley to go out to try to break up the opposition—in this case, Rileys—and for the other two to drive to rule. Whenever Handley appeared in the team, it was considered expedient to assign this role to him as, not only did he drive with considerable dash and verve, but he was none too amenable to pit discipline—so it was much easier to let him go.

From the point of view of pit control, the T.T. was always a very complicated race. Handicap was arranged, not only by differences of starting time, but by the allocation of credit laps as well. Thus, a fast car with a high handicap speed might start at a given time faced with completing the total number of laps of the circuit, while a slower car might start some minutes *later*, but have one, two or three laps less to cover. This meant that in the early stages of the race lap speeds were adjusted by conjecture until such time as all cars had started, had covered sufficient laps to begin to show their form, and the wizards of the slide-rule in the pit had had time to assess this form in terms of their own particular handicap times.

Early in the race it became apparent that the challenge to the MGs might well come from the largest cars, a Rolls-Bentley driven by E. R. Hall and two Lagondas. These were getting round the course at speeds in the region of 80 m.p.h. which, if they held it, would cause real difficulty. On the other hand, no panic measures were to be taken at this early stage because cars of this type in those days were frequently lone entries, driven on the 'win or burst' principle; private battles often developed between them which usually did them no great good; and their rate of tyre wear was not always predictable so that the number of stops for wheel change was unknown. On the other hand, the MG camp knew Hall, knew the usual excellence of his pit control, and could rely on him not being misled into doing anything silly.

F

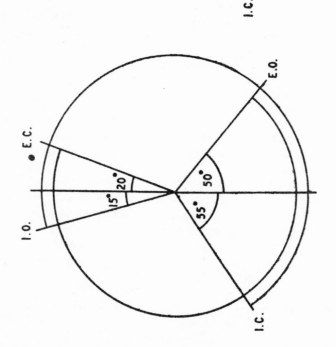

Fig. 9.

Handley lost his third gear quite early on, but it did not seem to have much effect on his speed. For several laps he made times which successfully produced a crop of 'faster' signals from rival pits and, having thus discharged his duty, he crashed in a blaze of glory, happily without injury. Before this, however, a good deal of excitement had visited the MG pit. Dodson and Eyston were up among the first six in the race when, shortly before half distance, one of Everitt's rear wheels collapsed with irreparable results to his brake drum and gear. Examination of the wheel showed it to be an ordinary one and not one of the racing wheels which had been specially tensioned for the event. It was apparent therefore that the wheels had become mixed during practice or before, and it was possible, if not probable, that some of the weaker wheels were on the other race cars. For safety, it was imperative that all these wheels be changed.

Practice had shown that one change of rear tyres would be necessary during the race and the pit personnel had been drilled accordingly. No routine had been worked out, and no practice done on the changing of front wheels. Fuel carried was sufficient for the cars to go half the race distance plus one lap and, on the pre-arranged plan, Dodson was due to be called in for replenishment—and change of rear wheels—at half distance minus one lap, Handley at half distance and Eyston at half distance plus one. Cousins worked out a sequence for the front-wheel change and, as Dodson was at that moment leading the race, decided to change the order, call Eyston in first and practise the routine on him, in the hope that a few seconds could be knocked off the time when Dodson's car came to be dealt with. When all was ready and at the appointed lap, Eyston was called in. Obedient as always to pit orders, he arrived, somewhat out of temper, however, at the departure from agreed routine, and consequently inclined to be argumentative. Cousins was in the middle of an attempt to quieten him down when, without prior warning, Handley arrived in the pit area to deliver himself of a few well-chosen words about his gearbox. For a few seconds, pandemonium reigned. Then Handley was swept out of the way and Eyston's car made ready in comparative peace. As a result, when Dodson was dealt with on the next lap, his pit stop was seven seconds shorter than Eyston's.

From this point on, the atmosphere of the race was tense, as Hall and Brian Lewis' Lagonda were having a ding-dong struggle on level terms, and Dodson was abreast of them, within a few seconds, on handicap. Wheel changes, for the second time and late in the race, on both the large cars gave Dodson a lead of just over two minutes, and the last few laps witnessed his attempt, driving all he knew, to retain it. With three laps to go, his lead was down to 2 mins. 11 sec., Hall lapping at 81 m.p.h. and Dodson at 76 m.p.h. One lap later, the difference was but 90 sec. and, at the start of the last lap, 55. This was a real scrap, a

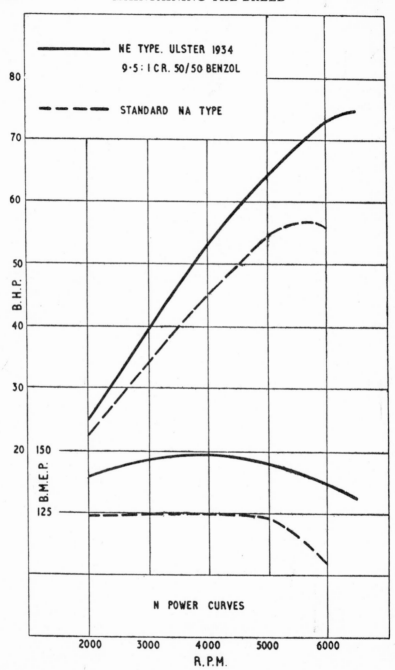

Fig. 10.

real drama, and it was clear that the issue would not be decided until the last few hundred yards. All round the course every spectator who had a stop-watch used it on that lap, checking the narrowing gap between the two cars—31 sec. at Comber; 26 at Ballystockart; 22 at Dundonald. Even here it seemed possible to the onlookers that Hall might still catch the flying Dodson, but this he failed to do by a mere 17 sec. So MG won their third T.T. and once again demonstrated the paramount importance of the pit.

CHAPTER IX

P, Q AND R

THE limiting feature of the J Type engine was its two-bearing crankshaft. Even the fully counterbalanced J4 shaft, with its 1⅝-in. diameter crank-pins, restricted the supercharge pressure which could be applied before serious whip set in. And on the J2 the shaft bent perceptibly, unsuper-charged and with only modest compression ratios. So the next develop-ment in the Midget was, quite obviously, the insertion of a centre bearing. The design of the L and K engines had incorporated highly satisfactory intermediate mains, and the diameter of the camshaft had been increased, compared with previous types, the associated valve gear being redesigned accordingly. From the designer's point of view, therefore, the new Midget engine was a gift, all that was necessary, in principle, being to take the K engine and chop two cylinders out of the middle of it. Such was the basis of the engine which was to be the heart of the P, Q and R Type cars, but, for the sake of uniformity and clarity, we will treat each type separately, and in the order named, starting with the PA Type.

Shrewd readers will have sensed from this that the thorny problem of nomenclature must again rear its head. Last time this was men-tioned, the convenient arrangement had been made that cars of similar type would be designated by letters, shades of difference being indicated by suffix *numerals*. What, then, can PA mean? It is a long and boring story, but the essence of it—which should have been faced in Chapter VII—is that in the K range there were three chassis, the K1, the K2 and the K3, in which the changes were rung with *four* engines, the KA, the KB, the KC and the KD. It was all very confusing. And when, subsequently, the K1 chassis was fitted with the N Type engine, and came to be known as the KN, the adherents of the suffix numeral finally abandoned their cause. From then on, each new model auto-matically took the suffix A in anticipation of subsequent variations. The PA Type was such a case.

In general form, the new car followed the J fairly closely, the principal chassis alterations being an increase in wheelbase to 7 ft. 3½ in., and the incorporation of the J4/L Type 12-in. brakes. The engine retained the normal bore and stroke of 57 × 83 mm. giving a capacity of 847 c.c. and had, in addition to the centre main bearing, a cylindrical white-metal front main bearing, in place of the ball-race of the J Types. The detailed arrangement of each individual bearing was, in fact, exactly the same as the corresponding one in the K3. The PA was produced concurrently with its 6-cylinder counterpart, the NA, and on both these models a change of combustion chamber shape was made from that which had obtained all through the range up to 1934. On the PA, the compression ratio was 6·2 to 1 and the engine gave 35 h.p. at 5600 r.p.m. The chassis carried two-seat and four-seat open bodies, the complete car with the former weighing 14¾ cwt. The weight of the Midget was going up.

The model proved to be very popular. It handled extremely well, had a quite creditable performance, and could, moreover, be thrashed unmercifully for miles on end without adverse effect. But there was a good deal of call for more power so that, after it had been in production for eighteen months or so, a new version appeared, the PB, with an engine 10 per cent larger. This increase was obtained by opening out the cylinder bores from 57 to 60 mm., the engine remaining in all other respects dimensionally the same. Retention of the existing size of combustion space automatically raised the compression to 6·8 to 1, a ratio still well within the capabilities of the engine on the fuels which were then currently available from 'the pump'. Initially, the improvement of power output derived from these changes was disappointing, and it is interesting that this was rectified merely by an alteration in the width of piston ring. The rings used on the original tests were 0·078 in. wide and the resulting power was 39·9 at 5500. Substitution of rings 0·093 in. wide improved this to 43·3 h.p. at the same engine speed.

The PA and the PB were both sports, not racing cars, but we have given some space to a description of them because the PA was used officially in the Le Mans 24-hour race of 1935. Kimber had had his eyes on the Rudge-Whitworth Trophy for a long time, but this was a biennial award, it being necessary to qualify in one year to be able to compete for the cup in the succeeding year. Obviously, reliability was of first importance for the qualifying year and, as the minimum speeds required for each class were quite modest, a rugged, uncomplicated, unsupercharged car, such as the PA, seemed to be a good choice.

The details of the preparation of the cars and the conduct of the event stand out in the memories of the members of the MG Competition Department for two reasons. One is that it was the first time in their racing history that they had had sufficient time to prepare the cars to their own entire satisfaction. The other, that it was the last because, when they returned from Le Mans expecting to find everyone jubilant at the success, they found little but apathy and dejection, the ban having fallen, during their absence, on the construction of racing cars and on official MG support for racing. The irony of it was extreme, the whole event having been run without any major hitch and very few minor ones, and providing three perfectly good qualifications for the following year which it would not be possible to utilise.

The cars were made available several months before the race and the work of their preparation was carried on unhurriedly and methodically. Engines were run-in on the test bed, tested for power and then dismantled for a final check. All fitting in the rest of the chassis was examined in detail and all nuts pinned or wired. The sole constructional departures from standard were the fitment of cycle-type wings, stoneguards to headlamps and the cutting away of portions of the front apron to assist oil cooling. Tail lamps were duplicated and fitted with a change-over switch, tell-tale lights on the instrument panel being wired in series with each. Instrument lights were operated by a push button on the steering wheel. All cars were completely ready, stored away and sheeted by the end of March, two clear months before the race.

George Eyston selected a complete team of ladies for the event, all of whom were of known driving ability, but to whom a wheel in a twenty-four hour race was a new experience. Miss Doreen Evans and Miss Margaret Allan had handled an NE apiece in the 1934 Relay Race, and for Le Mans the former was teamed with Miss Barbara Skinner and the latter with Mrs. Hugh Eaton. The third car was driven by Miss Joan Richmond and Mrs. Gordon Simpson. As was to be expected, the ladies and their cars were very much photographed prior to the event, but most of them would have liked to have been able to lay hands on the wretched journalist who dubbed them 'George Eyston's Dancing Daughters' and produced a headline in the daily Press to that effect. The name caught on and has, in fact been common currency in the MG factory ever since, when occasion has arisen to refer to the 1935 Le Mans.

The selection was a complete success from every point of view, particularly that of team management and pit control. Galling as it may be to the male sex to read it, discipline could not have been better, and to the MG pit personnel it was a complete novelty to find all drivers arrived, for instance, for practice at the appointed hour. The set minimum average speed for cars of the engine size of the PA was quite modest and, on the rather complicated formula, worked out at 47·38 m.p.h. This was well within the car's capabilities, and pit control's main problem would be to keep speeds *down*. The race regulations needed a careful eye, too, as an instance of which the following extract, from the instructions issued by Eyston to the pit staff, is interesting.

"Any laps done in excess of 136 *must* be at an average speed faster than the set minimum. Zero one watch when the car completes 136 laps and use schedule again to see that this rule is complied with."

(The schedule here referred to consisted of a list of times for the completion of each of the 136 laps worked out in advance and based on the set minimum speed.)

"Any car taking more than thirty minutes to complete the lap on which it is engaged at the expiration of the 24th hour will be excluded. If a car is crippled, but has completed its minimum distance, keep working on it at the pits, but don't start another lap."

In due time, cars, drivers, mechanics and pit staff left Abingdon for the journey to Le Mans, drivers taking turn and turn about in order to accustom themselves to their vehicles. Arrived on the course, practice was concluded without incident, and without any work on the cars being necessary beyond routine adjustments, change of oils and so on. The smooth routine persisted through the race itself, when a set schedule in excess of 53 m.p.h. was maintained by all cars, the only replacement necessary being one tail-lamp bulb!

Such was the stout, though isolated, contribution of the P Type to official MG racing history. Its main claim to fame, however, came in the indirect sense that its engine provided the basis for the new racing Midgets. Previously, the production sports car and its racing counterpart had been of similar dimensions, as in the case of the D and C Types in 1931, and the J2 and J4 in 1933. It was felt, however, that the J4 was just about as fast as a car of its size could be, consistent with stability and reasonable safety. For its successor, the Q Type, it was decided to increase the wheelbase and track on the basis that the increased power expected would more than compensate for the additional weight which would be inevitable. The wheelbase was made the same as on the K3, and N Type axles—3 ft. 9 in. track—were used.

The centre crankshaft bearing had been adopted in order to permit higher blower pressures, and these were secured by the adoption of a Zoller supercharger driven at 69 per cent of engine speed, and delivering 25 to 28 lb. per sq. in. The blower was specially developed by its manufacturers in collaboration with the MG designers, and it can be said that, for the first time, engine and blower were designed together as an entity. The results achieved have already been mentioned in connection with the Magic Midget, in which one of these units was ultimately installed, and reference to *Fig.* 6 will show the power given. For the first time, 150 b.h.p. per litre became a reality.

Such power was likely to give the back axle a rough time, particularly as a Wilson pre-selector gearbox was used. On the K3, axle failure had been overcome by stiffening up the final drive, but this was not possible on the Q Type, which had the much smaller N axle. Remember, too, that the 746-c.c. engine was now giving almost as much power as the 1100-c.c. K engine of a year before. The possibility of trouble was eliminated by an elegant safety device, in the form of a clutch built into the flywheel in the ordinary way, but provided with no pedal or other means of operation. The clutch was designed to slip, when hot, at 1·25 times maximum engine torque and this, when multiplied by the bottom gear reduction ratio, was just safely within the capacity of the rear axle. Thus, when changing gear and taking full advantage of the potentialities of the self-changing gearbox, the inertia loading of crankshaft and flywheel caused the clutch to slip momentarily and no damage was done.

The car, in general layout, followed the 1934 K3 very closely. In fact, in side elevation it was not easy to tell the two cars apart. There were differences, however. The twin brake cam lever was not adopted for the Q Type, but a composite steel brake drum was introduced; the fuel tank, of 19 gallons capacity, did not form part of the outer skin of the body, but was all enclosed. Battery and coil ignition was used and no provision was made for any electrical equipment beyond the fuel pump and starter, as road-racing equipment, wings and lamps, were not supplied. The rear suspension was controlled by hydraulic shock-absorbers in place of the twin duplex friction types of the K3. And, finally, 18-in. road wheels with 4·75-in. tyres were used, as compared with 19-in. wheels of the K3, with the final drive ratio—straight cut, of course—of 4·5 to 1. 4·875 to 1 was available as an alternative. The complete car, ready to go, turned the scale at a few pounds over thirteen hundredweight.

It is an odd thing that just as the J4 achieved its main successes at the hands of one man—Hugh Hamilton—so the Q showed its paces under the guidance—or domination—of his friend and business associate, Bill Everitt. The final track-testing of the car was entrusted to him, and on Whit Monday he broke the Class H Brooklands Mountain lap record at 69·97, first time out. He then went to a Donington Park meeting, collecting one first and two seconds at speeds up to 65 m.p.h., and next, on August 1 at Brooklands, broke the standing kilometre and standing mile records at 69·75 and 79·88 m.p.h. respectively. This was a direct measure of the improvement of the Q, as these records were taken from E. R. Hall who, in a J4, had held them since the previous year at 67·21 and 74·74 m.p.h. Not content with this, Everitt was out again in October, to raise the Mountain Lap to 75·58 and the standing kilometre and mile to the remarkable figures of 75·42 and 85·59. It is noteworthy that the Mountain speed was almost three miles per hour faster than the then 1100-c.c. record, held by Seaman on the K3, and that the Standing Mile beat, by a small margin, Horton's 1100-c.c. record, on the special K3, made two months earlier.

The general consensus of opinion was that the Q Type was just about as fast as a 750-c.c. car could be, and even so, all the available acceleration could not be used because of wheelspin, so the problem arose—What next? Pre-occupied though they had been with the intensive development work in their own particular sphere, the MG designers had watched—from some little distance—the experiments

which were being made by other manufacturers—chiefly Continental—
with independent suspension. It seemed that the only way in which the
Midget could be persuaded to keep its feet on the ground, under the
fierce acceleration and high speeds now being obtained, would be by
means of a serious attack upon unsprung weight, and this, among
other things, was what independent suspension achieved. The designers'
knowledge of this, let alone their practical experience, was, to say the
most, very little, but this did not deter them from embarking on a highly
ambitious project. For the first time in the history of the Company it
was decided to design and build an out-and-out racing car, having no
sports counterpart, and no ready-made major components except the
power unit. An intensive study of the whole new field was embarked
upon, the designers purging their minds of all pre-conceived ideas of
orthodox construction and starting—almost literally—with a clean
sheet of paper. The object was to design and produce a single-seat
racing car, using the Q power unit, having independent suspension on all
four wheels, the complete projectile being no heavier, and preferably
lighter, than the Q. It was a bold concept, and some there are who, in
retrospect, will say that the designers over-reached themselves; that it
would have been more prudent to make haste slowly and retain an
orthodox rear axle until experiment should prove the new designs a bit
at a time; that if this had been done, the result would have been a world-
beater. Unfortunately, for reasons already touched upon and which are
in part explained in the intermission following this chapter, we shall
never know.

In all previous Midgets, incorporating the orthodox front axle
beam, the chassis frame had been designed to be torsionally flexible as
part of the means of ensuring front end stability at speed. One of the
first requirements, with independent suspension, was that the chassis
should be as rigid as it was possible to make it. So, from very first
principles, a complete change of ideas was necessary, and the frame
finally decided upon was a box-sectioned affair of highly stressed sheet-
metal, shaped in plan view rather like a 'Y' with its forked end forward.
This can be seen from the pictures in *Plates XVII* and *XVIII*. The prototype of this frame stood for some weeks on a pair of trestles in the
experimental shop at Abingdon, while the rest of the car was designed
and built round it. H. N. Charles, the chief engineer, was in and out of
the shop all day long and seldom failed, on entering, to stand on the
frame and jump his considerable weight up and down remarking, to himself or to the world at large, "Like standing on the floor". This almost
invariable performance rather tickled the mechanics who, after a few
days, started to make a chalk mark on the wall every time this comment
was uttered. By the time a fortnight had passed, the row of chalk marks
extended for three sides of the room, and it was not long before Charles
enquired what they were for. That cured him.

The front wheel hubs and swivel pins were coupled to the frame by means of wishbones of unequal length in the now familiar manner which ensures that track width is maintained regardless of the deflection of the suspension. Long torsion bars extended backwards to the mid-point of the chassis frame and terminated in trimming adjustments. The rear arrangement was similar in general layout, but the arms were of equal length, top and bottom, so that the rear wheels worked on a parallelogram. Again, torsion bars ran forward to terminations amidships, adjacent to those of the front bars. The lower pair of wishbones on each side were connected to the torsion bars and therefore carried the weight of the car, while the upper pair merely constrained the wheel into the vertical. The dimensions of all these parts were very carefully calculated and everyone was amazed to find that the upper arms, though admittedly made of high-tensile steel, were little more than $\frac{5}{16}$ in. in diameter. Such was the incredulity that Renwick's stress calculations were sent to Reid Railton for a check, but even after he had confirmed them, it was decided to thicken the arms up a bit because it was felt that no racing driver would relish the idea of entrusting his life to a pair of knitting needles.

The engine sat between the arms of the 'Y' in the orthodox position. As the car was a single-seater, the gear-operating pedal was placed on the left of the gearbox and means had to be found to carry the steering linkage clear of the power unit. The steering mast was therefore very short, terminating at the bulkhead between engine and driver, where a double steering box was mounted, feeding a drop-arm on either side of the car from which a straight push-pull rod went to each front wheel. The drive from the rear of the pre-selector box was carried to the final drive by means of an orthodox universally jointed propeller shaft as, not only did this avoid the necessity of designing a special shaft, but the universals would allow for any slight movements of the frame which might occur. The final drive housing was mounted securely to the rear end of the chassis frame and contained a normal crown and bevel and differential, but on either side of it, the drive continued to the road wheels by means of short universally jointed shafts. These were of similar length and parallel to the rear suspension links and were therefore almost entirely free from telescopic effects.

The final drive housing is worth special mention as it provides a means of introducing the subject of a ubiquitous alloy, known nowhere in the world outside the experimental department of the Abingdon factory, and named 'Pistominium'. In the course of development work, light alloy castings of one sort and another were frequently required at short notice and, there being no foundry, makeshift methods were adopted as a matter of routine. Certainly the casting of the first drive case for the prototype was somewhat ambitious, judged by previous pourings which had scarcely gone beyond the odd packing piece or body bracket, but, nothing daunted, a pattern was made, core box prepared and all made ready. Into the pot on the forge went all the scrap aluminium which could be found lying around and, as this consisted mainly of old pistons, 'Pistominium' was born. There was no furnace or bake-oven either, so core-boxes were invariably rather damp and pouring was a hazardous event. The boys tossed up for who was to pour and then, while every-one else cowered in corners, under benches and with their heads well pulled down inside overall blouses, the unfortunate winner got on with the business, keeping everybody informed of his progress with a running fire of humorous comment. You may smile—that is the intention, of course—but that final drive ran satisfactorily for many miles and is still in existence to-day.

But to return to the motor-car. The engine had to be modified in detail from that used in the Q Type. A vertical magneto replaced the distributor and, as there was no electrical equipment, the dynamo's entrails were removed (its shell and shaft had to remain, as it was the means of transferring the drive from crankshaft to camshaft). As there was no starter motor, one of the gears of the blower reduction drive was brought out through the side of its casing to engage with a sliding spur gear which received the starting handle. From a starting point of view, this was a mere formality, as everyone push-started anyway, but it *was* convenient for adjusting the tappets. The one electrical device which remained was the fuel pump, for which a small six-volt battery was included which had to be charged between races. There was a long-term plan to replace this with a mechanical pump, but this never had a chance to come about.

Over the whole of the front end, supercharger, carburetter and radiator, went a detachable cowl of a new MG registered design—looking rather like a Jersey cow, somebody said—but as much ahead oı its time as the rest of the car. A sleek single-seat body of which the outside of the fuel tank formed a part, completed a thoroughly work-manlike job which scaled 12½ cwt. It was beyond doubt that the MG engineers had produced a truly classic design.

The first time the model was out in force was in the J.C.C. Inter-national Trophy Race at Brooklands in April and this showed many things. It was obvious that, from the point of view of straight running round the outer circuit, something quite revolutionary in the way of a comfortable ride had been achieved. All the major bumps on the course were ironed completely flat, and an onlooker could see that the car seemed to float along over the roughest sections. That it came as a surprise, if not a shock, to the seasoned drivers is illustrated by the fact that Handley, after practice, was beseeching Charles to 'take it away and clamp a pair of half-elliptics on the back'. More likely, however, this comment was prompted by the car's behaviour on corners. With parallelogram action in the suspension, the centre of roll is on the ground and, the centre of gravity being some distance above this, the whole car heels over outwards on a corner, taking the wheels with it. This meant that the car adopted some highly unconventional and distinctly awesome postures and the sensation to the driver was, to say the least of it, novel once he had overcome his fright. But, for all that, all four wheels remained firmly on the ground under all conditions, it seemed almost impossible to make the car slide on a corner, a much greater proportion of the available engine power could be used for acceleration, and braking was revolutionised. Unfortunately, in this race, there was an unexpected epidemic of valve-spring trouble, although two of the cars completed the 260 miles, one leading its group and securing sixth place in the race at over 82 m.p.h. But the 'backbone' of the frame of this car was found to be split.

The next excursion was to the Isle of Man for the Mannin Beg, a race which was to prove to be as big a débâcle for the R Types as it had been for the K Types two years earlier—and for very similar reasons. Car after car, both in practice and during the race, broke the short propeller shafts between differential and rear wheels, and only one car finished. Investigation by the designers on the spot failed to indicate any stressing errors, the shafts themselves certainly being strong enough for their job. Obviously there was a catch somewhere. At one part of the course the road climbed steeply—a fast third-speed climb for most cars—and was crossed by other roads, at which points the gradient levelled out for a short distance and then began again. On reaching these intersections, the cars tended to leave the ground—or at least rise to the upward limit of their suspensions—and then smack down again, deflecting the springs to their bump stops. These stops on the R's were so placed that both the upper and lower limits of movement of the wheels were quite comfortably within the maximum operating angles of the universal joints of the drive shafts, yet it appeared obvious that these were being overloaded to breaking point. Subsequent investigation showed that temperature rise in the hydraulic shock-absorbers weakened their efficiency to the point where they permitted the wish-bones to strike their stops much more heavily than was originally envisaged in the design. As the stops were towards the in-board ends of these links, the latter sprung under the exceptional loads prevailing and allowed the drive shafts to be deflected beyond their critical angle.

The remedy, once the cause was known, was simple, but unfor-tunately, the opportunity to put it into effect never arose. With the acquisition of the MG Car Company from Lord Nuffield by Morris Motors Ltd., the racing activities came to an abrupt termination. From many points of view, it was an inglorious end to five magnificent years, and one is left to speculate upon what this revolutionary, yet basically correct, car would have become once the 'bugs had been taken out of it'.

INTERMISSION

When racing was stopped, a statement was issued which is here quoted from "The Sports Car" of August 1935.

"Lord Nuffield has said there are to be no more MG racing cars. This announcement came as a shock to all and sundry connected with or interested in the sport, for since 1931 one or other of the highly successful MG racing types has either won outright, or most certainly been well in the picture, in almost every British and Continental event for which the cars have been eligible.

"In fact, if the upholding of British prestige abroad can be laid at the door of any one marque that surely is MG.

"Why this decision? Some of those who assume the wisdom of experience have said 'What has happened to every other manufacturer who has raced to any extent?' 'Why, of course, their financial resources are at an end!'

"This reason can be discounted right away when it is explained that as a company we have never raced. Racing has always been left to the enterprise of the private enthusiast. Also our last balance sheet would satisfy the most critical shareholder.

"The real reasons for discontinuing the building of racing machines are as follows:—

"First of all, the Directors have decided that, at all events for the present time, racing for the purpose of development has, in our case, served its useful purpose.

"Another reason, rather more obscure, purely concerns racing itself and has no bearing on the commercial aspect, namely, that we are handicapped out of British racing, through no real fault of the handicapper. It is simply a case of carrying a fundamentally unsatisfactory system to its logical conclusion.

"It stands to reason that a car which very frequently wins must inevitably have its handicapped speeds increased to a greater amount than the 'also rans', whose development and speed capabilities are to the handicapper far more nebulous.

"This attitude can better be understood when it is appreciated that MG racing cars are securing first places in almost all the Continental events in which they compete and which are run on a class basis without handicap systems.

"This is briefly the true state of affairs with MG racing and we are going, so to speak, to rest on our laurels. We intend to let the production type catch up with the extremely advanced ideas incorporated in the present

racing car, which is highly specialised and years ahead of its time when regarded from the point of view of applying its design to standard machines.

"There are many MG cars competing in races at present and they are likely to do so for several seasons, so the name will continue to appear in the racing programmes until such times as we may be ready again to use the field once more for development."

All this was quite true and made good sense, but the statement did not give what is perhaps the main reason for the decision. Both the MG Car Company and the Austin Motor Company were spending large sums of money designing and building very small quantities of highly specialised vehicles for the primary purpose of competing against one another. In the 750-c.c. class, nobody else could get a look-in. It was all great fun, but commercially there was no future in it and so, through a private truce between the two companies, it stopped.

The beginning of the book will have made it clear that the MG Car Company came into being on a wave of enthusiasm, and it may be thought that it was kept on the crest of this wave only by its continual successes in the competition world. Had this been so it would never have ridden the blow which the cessation of racing delivered. By then, however, the roots had gone far deeper, and although it is true to say that those who were intimately connected with the racing game felt at the time that their world had ceased to exist, the enthusiasm survived and found its outlet in the continual struggle for improvement of the sports cars, and the vigorous solution of the innumerable problems which arose from day to day.

George Eyston visits his tailors for a 'fitting' of EX 135. He had been 'measured' some weeks earlier.

EYSTON in the car at Montlhery, with the track body. Colours: cream and brown—hence 'Humbug'.

The complete car in Road-racing trim.

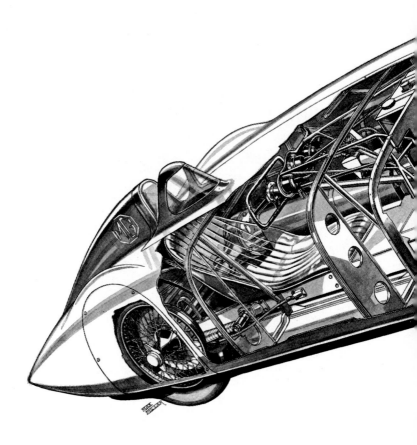

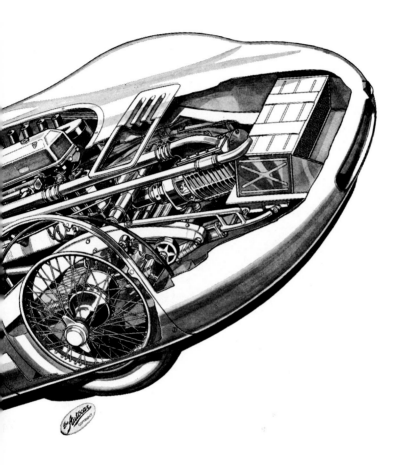

Drawing of EX 135, reproduced by courtesy of *The Autocar*

The NE Type was introduced to defeat the supercharger ban in the Ulster T.T. of 1934.
Above: DODSON, the winner, passes the grandstand for the last time.

Photo by Barratts

The Brothers Evans in close company at Quarry Corner in the 1935 Race.

EX 135 in its modern guise. The photograph shows GOLDIE GARDNER driving, on the occasion when he achieved over 200 m.p.h. at Dessau in 1939.

CHAPTER X

EX 135

THE ban on racing activities called only a temporary halt to the business of record-breaking. But for this, the story of EX 135 would have been brief.

Late in 1933, the first year of the K3, George Eyston ordered from Kimber a special car, to be based on the K3, and to be an International Class G version of the by then famous Magic Midget, EX 127. The fundamentals of the specification were that the car was to have maximum power with minimum frontal area and drag, for record-breaking purposes, and was to be suitable in addition for road-racing, for which an alternative and interchangeable body was to be provided.

Eyston visited the factory at Abingdon and was literally measured for his car. He sat in various postures in front of a large vertical drawing board and his silhouette was sketched. The design staff looked at their register of experimental projects and, as the next available number was EX 135, this became the official designation of the car. Charles has commented on the high proportion of small car drivers who are big in stature, and Eyston was a case in point. Experience with EX 127 had shown that to reduce the frontal area to a minimum, it was essential for the seat to be between a chassis side member and the propeller shaft, and this automatically dictated an offset transmission line. In order to secure an optimum overall shape, it was decided to lengthen the wheel-base, compared with the standard K3, to 8 ft. 3 in., and to adopt an angle of offset of 6°. The rear axle was built of light alloy castings and steel tubes, the final drive being as near to the left-hand end of the axle as it would go, the otherwise straight chassis side member being cranked so as not to interfere. From the rear axle pinion the drive ran forward in a perfectly straight line, at an angle of 6° to the centre-line of the car, through propeller shaft, gearbox, crankshaft and supercharger drive. To provide sufficient rigidity, the chassis side-members, which on the K3 were of open U-section, were boxed, plates being welded along the entire length of the open side of the channel.

A standard K3 front axle was used, incorporating the scissor-type brake gear, but this latter was made easily removable as it was not intended to carry front brakes when the car was used for record-breaking. Very stiff road springs were used, damping being provided by semi-rotary hydraulic shock-absorbers, those at the front being mounted high up on the frame, housed within the body framework, and connected to the axle by long vertical links. The rear damping was assisted by a pair of friction type shock-absorbers having long arms, and so arranged that they acted as radius rods and relieved the rear road springs of drive and braking torque. Normal K3 Type torque reaction cables were fitted at the front.

The fireproof bulkhead behind the engine provided a mounting point, on the engine side, for the reserve engine-oil tank and an independent oil supply for the supercharger. A lattice structure on the driver's side carried the instrument panel and the hand air-pump for the fuel feed, the fuel tank being behind the driver. A normal K3 power unit with Powerplus blower was used, the radiator being specially constructed to conform to the contours of the track body. As with EX 127, the engine cover—which formed the entire forepart of the track body— was arranged to have an adjustable opening at its junction with the body proper, by means of which the volume of air passing through the radiator could be controlled.

The track body, which had smooth contours with few excrescences, was painted in the MG Company's colours, cream and brown, in stripes and this rapidly earned the car the nickname 'Humbug'. The road-racing body was considerably flatter in side elevation than the track body and had a large open cockpit to afford the driver better visibility and greater freedom of movement. This body was—by reason of a difference of opinion with the Experimental Department's sheet metal worker who refused to work week-ends—constructed by Jackson and Marney, whose skill as panel-beaters was attained more by adoption than by training. Perhaps it was a little unfair to the finished article that it should, in consequence, have come to be known as the 'Coal Scuttle'. The car, with its two bodies, is shown on *Plate XIII*.

Its first public appearance was in the Mannin Beg race of 1934, when, with road-racing body, it took third place at 69·93 m.p.h. behind Black and Dodson's standard K3s. In the process, it gave a convincing demonstration of its potentialities by breaking the Class G lap record at 74·40, but plug trouble held it up. There was little surprise, therefore, when it won the B.R.D.C. British Empire Trophy at Brooklands a month later, in the same trim.

The track body was given an airing in September when the car was entered for the B.R.D.C. 500-mile Race, again at Brooklands. It created a sensation by lapping comfortably in excess of its handicap speed and piling up a commanding lead by half-distance, at which time it had averaged over 113 m.p.h. Shortly after this, while it was being driven by Wally Handley, its relief driver, it came off the home banking in a terrific skid, ran sideways for some 200 yards and finished up on the grass on the inside of the track. Handley reported that 'something had locked up', but this story was discounted in view of the fact that Handley had already made quite a few spectacular exits from the running during this and the preceding season. The suspicion was confirmed when Jackson *drove* the car back to its stable after the race. Handley was insistent, however, and there was a greater inclination to listen to him when a large flat was discovered on the tread of one of the rear tyres. Further examination disclosed a well-blued rear hub ball-race, which both explained the skid and exonerated Handley.

Back at Abingdon after this race, preparation work began for a series of record attempts to be made covering all Class G records up to one hour. Nothing was envisaged beyond a careful check of the whole car, the engine being bench-tested just prior to shipment.

At about this time, MG's had begun to toy with the Zoller supercharger, and Harold Robinson was in charge of installation and tests on a K3 engine. While engaged on a run with this engine he saw a torque reading which was equivalent to 200 h.p. The news was treated with the utmost scepticism by the rest of the boys in the racing shop, but Robby was adamant and conveyed the news to Charles who, in turn, told Kimber. Exactly what was said at the time is not recorded, but Jackson, who was engaged in putting the final touches to Eyston's car prior to departure for Montlhery, was horrified to receive instructions from Kimber to install the Zoller blown engine in the car, and to learn that the purpose was an attack on the World's Hour Record—that is, the hour record for cars irrespective of engine size and which stood at that time at around 134 m.p.h. The idea was doubtless born of great enthusiasm, but for many reasons it was not only over-ambitious, but perhaps also not in the best of taste. The car was Eyston's property and he was sponsoring the record attempt. Moreover, he was interested both technically and financially in the manufacture of Powerplus superchargers, and could only be expected to care rather less than nothing about the Zoller. Apart from these ethical considerations, the car had not yet achieved 120 m.p.h. over a short distance, let alone 140 for a solid hour, and there was a wealth of difference between a momentary flash of 200 h.p.—even assuming this had, in fact, been achieved and nobody had made a mistake—and the maintenance of a steady, say, 175. However, the arrangements went ahead; Jackson persuaded Kimber to let Robby go with him to Montlhery to tune the engine; Eyston was pretty put out about the whole affair.

At Montlhery, it seemed to be impossible to make the engine run clean. It was tuned, tested and tuned again, but despite occasional bursts when it showed its latent possibilities, the engine misfired, banged off through its release valve, and generally exhibited a disinclination to behave. Leaded fuel was being used which made it difficult to read the plugs and deduce the mixture condition. While all this was going on, Robinson was having his leg pulled unmercifully, and among the many gratuitous suggestions offered by the other mechanics was one from

Denly that Robby had put the wrong pistons in. Before long it became necessary to take the head off, as certain cylinders were losing compression and, while Robinson scrutinised the head, Denly noticed that Nos. 1 and 6 pistons were about ⅛ in. down their cylinder bores compared with the remaining four. It appeared that Denly's theory—far-fetched though it sounded—might have some substance. When the sump was removed, however, it was found that the two end connecting rods each had a double set which shortened their effective length by this very large amount. It was apparent that the detonation over the preceding few days had been sufficient to bend the rods, which explained also other connecting rod failures, which had occurred on the test bed, despite their being strong enough for their theoretical job and devoid of cracks or flaws.

It was thereupon decided to fit new connecting rods, touch in valves, re-assemble and make one more test. This was done and the car covered three laps of the track with only a moderate amount of misfiring—but then lapsed into silence amid a large cloud of smoke. With the engine cover removed, the blower casing was found to have split and Eyston's consequent remark—"Thank God for that"—was doubtless as pardonable as it was, perhaps, uncharitable, for the failure was the answer to most of his current difficulties.

So ended the ill-fated attempt on the World's Hour Record—literally in a puff of smoke. Now it was possible to get back to the original project and go for records in the way which had long since been carefully planned. It took rather less than a day to re-install the Powerplus blower and, after tuning, the engine ran perfectly clean on its first test run. On October 27, Eyston took the car out, captured the flying mile and kilometre records at 128·7 m.p.h., and went on up to ten miles which distance was reached at 128·53. Next day, he went for the Class G one-hour record and achieved his primary object by covering 120·88 miles. The consistency of the running may be judged from the speeds at which the intervening records fell, remembering that the One Hour is taken from a standing start: 50 kilometres, 119·84 m.p.h.; 50 miles, 120·72; 100 kilometres, 121·65; 100 miles, 121·13; 200 kilometres, 120·82.

This was the first and last appearance of EX 135 as a record-breaker in the hands of George Eyston. The following year, MG's racing axe fell. Eyston sold the car and, but for an entirely independent chain of circumstances, that might well have been the last to be heard of it altogether.

The other outstanding contemporary K3 was the offset single-seater owned by R. T. Horton, and prepared by R. R. (Robin) Jackson of Weybridge (not to be confused with R. C. (Reg.) Jackson of the MG Car Company). This car, it will be remembered, had held the Class G One Hour at 117 m.p.h. prior to Eyston's run, and had also taken the standing start mile at 83·2. Shortly after these achievements, Horton had retired from racing, and had sold the car to Major A. T. Goldie Gardner. It first re-appeared in the hands of its new owner at the Brooklands Bank Holiday meeting of August, 1936, where it established a new Class G outer circuit lap record at 124·40 m.p.h., which was particularly remarkable because it came within reasonable speed of the accepted maximum for the track. On the following day, in the course of attempts on British records—which were subsequently disallowed because of a misunderstanding with the timekeepers—he covered 50 miles at over 119 m.p.h. These events, coming after some twelve months of MG inactivity, fired Kimber's enthusiasm again, and he agreed with Gardner to prepare the car and put the services of Reg. Jackson at his disposal for his next attempt.

The preparation of the power unit remained in the hands of Robin Jackson, who introduced a series of important changes in the engine. Profiting from the experiences of Bobby Kohlrausch, who had had a cylinder head for the Magic Midget cast in bronze by Robert Kramer of Cologne, a six-cylinder head, in similar material, was made for the K3. Robin Jackson abandoned the MG method of securing engine valves with circlips, and returned to the time-honoured split cotter, seating the valves directly on to the bronze. He designed a special camshaft, to make the best use of the high blower pressures intended, and installed a No. 10 Powerplus blower which was specially built, incorporating ports of a size appropriate to the next larger blower, the No. 11. The engine thus modified having given a satisfactory showing on the test bed, the car was shipped to Weybridge for installation, and arrangements made for a run on the Autobahn at Frankfurt in June.

During the preceding two years Eyston's kilometre and mile records had been raised, by Maserati, to 131 and 138 m.p.h. respectively, so Gardner had quite a task in front of him, but these proved to be relatively easy meat, speeds in excess of 142 m.p.h. being returned for both distances. Well satisfied, the party moved on to Montlhery to essay the longer distances up to one hour. Misfiring at high speed had persisted during the running at Frankfurt, and continued at Montlhery, the blower outlet manifold splitting before a run could be undertaken. With this repaired, the run began, but after taking a few records up to 50 kilometres, the manifold split a second time and further attempts were abandoned. The work done had sufficed, however, to show that the engine changes were very much in the right direction, and that it would not be very difficult to improve on even these new speeds. The goal, obviously, was 150 m.p.h.

In the intervening four months, before the car went out again in October, further changes were incorporated in the engine. The Zoller supercharger came back, this time with a chain and sprocket reduction gear at its front end, a long shaft running forward from the front of the engine. Robin Jackson also introduced a new induction manifold on which the gas entered at the *centre* instead of at one end as on the K3. But even with these alterations and with a change of fuel, the car again misfired at speed when it next arrived in Frankfurt. Despite much tuning, this persisted until Reg Jackson drove the car in order to try to discover at first hand what was amiss. Never having driven the car at speed before and in any case being very much pre-occupied with the engine and the revolution counter, he completely misjudged the length of road which had been made available for the record and arrived, beyond the far end, at a point where a German cinema unit was busy making a film; actors, extras, and film paraphernalia being spread all over the highway. Somehow they melted away at his approach and there was no mishap, but the car had run substantially clean. Goldie took the car over at once and broke his own mile and kilometre records at over 148 m.p.h., fast enough to take the records but still short of 150 m.p.h. On the next run, however, the blower drive disintegrated.

These last records were important because they were made on the occasion of the German Record Week, when, it will be remembered, Rosemeyer drove the Auto Union at 257 m.p.h. The world of European motor sport was there, and all were much impressed by the high speed of Goldie's diminutive machine. Chief among them, from the MG point of view, was Eberan von Eberhorst, Chief Engineer of Auto Union and collaborator with Dr. Porsche, who in discussing the MG expressed the view that the next logical step in its development for record-breaking was to provide it with an all-enclosed body, such as on the Auto Union. This aspect was fully discussed between Gardner and Kimber, and on their return to England they approached Lord Nuffield to secure his blessing on the project. Before long, it was announced that a new car was to be built, the object being to achieve 170 m.p.h. with an 1100-c.c. engine, thereby securing for Britain world supremacy in the small car field.

The broad outline of the plan took shape very quickly, and it was considered desirable to locate EX 135 and buy it from its owner, to use it as the basis of the new car. Once this was done, the outlining of the body was entrusted to Mr. Reid Railton, who had at that time just completed a beautiful job on Mr. John Cobb's car for the World Land Speed Record. The rebuilding of the chassis and the construction of the body was undertaken by the Abingdon factory, and it was arranged that Robin Jackson would continue with the development and preparation of the engine of Gardner's own car for ultimate installation in the new machine. Work began on this basis.

In plan, the main measurements of the body were controlled by the existing chassis dimensions. It would have been possible to reduce the overall size of the finished car only by a substantial re-design of the chassis, and it was considered safer to adhere to the already well-tried foundation. Concessions were made, however, by the use of special road-wheels, which reduced the effective track to 47 in. at the front and 46½ in. at the rear. The steering movement of the front wheels was then deliberately restricted to 18° and the waistline of the body drawn so as to give but ¾ in. clearance to the tyres when on full steering lock, nose and tail being blended in to the best advantage.

The side elevation was next schemed with the driver sitting but 7 in. off the ground. Goldie Gardner is well over 6 ft. tall—another instance of the big man in a little car—and it was found that, if he adopted the normal upright driving position, the total frontal area of the car worked out at a great deal more than the desirable maximum. After some considerable discussion and experiment, he agreed to the use of a hammock-type seat, of which the back-rest lay at an angle of 45°. He was therefore to drive the car in a half-lying position, and this enabled the frontal area of the car, including the driver's windscreen and the protruding portions of the road wheels, to be reduced to the very satisfactory figure of 11 sq. ft., the driver, from seat to shoulders, being compressed into a vertical height of only 22 in.

With the plan and side elevations decided, the overall shape of the body was then worked out in order to provide the smoothest possible air flow over its surface, consistent with the maintenance of good directional stability and—most important—absence of any tendency to 'take off' at speed. In aid of this latter, the nose of the body was designed to have a fairly steep fall-off towards the front, a feature which was subsequently found to be covered by the German 'Jaray' patents. In addition, the underside of the body, which was dead flat between the axles, was tipped downwards into the wind, such that the ground clearance under the front axle was 5 in. and under the rear axle 7 in. The combination of these two features led the aerofoil shape into the wind with a negative angle of incidence, which successfully eliminated all tendency of the front of the car to lift at high speeds and at maximum engine torque.

It was also desirable to shape the body so as to be subject to as little disturbance as possible from cross winds. The ideal requirements for purely forward motion indicated that the fairings over the front wheels should be run straight through the length of the car to join up with the rear wheel fairings, but this would have had the effect of increasing the area of the side of the car and of presenting a large flat surface to side winds. A small concession to forward efficiency was therefore admitted, the wheel fairings were made discontinuous, and the sides of the body radiused considerably, top and bottom.

The driver's head protruded through the top panelling where it was covered by a removable moulded perspex windshield. An upholstered pad was placed behind his head and streamlined off into the body tail. The top panels closed fairly closely on to the driver's shoulders, but were left springy at this point to accommodate any vertical movement which might arise from road inequalities. In this original design, the driver was not completely covered in, as it would have been necessary to increase the size of the windshield and fairing to allow for this move-ment. Accordingly the dome was left open over the driver's head, and provided with a sponge-rubber guard around its edge.

Integral with the body, provision had to be made for ducting the cooling air and the air supply to the carburetters. It had been decided to adhere to the well-tried honeycomb form of radiator, and this was placed low down on the front of the chassis. A slot was provided in the leading edge of the nose and the air conveyed by a tunnel, through the radiator and emerging by a louvred grill placed at the bridge of the nose. To one side of the slot, an air intake port connected to another duct feeding the carburetters. This port projected some 3 in. in front of the main line of the body in order to eliminate the possibility of starvation from eddy effects. It is to be noted that the engine compart-ment was thus sealed off, neither cooling air nor the intake leading to the engine itself.

Each of the four road wheels was completely enclosed in a box constructed internally to the body, only the lower edges of the wheels protruding through on to the road. This was done to reduce pumping losses. The outside of each box was made detachable to enable the wheel to be removed.

The complete exterior shape of the car was set down on paper in the form of a series of transverse cross-sections taken every 6 in., much as is done in boat-building. Pursuing this practice a stage further, a full-size wooden jig was made, $\frac{1}{2}$-in. plyboard being cut to drawing and mounted, each 6 in., on a central longitudinal member. This done, locations were provided for the top cover, windshield, undertray and wheel covers and the entire former then shipped to the sheet-metal works for the panelling to be made. This was carried out in 18-gauge aluminium sheet, hand-beaten in sixteen separate sections which were then welded together on the fixture.

While the body-shell construction was in progress, a second jig was in use as a foundation for the framework, which was constructed mainly from 20-gauge Duralumin flanged U-channel, the flanges being outwards to facilitate attachment of the panels. Seven rings, conform-ing to the shape of the body, were first constructed and spaced out along the length of the car, these being tied together by a cruciform arrangement of channel down each side. Four of the rings carried light steel plates attached to their undersides to act as mounting brackets to the chassis, and one was blanked in completely to provide a firewall between engine and driver. Cross-bracing was applied as necessary to prevent lozenging and the entire framework, assembled with $\frac{3}{16}$-in. Dura-lumin rivets, proved to be extremely rigid, though weighing but 52 lb.

The design arranged for the entire body shell to be welded up into one piece, but to permit assembly, the last weld—all round the centre of the body—had been left undone. The two halves of the shell were now pushed over the framework from front and back and the final weld completed. Holes for riveting the shell to the framework were punched through from the outside, thereby countersinking the rivet heads and providing a degree of natural interlock between panel and frame. Ingress for the driver and access to engine and chassis parts were afforded by making the top panel and the undershield detachable and these, together with the wheel covers, were secured with flush-fitting Dzus aircraft fasteners. The complete body, on its framework, and including all these covers, weighed 228 lb. and could be lifted on or off the chassis quite easily by two men.

It is, perhaps, remarkable that no wind-tunnel checks were taken in the course of the design of this body. Partly, there was a degree of urgency for the car, which was required for record attempts by the end of the summer. But, what was more pertinent, Reid Railton was so sure of what he was doing, based on his previous knowledge and experience, that he felt that wind-tunnel tests could be dispensed with. His confidence has since been completely justified by the performance of the car, its speeds in relation to the horse-power known to be available showing it to approach very closely to the ideal shape for a car of that frontal area.

The chassis remained basically as it had been originally built for Eyston, with a wheelbase of 8 ft. 3 in., and the engine and transmission set obliquely across the car at an angle of 6°. Certain detail changes were made, however.

As the car was to be used only on selected roads where freedom from surface inequalities would be a primary consideration, it was felt desirable to restrict the vertical movement of the axles as much as possible in order that a very small ground clearance could be used with safety. Upward movement was therefore limited to 1 in. at the front and 2 in. at the rear. Again, as riding comfort would be assured by the even road surfaces, the hydraulic shock absorbers were dispensed with and two pairs of duplex friction dampers fitted to each axle. The front springs had a rate of 475 lb./in., and the rears 227 lb./in. The weight of the complete car, with driver, ready for a run, was 2000 lb., 55 per cent of which was on the front axle.

As originally, when used for track work, no brakes were fitted to the front axle. Although considerations of wind resistance did not now arise—the front axle being completely enclosed—the reduction in unsprung weight could but have a beneficial effect upon any tendency for the front axle to 'tramp' at high speeds. With the same end in view, road wheels and tyres were balanced to a high degree of accuracy. Tyres were specially built by Dunlop and consisted of a few layers of cord covered by an extremely thin rubber tread, no more than 3 mm. thick. They were run at the high-sounding pressure of 60 lb./sq. in. and were remarkable in that, at the estimated speed of the car, they attained a rolling radius equal to their static unloaded radius.

Fuel was carried in a 7-gallon tank mounted alongside the driver, and fed by means of air pressure, a large air reservoir being provided in the tank so that it could be pumped up before a run and hold sufficient pressure to permit a record to be taken without further pumping. An air pressure gauge was included among the few instruments, the others being engine speed indicator, oil pressure gauge, supercharger pressure gauge, and oil and water thermometers. These were mounted on a panel secured to the chassis by a light tubular framework, independent of the body, the panel being bent at an angle to bring the dials as nearly as possible into the driver's line of sight. Also of interest is the fact that the steering wheel, of oblong shape and reduced in size to a mere 10 in. across its larger diameter, was made quickly detachable to enable the driver to get in and out more easily.

While this work was going on—the car was completely dismantled and all components crack tested—Robin Jackson was pushing ahead with the engine development. Jackson (Reg) and Enever had been down to see the engine on test and were not altogether happy about it. The misfiring which had shown itself on the occasion of the two previous runs with the ex-Horton car still persisted, and Enever formed the opinion that the test house was not large enough. When flat out, the engine needed between 100 and 200 cu. ft. of air per minute and if, as was usual, the exhaust discharged into the same room, a high degree of pollution rapidly ensued. In fact, after the engine had been running for some little time, it was necessary for those conducting the tests to wear gas-masks in order to adjust the engine or brake. Kimber was consulted and he finally agreed with Robin that the engine should be brought to Abingdon, where a very large test house was available, and that any further engine development should continue alongside the preparation of the car. But even here, the misfiring continued and the cause had to be sought elsewhere.

Robin Jackson had done a fine job on the engine to develop it to the pitch which it had attained at this stage, and probably his greatest single contribution was the camshaft, which remained in use for many years, and which, it would appear, is difficult to improve upon. The timing, which is rather extreme, is shown at *Fig.* 11. The large overlap of 81°, together with the high inlet manifold pressure, permits an almost complete 'blow-through' at the end of each exhaust stroke, ensuring that the cylinders are filled almost completely with fresh mixture though obviously at some expense in fuel. This action also assists in cooling the exhaust valve, the opening of which is, additionally, left very late in order to allow the maximum time for burning of the huge quantities of fuel involved and to permit the combustion temperature to drop as low as possible before exhausting begins.

The transfer of the engine to Abingdon gave Enever the opportunity to put into practice many of the ideas which had been turning over in his mind for some time, and to him must go the lion's share of the credit for the successful further development of this and the subsequent series of engines. He would be the last person to admit to being a genius—or even to being creative though there are some who regard

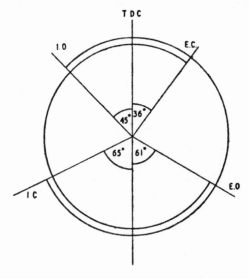

VALVE TIMING — EX135
Fig. 11.

him as both. But he has the happy knack of being able to ferret out the people who know—whatever the problem—to pick their brains, and to translate the result into practical applications. He is, moreover, a great believer in fundamental principles and invariably refers, in the first instance, to the standard works on engineering of half a century ago for the basis of the solution to a problem on these engines of such high power and performance that they could have had no place in the highest flights of the author's fancy.

Engine test at Abingdon, where it was possible to run the engine without exhaust manifold and watch the valves directly, showed that, despite the extreme valve timing and the cooling value of the fuel, misfiring was caused by exhaust valve incandescence. This direct observation of the valves was quite an experience, because one was exposed to the direct blast of the exhaust and the noise was deafening. The remedy of the trouble was to resort to sodium-filled valves (e.g. valves with hollow

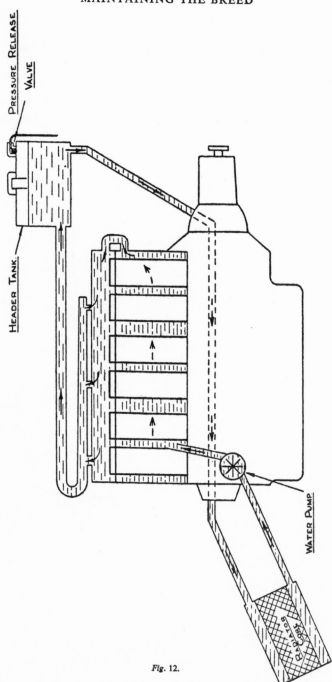

Fig. 12.

stems partly filled with metallic sodium which melted at running temperatures and helped to transfer heat from valve head to stem) and to use bronze guides extending close up to the head of the valve. These cured the misfiring but the close inspection of the engine while under power had shown that, at maximum speed, a fan of water spurted from the cylinder head joint. Enever considered that this, the most important joint in the whole engine, was, as always, unduly weakened by the presence of the innumerable waterways cored in the cylinder block at this point. It was felt that, if an alternative water-course could be found, not only could the joint be strengthened, but any slight remaining tendency to blow would be relatively innocuous. A cylinder block was therefore introduced in which the cooling water, fed in by the water pump to the bottom front of the block, was taken out at the top back, whence a short transfer pipe carried it into the back of the cylinder head, no water passing through the gasket face at all. The general layout of the cooling system is shown at *Fig.* 12, from which it will be seen that the water emerged from the head through a series of graduated ports so arranged as to constrain the bulk of the water to pass through to the front. This was further ensured by the use of a composite water outlet pipe so arranged that a head of water was constantly maintained forward of the engine, despite the fact that the 'header tank' was situated behind and above it.

The only other major change to the engine was to the inlet pipe. The original K3 had used a pipe fed at its front end by the supercharger and connected by six short branch pipes to each cylinder. Robin J. had seen the shortcomings of this and had fed the pipe centrally. Enever went one better and, profiting from experience on the L and NE Types, used *two* feeds, each one placed centrally between the end pairs of cylinders.

While this work was going on, the clutch had to be considered. The pre-selector gearbox of the standard K3 was not to be used, partly because good performance on indirect gears was of little consequence, partly because it was heavy and partly because of its inherent drag. A clutch, therefore, had to be designed from scratch. This was no light task as the anticipated torque was of the order of 150 ft./lb. at 6500 r.p.m. and, with normal MG flywheels and clutch housings, there was not much room. The problem was finally solved, with the co-operation of the Borg and Beck Company, by securing the outer cover of one of their normal 10-in. clutches to the periphery of the flywheel. Countersunk setscrews were used and there was a mere $\frac{1}{16}$-in. clearance between them and the housing. The use of a clutch of such large diameter ensured that the operating pedal required no higher pressure to disengage than on an ordinary car.

Supercharging was provided by a 'Centric' positive displacement compressor designed to give an induction manifold pressure of 26 lb.

per sq. in. From *Fig.* 14 it will be seen that, in this type of supercharger, the vanes are secured, through ball-races, to a shaft mounted concentrically with the outer casing. It is therefore possible to leave a small but definite clearance between the vanes and the outer casing, and seizures between vane and casing, a frequent cause of failure in some other types, is eliminated. Both angular and radial movement of the vanes relative to the rotor is facilitated by the insertion, in the rotor, of hard-wearing non-metallic trunnions.

The porting of the outer casing was so arranged as to provide pre-compression within the supercharger, prior to the opening of the delivery port, of 18·6 lb./sq. in. This high degree of pre-compression is very effective in reducing power absorption and temperature losses which would otherwise be high by reason of excessive fluctuation of gas flow when using high induction pressures. The rotor was driven through an internally toothed ring gear from a main pinion, giving a reduction of 0·66 to 1. On the rear of the casing and external to the supercharger itself a further reduction of 0·6 to 1 was provided, giving an overall reduction of 0·396 to 1. The swept volume of the compressor was 3200 c.c. per revolution of the rotor.

In this form, the building of the engine was completed and it was made ready for bench test. Some little work was done to discover the optimum carburetter setting, but otherwise there was nothing by way of last minute snags or difficulties. The whole test was ominously easy, the unit showing, and holding, 194 b.h.p. at 7000 r.p.m. without any trace of misfire. Maximum b.m.e.p. was 342 lb./sq. in. at 6800 r.p.m. and maximum torque 148 ft./lb. at 6500 r.p.m. (See *Fig.* 13.) At this power 170 m.p.h. was confidently expected, with an axle ratio of 3·6 to 1, and the test was so satisfactory that the engine was removed from the bed, installed in the car, and not run again until the morning of the record attempt.

At the beginning of November, the car with its spares, fuel, oil and accessories, was loaded into its lorry and transported to Frankfurt; Gardner, Kimber, technicians and pressmen accompanying it in a considerable convoy. Arrangements had been made with the German motoring authorities for the closing of the Autobahn and the provision of timing facilities, but for four days weather conditions were such as to preclude any contemplation of the attempt. In consequence, and on the basis of the official weather reports, the party disbanded temporarily, the only casualty from the ensuing jollification being one who, one dark night, mistook an artificial ornamental lake for a wet, black asphalt path and spent the evening in borrowed pyjamas, while his clothes were dried. All reassembled at dawn on Wednesday, November 9, in cold but otherwise perfect weather conditions.

The car was unloaded, filled with fuel and pushed off to do its warming-up run, this being the first time the engine had fired since it

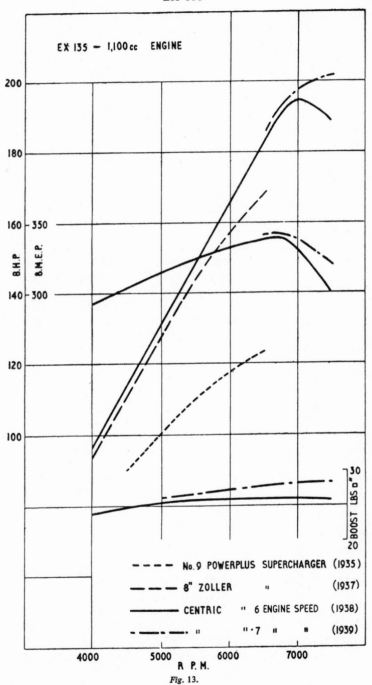

Fig. 13.

had run on the test-bed. It shot off down the road but, no sooner had it gathered speed than it spluttered to a standstill, and was hauled back to the start, while the technicians scratched their heads as to what the cause might be. They came to the conclusion that the only difference in the conditions between test-bed and car was that the carburetter intakes were subjected to the pressure built up by the air on the front of the car, and that this was not balanced to the float chambers. It was accordingly decided to remove the internal ducting leading from the intake hole on the body to the carburetters. This involved partial dismantling of the carburetters themselves, and great was the surprise when, after disconnecting a fuel line, a piece of wood, $\frac{1}{2}$ in. long and the diameter of a pencil, floated out with the fuel. Obviously it had been used to plug something somewhere, but nobody knew what. It was, however, a simple matter to re-establish the fuel supply, although the removal of the ducting was completed as a precaution before Gardner was pushed off again.

All this time, Jackson had been waiting, 'in the cheerless dawn', thirteen kilometres away down the Autobahn. He was very cold. His sole companion was a member of the German Signal Corps, who manned the telephone, and whose contribution to history was to apologise to Jackson for his inability to speak English and to explain, in all seriousness and with impeccable grammar, that he spoke only American! The amusement caused by the retailing of this story was tempered only by the background of the Munich crisis—not yet three months past—which caused a certain reticence in any dealings with a Nazi uniform, however lowly. After waiting almost two hours, Jackson saw the car coming, ran into the road and waved his arms. Goldie applied his brakes—hard—for the first and last time. Devoid of cooling, and, in any case, designed for use from speeds of 120 m.p.h., the rear brakes reacted unfavourably when smacked on at 170 or so. It was a nasty moment, but Gardner held the car and brought it safely to a standstill. His first words electrified Jackson—"Look! Tell me! What gear am I in?" In the middle of the run, he had seen the tachometer on 8000 r.p.m. and had lifted his foot for fear of damaging the machinery. It had occurred to him that the clutch might be slipping, but in the remaining moments of the run he had so convinced himself that he had come through in third gear that he apologised to Jackson for making a mess of things. A phone call to the timing box disclosed that his speed had been 288·692 k.p.h. from which, without bothering to convert to miles, it was quite clear that the car had been in top.

Fuel was low, because of the trouble at the start, and fresh supplies had to be brought from the other end of the course. Meanwhile, Jackson had a look at a couple of the plugs, to reassure himself as to the mixture, turned the car round and filled it up. His final advice to Goldie was to go back the way he had come, but with his foot flat down all the way. He figured that, even if the engine flew to pieces half-way through, the car would coast the rest of the way fast enough to take the record. There was nothing to lose. Goldie did as he was bid—he always did, which is one of the secrets of his success—with the result that his return speed exceeded 196 m.p.h., giving a mean record speed of 187·61 m.p.h.

Such was the jubilation that Jackson was forgotten until he telephoned and was retrieved—colder than ever—by Kimber and Pomeroy, the latter's Teddy Bear coat being transferred to Jackson on Kim's *instructions*! Some discussion as to the possibility of a further run, with a view to establishing a *mean* 196, was brought to a sudden conclusion by the discovery that the plugs were coated with aluminium dust, subsequently shown to be caused by the supercharger vanes scraping an end-cover. And so, finally, there came the official measuring of the engine by the international authorities, an inevitable occasion which has an atmosphere all its own. No matter how carefully the engineering has been carried out, and no matter how confident the technicians that the dimensions are within the prescribed limits, there is always a haunting fear that something will have grown mysteriously since last the head was off; that perhaps a mistake has been made somewhere; or even that the foreign dignitary with the micrometer will himself make a mistake and be prepared to be pig-headed about it. It hardly ever happens, but always a reverent silence falls over the party until the rites are completed.

For this performance, Goldie Gardner was awarded the Segrave Trophy, presented annually for the most outstanding performance in the realm of transport, whether by land, sea or air. Certainly, the extraction of such a speed from so small a car was an achievement of first importance which, apart from anything else, enhanced the prestige the world over, not only of the *marque* MG but of British automobile engineering in general.

From the result it was patently obvious that the body was a good deal better than even the best estimates which had been made of it, and that the achievement of 200 m.p.h. was purely a question of axle ratio. But, because of the aluminium, the engine was suspect and, in any case, an alternative ratio was not then available. Moreover, the previous record speed had been handsomely exceeded and there was no need to hurry. So the party returned to England and the car went off on an exhibition tour prior to its return to Abingdon. There, with the body off, the chassis and engine were dismantled and inspected in every detail. Apart from a complete renewal of the brakes, nothing needed replacement and the car was stored away until it should be needed again. The aluminium dust had caused no damage and a slight increase in the end-clearance of the blower vanes removed the possibility of future trouble of this kind. As it was confidently expected that the next outing would be an attempt to achieve 200 m.p.h. all available data were collected

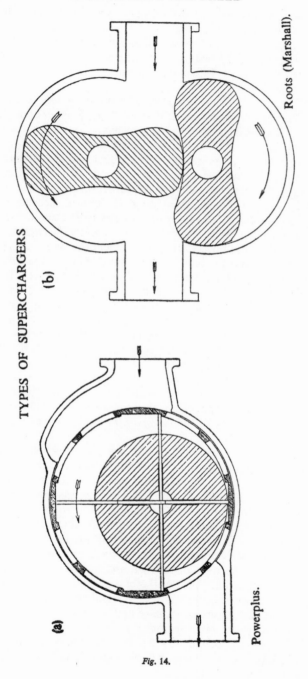

TYPES OF SUPERCHARGERS

(b)

Roots (Marshall).

(a)

Powerplus.

Fig. 14.

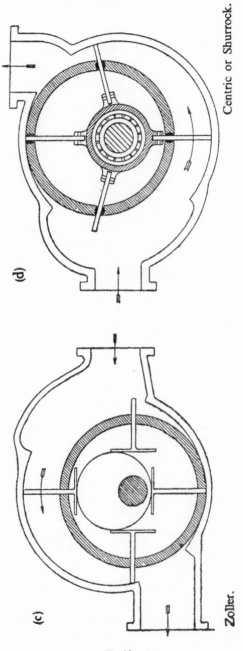

Centric or Shurrock.

(d)

Zoller.

(c)

Fig. 14.

and a calculation made to determine the desired axle ratio. As a result, the manufacture of a fresh pair of final drive gears of 3·09 to 1 was put in hand.

Early in the New Year, news was received of the opening of the Autobahn at Dessau, part of which had been built particularly level and straight to provide a suitable venue for motor record attempts. It had originally been intended to use this road for the record run of the previous year, but it was not ready in time. Negotiations were now begun again through 'ONS', the supreme national office for motor sport in Germany, and arrangements made for June. There was little to be done in the way of further preparation of the car, and the only alteration made to the engine was to re-gear the supercharger so as to provide a 17 per cent increase in blower speed. The engine ran extremely well on the test bed, giving off 202 b.h.p. at 7500 r.p.m. as shown at *Fig.* 13.

War fever was running high in Europe at the time the party crossed the Channel. With an enormous military machine which, at that moment, had nothing particular on hand, the Germans were able to spread themselves in the matter of organisation and personnel. Those who had been so helpful on the previous occasion now had at their disposal almost unlimited men and equipment, and the party on arrival at Dessau found a beautifully equipped lorry containing the timing apparatus, a refreshment van, a mobile loudspeaker van which produced music to while away the periods of waiting, a fire tender, a complete German Army meteorological unit, and police and military in profusion. The yard and garage of Dessau Police Station was at their disposal for preparation and housing of the car. On the morning of the attempt, some eight miles of two-way road were closed to all traffic and converted to a single track, with a black guide-line down the centre, by the simple process of removing about a thousand posts which normally stood on plinths on the black line. Even the method of the removal of these was impressive, if somewhat extravagant. At one moment there was a two-way road, straight as an arrow as far as the eye could see with a post every twenty yards or so dividing the tracks; the next, a single ribbon without a post in sight. At a signal soldiers had come on to the road, grabbed a post apiece and vanished into the hedges again—as quick and as simple as that!

The car behaved so faultlessly that it made the business of record-breaking look ridiculously easy. It started at the first push and disappeared into the distance on a warming-up run. On its return harder plugs were put in and Goldie was away. To those waiting at the start it seemed no time at all before he was in sight again on the return run, and he had hardly stopped before it was known that the magic figure of 200 m.p.h. had been exceeded. The speeds finally calculated were: Flying kilometre—203·5 m.p.h.; flying mile—203·9 m.p.h., and

5 kilometres—197·5 m.p.h. The highest speed recorded, in one direction, was 206 m.p.h.

But this did not finish the record-breaking. Without saying very much to anybody except Goldie and Kim, Jackson and Enever had brought with them a set of pistons ·020 in. oversize and a Van Norman portable cylinder-boring machine. They planned to bore the engine out, after it had been officially measured for the Class G record, to make it exceed the 1100-c.c. limit, thereby bringing it into the next class, F, which includes all sizes over 1100 but not exceeding 1500 c.c. This was to be done overnight, while the engine was still in position in the car, so that Gardner might attack the Class F records at dawn the following day.

Jackson and Enever each assumed that the other had used the boring machine before—it was in fairly common use at Abingdon. Doubts had entered Jackson's mind in the middle of the preceding night and he wakened Enever to ask him. The response was not everything it might have been, but he did learn that Sid had brought the instruction book—so he went to sleep. The first difficulty on the morrow, however, was that the boring bar took 220 volts 3-phase, whereas only 110 volts were available in the police station. Accordingly, the authorities called in a unit of the German Army signals, who ran a cable on poles several hundred yards to the police station from the nearest 3-phase supply. This done, the two boys sat on a box and began to figure out how the darned thing worked: there was plenty of time and, in any case, they were probably a little slap-happy from the success of the morning. The machine lay on the floor in front of them, and they succeeded in connecting it to the supply. To verify this they switched it on, whereupon the torque reaction of the motor took charge and trundled the device all round the room. As the switch was mounted on the motor, it was quite a job to catch it and switch it off again, and they were quite convinced that they had ruined it for good and all. Detailed examination failed to disclose any damage, and so they erected it on number one cylinder, set the cutter, switched it on and hoped for the best. A beautiful bore, dead to size, resulted. Between each bore it was necessary to sharpen, and therefore reset, the cutter, and there was a great deal of apprehension when the cutting noise in number two bore was very different from what it had been before. The explanation of this proved to be that the cutter had been put back to front, and number two cylinder exhibited all the qualities of a fine screw thread. It was within size, however, and responded well to the judicious use of a hone. Extreme care with the remaining bores ensured that they resembled number one, and reassembly of the engine, now 1106 c.c., proceeded.

While the cylinder head was being refitted, it was discovered that the front camshaft bearing housing was broken. Such an obscure failure had not even been considered as a possibility, and no spare had been brought, so it was a question of 'make do and mend' or abandon the further record attempt. It so happened, however, that the man in charge of those responsible for the measurement of the engine was the Herr Direktor of the nearby Junkers factory, and, he having offered to have it repaired, Enever went with him to the works. Enever tells of the considerable discussion which ensued before he was allowed to enter; how finally he was instructed to look neither to right nor left on his way through the works; of the obvious intense military activity everywhere; and of his arrival in the Direktor's office where he remained all the while the repair was effected, the passing of time being accelerated with the aid of great bowls of brandy. Herr Direktor having pressed innumerable buttons and having interviewed and instructed a cavalcade of heel-clicking ober-something-or-others, a very passable repair was made and in a very short time. Thereafter assembly of the engine was quickly completed and the car sheeted and locked up for the night.

In the morning, the car was taken to the start-line, Goldie climbed in, took it for its customary warming-up run, and thereafter went straight off to take the records without any preliminary running-in whatever. The engine note was clean and crisp, and he returned speeds just fractionally higher than on the previous day, and completely consistent with the slight increase in engine size. The speeds were 204·2 m.p.h. for the kilometre, 203·9 for the mile (exactly the same as for Class G), 200·6 for 5 kilometres, and with a fastest one-way speed of 207·4 m.p.h. Thus ended an entirely satisfactory venture which, from every point of view—design, preparation, driving and organisation— could be regarded as model.

From the time of the first successful run at Frankfurt in the November of 1938, plans had been gently taking shape for a 750-c.c. power unit with which the car could attack Class H records.

It was decided to construct a six-cylinder engine, using as many of the K3 components as possible, but before design had gone very far it became apparent that most of the major components had to be manufactured specially. An N Type cylinder block was cast with special cores, so as to leave the bores thick, permitting them to be machined to 53 mm. diameter. The crankshaft was similar in its general dimensions to the K3, but with a stroke shortened to 56 mm., the original connecting rods being retained, and the pistons having a greater compression height. The shape of the pistons was, in fact, quite extraordinary as, with the smaller swept volume of each cylinder, it was necessary to recover as much as possible of the original atmospheric compression ratio. In practice, it was found impossible to exceed 5·1 to 1. This engine was built, but never tested, as all work came to an abrupt stop with the outbreak of war.

The car and engine were therefore partially dismantled, thoroughly treated with preservative, and stored away at Abingdon. As a result of war-time activities, the MG Car Company took additional temporary premises in the town for storage purposes and the record car and its components were transferred there, but in 1944 these buildings caught fire and were partially destroyed. The chassis and body were removed in time to avoid damage and the 750-c.c. engine was in a part of the premises which was unaffected. But the 1100-c.c. block, all the alternative final drive gears, and all the loose components including the superchargers and carburetters, were damaged beyond hope of recovery. So, when war was over and interest in quick motoring revived, the style of those anxious to take up where they left off in 1939 was somewhat cramped.

A new blower had to be designed and this was undertaken by Chris Shorrock, one of the designers of the pre-war Centric, and the Sterling Engineering Company. Known as the 'Clyde', it followed the layout of the Centric very closely, except that the internal reduction gearing was of different design and the ports re-arranged, bringing the carburetters on to the opposite side from that which they had previously occupied. The blower was driven at 0·392 engine speed through a single pair of gears, and an increase in size of carburetter was introduced, two instruments each of $2\frac{3}{16}$ choke diameter being used.

For maximum power it was considered desirable to extend the engine speed range beyond the 8000 r.p.m. limit of the 1100-c.c. engine, and attention therefore focused on the valve-gear—the limiting factor. An intensive study of valve springs was embarked upon, a bench rig being constructed whereby the valve-gear could be driven, through a four-speed gearbox, by a variable speed electric motor, and the behaviour of various arrangements of valves, springs and rockers observed by stroboscopic and other means. Quite early in these tests it was discovered that the constant running was damaging the bronze valve seats, and a change was made—for tests only—to a cast-iron head, but not before the wrong gear in the driving gearbox had been engaged and the valve-gear run accidentally at a speed equivalent to 12,000 crankshaft r.p.m.! In the end the target of 10,000 r.p.m. had to be foregone, and a compromise 9000 accepted.

The power developed was a little disappointing when compared with the 1100-c.c. version (see *Figs*. 13 and 15), particularly having in mind the improvement which had been made in the valve-gear, but this was inevitable because of the reduced nominal compression ratio.

By the time the construction of the engine was well advanced, the question arose as to where to run the car. Germany, in 1946, was in much too much of a mess to be contemplated and Italy was similarly afflicted, though to a lesser extent. Gardner was in correspondence with the leading motoring organisations in both countries, and ultimately a report came that a stretch of the Brescia–Milan Autostrada could be used. A meeting was accordingly arranged there for July.

The attempt proved to be abortive, and presents the only grey spot in the life of the car to date. And this was due solely to the unsuitability of the road. The measured mile was straight and in reasonably good condition, but there was a very considerable bend in the run-in distance, the surface of which had, furthermore, suffered not a little from the war. In addition, the car was of the same weight and dimensions, but, with rather less than 75 per cent of the engine power which it had had on its previous runs, and therefore took a longer distance to wind up to its maximum. This meant that on each run Goldie had to fight the car through the bend in an endeavour to come out of it sufficiently fast to take the record. Similarly, on the return, if he kept power full on until he crossed the finishing line, he arrived at the bend very fast. In the first place, the car had little in the way of brakes and, in the second, it will be remembered that the steering lock had been restricted and Goldie would have had little chance of doing anything very much about a rear-wheel slide if one developed. Very courageously, he made several attempts, but was either not fast enough or had to lift his foot, in which case the engine spluttered when he opened it up again.

It was then decided to lower the back-axle ratio in order to increase the overall acceleration and permit the bend to be taken in less exciting fashion. This was an improvement and one run exceeded the record speed. By now, however, the car had done a great deal of running and, on the return, the blower seized solid. This was something of a relief to Goldie, but not only was a spare blower available, but the nearby Alfa-Romeo works were at their disposal, and it is to Goldie's very great credit that he left the decision as to whether or not to carry on entirely to Jackson and Enever. Sid was deeply interested in the running from a technical point of view and was half-inclined to try again. Jacko, however, felt that what had not been achieved in a week was unlikely to succeed in a fortnight, even with a new blower, and so the attempt was called off.

A few days after their return to England, Jackson was in conversation with an acquaintance who during the War had been stationed near a place called Jabbeke in Belgium, and who expressed the opinion that they had been crazy to trek all the way to Italy in search of a road when the Perfect Thing existed just across the Channel. It was stated that near this town, there were 'miles and miles' of straight, level, brand new concrete road, which would be ideal for record breaking. This information was phoned to Gardner, who relayed it to his friend Jean Simons, in Belgium, requesting a report. Simons was a sporting motorist associated with the R.A.C. of Belgium, and his acknowledgement of the request indicated that even he knew nothing of this road, so that, at this stage, it all sounded rather like a fairy tale. His next communication, however, restored the highest hopes and accordingly Gardner, Jackson and Enever went to Belgium to reconnoitre.

The road proved to be one section of the very beginnings of the projected road from the Channel ports to Istanbul. It started nowhere in particular and petered out at its far end, so carried only a small amount of purely local traffic. It was, however, in excellent condition, the centre section, some eleven kilometres long, being as straight and flat as had originally been said, and constructed on the lines of an Autobahn, completely devoid of side turnings. In short, it was as near perfect as could be desired.

The co-operation of the Belgian authorities was readily forth-coming, and Goldie selected a section of five kilometres on a stretch where the maximum protection from side-winds was provided, and where a straight run-in of some four kilometres was available at each end. A date in October was settled for an attempt, and the R.A.C.B. agreed to have everything prepared by then. It must be stated, how-ever, that the Belgians had not previously participated in any record meetings of this kind and, in short, 'did not know the drill'. It was not expected, therefore, that the meeting would run with such clockwork precision as, for instance, at Dessau, where the Germans had made fast motoring on the straight a national institution. They did extraordinarily well, however, their hospitality was as lavish as their co-operation was intense; and this pioneer effort of Gardner's established Jabbeke as the principal venue for events of this kind in post-war Europe.

Goldie broke the records held by Kohlrausch on the Magic Midget since 1936—and by a clear 18 m.p.h., which was not bad going. But this particular venture showed that the long interval of war had made its mark in many places. Old hands had not yet found their touch again.

The facilities of the Abingdon factory had not been available to Goldie on this occasion, though he still had the services of Jackson and Enever. Through the generous help of the Sterling Engineering Company, the blowers had been developed and the engine tested, but the components of the engine had been produced piecemeal and, though it is easy to be wise in retrospect, it is now clear that, for instance, the cylinder head should have been re-designed to suit the small displacement, and that, probably, a four-cylinder engine would have been a good deal better. Furthermore, the car, with a 4·1 to 1 rear axle and 19 × 4·75 tyres, was over-geared, the maximum engine speed reached during the records being 7750 r.p.m., although the valve-gear had been designed for 9000. Best utilisation of the power known to be available should have yielded speeds of the order of 175 m.p.h., whereas those actually achieved were 159·09 for the kilometre, 159·15 for the mile and 150·46 for 5 kilometres. The fastest speed one way was 164·72, which is quite quick for a 750-c.c. machine, but not fast enough in relation to the other performances of the car.

During some of the engine tests, Chris Shorrock had suggested that it might be fun to disconnect two cylinders and 'see how she goes

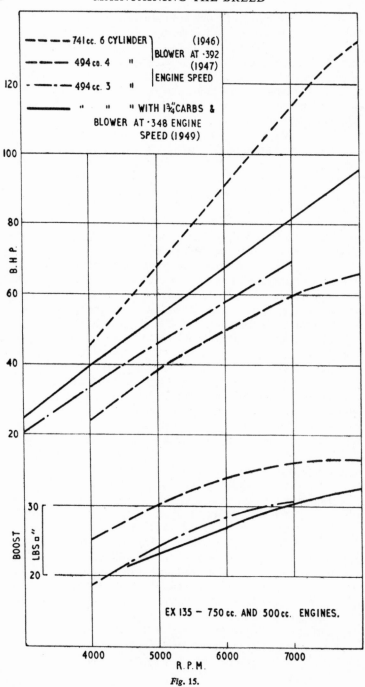

Fig. 15.

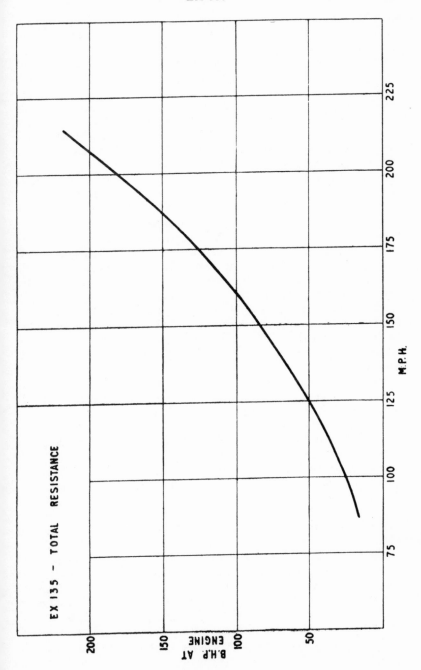

Fig. 16.

as a 500'. Nothing was done at the time, but Enever prepared two special pistons with large holes bored through their crowns, and brought them with him to Jabbeke. With the Class H records safely completed, these pistons were inserted into numbers 2 and 5 cylinders, the valve rockers of these were removed, and Goldie made a test run using third gear. Although the engine sounded distinctly erratic at slow speeds, it smoothed out once it got going, and 100 m.p.h. was exceeded, getting within 3 m.p.h. of the existing 500-c.c. record. It showed the possibilities.

From the data accumulated from the various runs it had been possible to plot a curve of the total resistance to motion of the car. As soon as it had made its first run at Frankfurt in 1938, Enever adding a certain amount of guesswork and clairvoyance to the established facts, had drawn a rough graph, and this he had modified and corrected in accordance with fresh information as it became available. In addition to the actual record runs, Goldie had on several occasions made extra runs purely for data purposes and the correlation of all the powers and speeds had ensured that the curve had, by this time, acquired a high degree of accuracy. The current version is reproduced at *Fig. 16.* By plotting a power curve to the same vertical scale as this, superimposing it and moving it laterally, the point of peak power may be made to intersect the resistance curve. From this one may not only read off the road speed but, also by comparing this with engine speed, calculate the optimum overall drive ratio. A fair selection of rear axle gears can be supplemented by a variety of wheel and tyre sizes by means of which any desired ratio may be approached very closely. Experience has shown that the best procedure is to fit to the car the axle next below that indicated by the curve, using the smallest available wheels and tyres. If all goes well, it should then be possible to increase the tyre size, on the spot, as practical experience dictates.

At the end of 1946, the 500-c.c. records stood to the credit of Johnny Lurani's Guzzi-engined Nibbio at speeds around 106 m.p.h. It was known in advance, therefore, that a minimum of rather less than 40 horse-power was necessary if this record were to be beaten, and, pro rata to the performance of the larger-capacity engines, this looked fairly simple. At this time, however, there was a disagreement on questions of principle between the MG Car Company and Colonel Gardner, as a result of which the preparation of the car and engine could not be undertaken at Abingdon. Goldie therefore determined to have the six-cylinder engine built with numbers 2 and 5 cylinders inoperative, in much the same trim as had been tried on the occasion of the last visit to Jabbeke, and this work was undertaken by Enever and Jackson, working week-ends at Goldie's works at Croydon.

Instead of using dummy pistons, the connecting rods were removed completely from the inoperative cylinders, and bob-weights of weight equivalent to the rotating mass of the rods fitted to the two crank-pins.

Up to this time, the camshaft had been driven through a vertical shaft incorporating no less than four small Woodruffe keys and a sheet-steel universal joint. The shell of the old dynamo, which had been retained to provide an upper steady bearing for the shaft, was now discarded completely, and the drive extensively re-designed eliminating three of the four keys and substituting splined connections which permitted vernier adjustment of the camshaft timing. In other respects the engine remained unchanged, but the size of the two carburetters was reduced to 1⅛ in. each. On completion of assembly, the power unit was taken for test to Harry Weslake, and the resultant power curve, taken with exhaust manifold and silencer fitted—because the test house was in a residential locality—is shown at *Fig.* 15. Disappointing, but adequate for 130 m.p.h. or so. The engine then passed to Messrs. Thompson and Taylor, who were to undertake its installation, having already prepared the chassis and fitted an enlarged and re-designed windshield so as completely to enclose the driver.

The attempt was to take place in July 1947. Goldie, with Bob Reading as chief mechanic, Kesterton of S.U. and others went over to Belgium with the car—now known as the Gardner Special—and Jackson and Enever were to follow, ostensibly on holiday. These two, however, sitting in the boat train as it pulled out of Victoria Station, read in their evening newspaper that Goldie had taken the records at 118 m.p.h. and, thereupon imagining that they really *were* on holiday, pressed on lightheartedly to Jabbeke. On arrival, they instituted an inquiry into the missing m.p.h. and learned that a loose union on a fuel line had run the mixture weak in the course of a run and that the engine thereafter had 'gone fluffy'. Abandoning holiday thoughts, they set to and took the head off, but though everything appeared to be in order and Goldie tried again the following morning, he was unable to improve his times.

For the following year, 1948, Gardner fitted a 2-litre un-supercharged Jaguar engine, with a view to attacking yet another series of records, this time in Class E (over 1500 c.c. but not exceeding 2000 c.c.). Just as reference to the resistance curve was necessary to determine the probable speed and the desired gearing, so from the knowledge that the car took these records at 177 m.p.h., does the curve show that the engine was delivering just on 130 b.h.p. at this speed. 65 b.h.p. per litre, un-supercharged! Pretty good!

During 1948, the 500-c.c. engine had worried Enever. The power was poor; the small bore six, with its 5 to 1 nominal compression ratio, had been consistently disappointing and temperamental; he knew there must be a better way of doing it. So with the dawn of 1949, and particularly with signs of the beginning of a *rapprochement* between MG's and Goldie, Sid started to scheme out an alternative. A poor 750 minus one-third equalled a poor 500. A very good 1100 divided by two was only a little more than a very *good* 500. Furthermore, three cylinders with cranks at 120° could have equal firing intervals and be substantially in balance. The clear answer to the problem was to use any three adjacent cylinders of the six and make sufficient slight adjustment either to bore or stroke, or both, as was necessary to get just below 500 c.c.

There are two ways of playing the record-breaking game: the one, as exemplified by Eyston, being to push each record up a little at a time, in the hope that someone will beat it, so that he might try again; the other adhered to by Gardner, being to smack the speed up as far as it will go and then sit back and watch the fun. Since the four-cylindered 500-c.c. run of 1947, Taruffi had been out in Italy with his Special and had carried the speeds to 129 m.p.h., so only the best possible, would suffice to beat him by anything like a good margin. Enever therefore reverted to the old traditional MG bore diameter of 57 mm., the size for which the head had been originally designed, and adjusted the stroke to 64·5 mm. to bring the three cylinders, taken together, to 493·8 c.c., it not being expedient to give away anything in terms of c.c. on an engine so small. The new stroke required a new crankshaft, and this was made with three 120° throws for numbers 4, 5 and 6 cylinders, the part normally occupied by throws 1, 2 and 3 being a plain bar extending forward through the first two main bearings to couple up to the supercharger drive. The only other special item was the magneto, which presented Lucas with a nice problem in that they had never made a 3-cylinder magneto before, but it was completed in such quick time in their tool-room that they had to have it back again after the record to draw it!

The engine was tested with the blower at 0·392 engine speed and with two 1⅝-in. carburetters, giving an output as shown by the middle curve of *Fig.* 15. This did not come up to expectations and it was clear that the supercharger was itself absorbing too much power, and that its pressure was considerably above optimum. It was accordingly re-geared to 0·348 engine speed and 1¾-in. carburetters fitted, and this produced the almost miraculous increase in output shown in the upper curve of the same figure. With the b.m.e.p. back up in the 300 region again, the record was a certainty, 150 m.p.h. more than probable and 160 m.p.h. not beyond the bounds of possibility.

So it was a very confident party which set off, in September 1949, for Belgium, the car once again bearing its MG monograms. The weather was foul; wind and rain causing a day-to-day postponement, the attempt finally being made on a day when a moderately strong wind blew obliquely across the course. This, in conjunction with the relatively low power compared with that of some of the earlier engines, gave rise to fairly sharp differences in speeds—9 m.p.h. or so—between the go and return runs. The record was, however, never in doubt and the mean speeds of 154·91 for the kilometre, 154·23 for the mile, and 150·51 for the 5 kilometres beat Taruffi's best speeds by over 20 m.p.h. The fastest recorded, for one direction, was 159·32 m.p.h., thereby fully justifying the original estimates.

At this stage, Goldie and his car had to their credit the fastest speeds ever recorded, anywhere in the world, in five out of the ten recognised International Classes—E, F, G, H and I. This would be rated an astonishing achievement in any circumstances, but when it is realised that Lt.-Col. A. T. Goldie Gardner, O.B.E., M.C., was, at the time of this latest record, in his sixtieth year, one can but marvel at his courage, even more than at his abilities. And even now, game leg and all, he is spoiling for more. That is why, as soon as this record was safely in the bag and the 'plombeurs' had measured the engine (they made it 57·3 by 64·3—497·367—which just shows how careful one has to be), the 1947 trick was repeated, one stage lower down the capacity scale, number 6 piston being removed in order to see what the Class J (350 c.c.) possibilities were. The result—a mile at 92 and a kilometre at 93·205 m.p.h.—with but 330 c.c. and without any correction of blower pressure or gear ratio showed that the existing record of 106 m.p.h. was in danger ere long.

CHAPTER XI

EX 135 (Concluded)

PERHAPS the story of this car so far, its preparation and its runs, has made the whole business sound too easy. On the other hand, to put in even a quarter of the available detail could have made the tale excessively boring. So let us consider that the time has come for a little diversion, and attempt a pen picture of the sort of thing that makes up the daily routine of test and experiment.

With a view to adding Class J to the list of 'fastest evers', early in January, 1950, Goldie booked the Jabbeke road for July 24. There seemed no valid reason for departing from the scheme which had been tried out during the previous visit to Belgium; the 500-c.c. 3-cylinder engine would be used with one piston removed.

And so, with but twelve weeks to go, the engine stands ready, though the blower has not arrived, and when it does there comes with it a message to the effect that the drive position has been changed, which in turn necessitates a modification of its mountings. Installation on the bed proceeds—a matter of routine by now—but the complexity of the associated plumbing, with water pipes, fuel lines, air pipes, and gauge tubes, never fails to be a source of wonderment to the casual observer. By the time all is ready, the fuel has not arrived—an infuriating business because the din of the exhaust is so terrific that tests can be conducted only at week-ends for fear of bringing work in the rest of the factory to a standstill. Meantime, an argument has started about the induction pipe; the engine has two cylinders working on a 3-cylinder 120° crank and therefore fires irregularly at 240° and 480° of crankshaft rotation. Shorrock considers that the spasmodic gas flow calls for a reservoir adjacent to the inlet ports, but Enever doubts it. Anyway, one is made. Finally, engine, blower, fuel, and a Saturday conspire together to make a run possible, the engine is switched on, the fuel pumped up, the starter pressed and—wonder of wonders—it fires on both and ticks over quite merrily but with the anticipated erratic sound. After a while the throttle is opened, but the engine fails to accelerate. Everyone waits patiently while Enever juggles with the butterflies and, after a minute or so, the note changes, the engine seems to shake itself, increase speed and, finally, away it goes straight up to 7000. At the first sign of life, those present take up their stations; John Crook at the brake with a streamlined left hand ready to pounce

Lt. Col. A. T. Goldie Gardner, O.B.E., M.C.

(a)

George Eyston, Syd Enever and John Thornley stand behind
the completed EX 179.

(b)

Eyston turns the wick up at M.I.R.A.

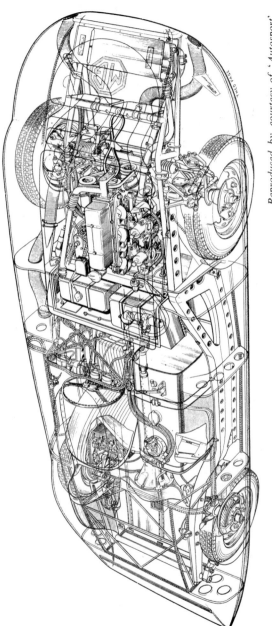

Reproduced by courtesy of 'Autosport'.

Theo Page's anatomical view of EX 179.

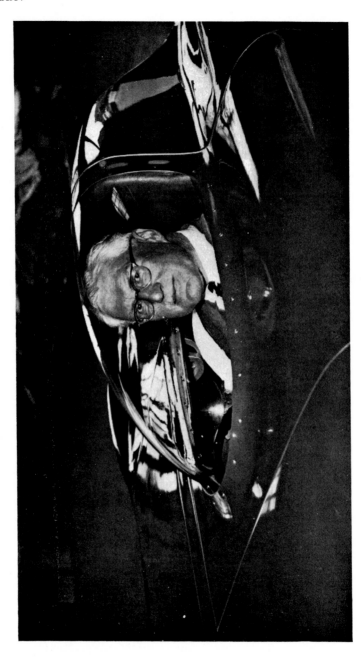

Capt. G. E. T. Eyston, O.B.E., M.C.

on the switch; Enever at the carburetters; Jackson standing back with
a hand on the air pump and an eye on the gauges; nobody, it will be
noted, in the plane of the cranks or flywheel. The power is low, the
blower pressure very high—37 lb.—obviously Chris Shorrock has done
a very good job. The fumes from the dope get in Enever's eyes and
temporarily blind him, and he runs, on a sudden, out into the open air,
forgetting in his pain that there is no return spring on the throttle.
The engine skies and Jackson makes a dive for the carburetters just as
Sid comes dashing back—and they bang their heads together. With
the engine shut off, the silence is intense. An adjustment is made to the
ignition timing and another run is taken. This cycle is repeated several
times, sometimes for ignition, sometimes for carburetters, sometimes
for plugs, and always there is the difficulty of getting the thing past its
tick-over speed of 1500 r.p.m. or so. In the end, it becomes quite
obvious that the blower must be geared lower. Even at tick-over with
the throttle wide it is absorbing so much power that there is none left
over for acceleration, even at no load.

There follows intense activity finding out the possibility of produc-
ing a new gear—and what is more, a new gear casing—and it is found
that, at best, this will take about ten days. Time is now precious and so,
in order to discover how the engine will behave with the slower supercharger, a TC. gearbox is rigged on the test-bed in front of the engine
so that the blower can be driven through this, in third gear. This puts
the blower another 2 ft. away from the engine and necessitates insertions
in the afore-mentioned plumbing to restore all the usual services,
H. and C. The engine is run again and this time there is less difficulty
in starting and power is much more encouraging: it is even now
sufficient for the record, but it is thought that there is more to be got.
More tuning, more runs. The expansion box is removed with no
apparent effect one way or the other, and then, with the engine running
flat out, there is a tremendous crash and everybody, with one small
corner of his mind always on the possibility of a broken con-rod or
worse, runs away or dodges for cover, but not before Johnny has
instinctively switched off. It is then discovered that the blast from the
exhaust stubs has dislodged the glass globe of an electric light fitting
hanging over the bed, and this has dropped smack on top of the valve
cover and burst.

It is noticed, in these later runs, that power falls off very gradually
after a few seconds at maximum, and numerous theories are advanced.
The induction pipe warms up a bit, but Enever believes that the cylinder
liners are moving. In any case, he is a bit concerned at the vibration of
the engine at low speeds and at 4000 r.p.m. and decides to try the effect
of a bob-weight on the idle crank-pin. This necessitates removal of
the sump and, as the oil is drained, it is seen to be an opaque creamy
brown colour and undoubtedly contains a lot of water.

J

As this oil is also fed to the blower and then absorbed in the gas-stream, the mixture obviously contains much more than its normal 2 per cent of water. Whether the effect of this is good or bad cannot be just now said. The bob-weight is fitted and tests continue, the engine now being much sweeter and, as soon as all possible data have been collected, tests stop and the engine is dismantled, The liners have moved and are $\frac{1}{16}$ in. lower than when they started. The bores look very dry. But this is only a slave block anyway; the proper one will be fitted up next week when, with luck, the new blower gear and housing will be available.

This, then, is a fair sample of life in the Development Shop at Abingdon and, to ensure that our story does not run into several volumes, we must return to bare essentials.

In its final form, the engine ran with pistons in numbers four and five cylinder bores, number six being sealed off. One of the large Shorrock blowers was used driven at a ratio of 12/46 and in this form yielded 45 h.p. at 7000 r.p.m. rising to 49·8 at 7600. The only noticeable peculiarity arising from the curious arrangement of firing interval was that an R.L.52 plug suited number four bore, whereas number five preferred an R.L.51.

In the first days of the New Year, the car itself had been shipped to New York where it formed a central exhibit in the British Automobile Show there. It arrived back in England towards the end of May. This involved working to a pretty tight schedule, as it was standard practice to strip the chassis right out and rebuild it before each record sortie. All was completed in good time, however, and the car loaded with all its spares and equipment in a large transporter which left Abingdon for the coast on the afternoon of July 21.

Monday dawned dry, but cold and somewhat blustery. By first light all was ready. The northern lane of the Jabbeke dual carriageway had been closed, the gendarmerie were in position and Goldie departed on his warming-up run. And the timing apparatus failed.

Failure of the timing apparatus is always a nuisance and can be very disturbing and even disastrous. The nerves of the whole record-breaking party, particularly those of the driver, are fairly well strung up by the time an attempt takes place, and the news that no time has been recorded comes like a slap in the face at a moment when one is least able to withstand it. Furthermore, a good deal of money is sunk in preparation for an event of this kind, all directed, in the ultimate, to the actual recording of a few seconds of time. In these circumstances it is to be hoped that as much care will be lavished on the preparation and checking of the timing apparatus as on the car itself. But at least three times has such a failure interrupted record attempts which are described in this book. Unquestionably, George Eyston was robbed of 120 m.p.h. with the Magic Midget at Pendine in 1932. On this occasion, in Belgium, the car had to make extra runs under adverse conditions of wind and the engine shed a piston before the runs were complete. And in 1951, on the Salt Lake at Utah, a whole set of records had to be abandoned.

But we digress. The officials of the R.A.C.B. soon reported that the trouble was beyond immediate repair and that part of the mechanism would have to be taken to Brussels. There was nothing to do but wait. The town of Bruges lay two kilometres to the north, but nobody dared be far away in case the timing apparatus was made to work again. As the day wore on the wind freshened and, by the time all was set again around six in the evening, it was blowing more strongly than Goldie liked. For at 120 m.p.h. or so the road does not seem to be very wide.

Nevertheless, the decision to make the attempt was taken and the east to west run was made in fine style, though Goldie found it some-what difficult to keep the car aimed at the far end of the road. On the return, however, things were not so good. Goldie entered the 5-kilo-metre stretch at 8000 r.p.m. and the mile at 8200, but at the start of the kilometre the cockpit filled with white smoke and, by the end of the stretch, the revs had dropped to 7600, so he switched off the motor and coasted to the end of the run. The difference in the figures for the two runs can be seen in the table below, particularly the ill effect upon the 5-kilometre figures:

1 Kil.	123·861 m.p.h.	117·056 m.p.h.	120·397 m.p.h.
1 Mile	123·397 m.p.h.	118·850 m.p.h.	121·048 m.p.h.
5 Kil.	122·249 m.p.h.	113·125 m.p.h.	117·687 m.p.h.

Since the previous 350-c.c. records were held by Count Johnny Lurani in his little "Nibbio" special at figures around the 106 m.p.h. mark the results, despite the frustrations of the day, were considered adequate and gave Goldie and his most versatile motor-car the honour of being the first pair to reach 120 m.p.h. in Class J.

It was therefore in an atmosphere almost of light relief, though the project was a serious one, that Goldie then took over Dick Benn's MG Y type 1¼ saloon. This car, in otherwise standard trim, had been fitted with a small belt-driven Shorrock supercharger kit blowing at some 8 or 9 lb., and it was hoped that 100 m.p.h. could be achieved. The figures of 104·725 m.p.h. for the mile and 104·680 for the kilometre were considered to provide a highly satisfactory conclusion to the Belgian venture.

This brought to an end also the use of the faithful old K3 engine. It had proved itself to be supreme in all the small car classes—1500 c.c., 1100 c.c. (its natural size!), 750, 500 and 350—and, although a great deal had been learned, there was, from a purely engineering standpoint, a faintly ridiculous tinge to the use of two odd cylinders. This had, however, served to keep Goldie and MG in association, and before the public eye, and had enabled the Abingdon team to exercise its ingenuity and keep its hand in. But the natural tendency now was to think in terms of more modern machinery and to endeavour to re-convert what had become purely publicity-seeking ventures to their original status of development projects.

The XPAG. engine had been introduced with the MG TB. in 1939, since when it had been steadily developed and used successively in the TC. and TD. Various methods of super-tuning its 1250 c.c. had been devised, and the effects of modest blowing, of the order of 10 or 12 lb., were well understood.

The existing "fastest-ever" for 1½ litres still stood to the credit of Goldie and the MG at 204·3 m.p.h. for the kilometre back in 1939. For 1951, therefore, the plot emerged to endeavour to show that the current engine, with push-rods, and designed originally for ordinary passenger car motoring, was as strong and as good as its O.H.C. predecessor which had been designed originally for supercharging. The venue would be the Bonneville Salt Flats in Utah, U.S.A., and the target would be 210 m.p.h.

A safari from England to the West-Central U.S.A. is a fairly expensive undertaking. Car, and possibly fuel, must be shipped and railed 5000 miles; Driver, Team Manager and mechanics must be transported and maintained; the promoter must foot the bill for the preparation of the course and for the transport and subsistence of the necessary time-keepers and officials of the American Automobile Association, who may have to be brought in from as far afield as Los Angeles and Chicago. The U.S. dollar being what it is, the whole thing adds up to a pretty penny.

This being so, and bearing in mind the statement attributed to H. N. Charles that there are some 4000-odd potential causes of trouble built into every motor-car, any one of which can bring it to a standstill, it was considered prudent to have an alternative target, a second string to the bow. To beam all this expenditure of thought, effort, time and money, on to two short bursts of some eighteen seconds duration just didn't make economic sense. The answer was to take alternative engines and axles, and assail the 1-hour record which stood to the credit of Bugatti at 119·01 m.p.h., together with the distance records, 50 k., 50 m., etc., which would be collected on the way.

To use the Salt Flats is not quite the straightforward matter it might appear to be. During winter, the whole area is a lake—only some six to eighteen inches deep, it is true, but nevertheless a lake. In late spring, evaporation starts in a big way, a process which may or may not be completed by mid-July. In early September there is serious risk of thunderstorms, which can flood the salt and render it unusable. So August is the only safe bet, and during that month everybody who wants to use it does so, including the American Hot-Rod boys who monopolize it for a whole week.

Furthermore, the surface is not necessarily dead smooth. Just as wind and tide determined the nature of the sand left by the receding sea at Pendine, so the wind, at the critical period of evaporation, determines whether the salt dries smooth or rough. If the latter, it may have to be scraped. 'Dry' is a relative expression, too. Some years, the water level may be only a few inches below the surface of the salt, in which case conditions can be very slippery—or, to use the local expression, the "salt is slick"—during the heat of the day.

As if this were not enough, the car had been committed in advance to appear in the Transport Section of the Festival of Britain from the 4th May until the Festival ended. By negotiation with the authorities it was agreed that it could be withdrawn on June 15, but even this necessitated an extremely tight preparation and shipment schedule, and caused the date of the attempt to be fixed later than the ideal. Fortunately, chassis and body overhaul had by now become a routine matter, and engine development and preparation could proceed without the car, but the modification of engine mountings and blower installation called for some fast work at Abingdon.

Two engines were prepared, both of 1250 c.c. The high speed engine had a compression ratio of 9·3 to one and 30 lb. boost, the blower running at ·544 engine speed. On the usual methanol blend with a valve timing of such overlap that each cylinder received a good, but extravagant, cooling blow-through once per cycle, it gave 213 h.p. at 7000 r.p.m. (*Fig.* 17), which was quite something for a crankshaft originally designed for 40 h.p. With a 2·8 final drive and normal tyres this would give 32 m.p.h. per 1000 r.p.m., sufficient for the job provided it would pull such a high axle. The second, or 'one-hour', engine had a more modest C.R.—7·25—and a blower geared at ·340 engine speed to give 10 lb. Output, at sea level, was 92 b.h.p. at 5400 r.p.m. and was to be used with a 3·4 axle to give 26.5 m.p.h. per 1000.

Note here the reference to sea level. The salt beds are at an altitude of 4000 ft. and the consequential loss of power was calculated to be 14 per cent. This was, of course, capable of correction at the blower, but the need for this was somewhat watered down by the knowledge that the same rarefaction of the atmosphere which produced the drop-off in power would also reduce the windage component of the total drag of the vehicle. The proportion of windage and rolling resistance to total drag were not known with accuracy even on concrete at sea level, let alone on salt at 4000 ft., and in this matter, therefore, Enever was feeling his way through a vast mass of information, much of it conflicting, which had been supplied to him by the cognoscenti and previous visitors to Utah.

Preparation was completed on the car, spare engine and blower, diffs., wheels, tyres and spare parts of all kinds, shipped on time. The schedule at the far end was that the car should arrive at Wendover

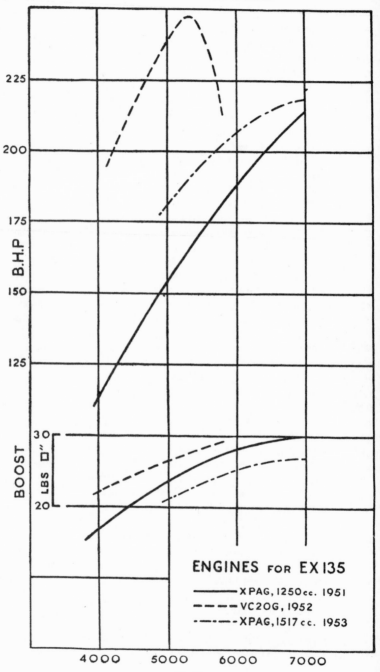

ENGINES FOR EX 135

———— X PAG, 1250cc. 1951
– – – VC2OG, 1952
–·–·– X PAG, 1517 cc. 1953

Fig. 17.

on Aug. 7, Goldie and the main party on the 14th, and that the first attempt, on the Hour, should be made on the 20th. When the main party arrived, there was no car—it was somewhere on the U.S. railroad in a freight car. Being 'green' to such exploits, nobody had thought to take the number of the freight car ex New York and the job of tracing it seemed almost hopeless. Whether it was actually found or whether it just turned up in the normal course is not recorded, but suffice it that, after three days of near panic, it arrived at Salt Lake City. Fortunately, it has always been a guiding principle that the best place to work on the car is at Abingdon, and it had therefore been shipped in such condition that, once uncrated, it was necessary merely to change its wheels, put in the fuel, top up its various levels, and it was ready for off.

Mention of fuel recalls that this had been shipped out from England in advance of the car. The red tape associated with its transport was quite extraordinary to the untutored mind, and misgivings as to the necessity of it all were underlined by its arrival at Salt Lake, rolling up and down inside an enormous freight car full of widely assorted and highly inflammable merchandise of all kinds.

The one-hour run, starting at first light on the 10-mile circular course, was pretty successful; not quite fast enough to put the record out of reach of anyone at Montlhery, but sufficient to beat existing records handsomely. Sixteen International and American National records fell, as follows:—

International Class	50 kilometres	127·8
	50 miles	130·6
	100 kilometres	132
	100 miles	135·1
	200 kilometres	136·6
	1 hour	137·4

American Class Records Flying Start:—

	25 kilometres	132·6
	25 miles	133·1
	50 kilometres	133·4
	50 miles	134·7
	75 kilometres	134·5
	100 kilometres	135·8
	75 miles	136·5
	100 miles	137·6
	200 kilometres	139·1
	1 hour	139·3

These are set down in detail because they are deserving of more than casual notice. In a run under International rules, one expects the speeds to improve with distance as the effect of the standing start wears off. The American National figures were, however, taken one lap later—at a flying start—and show how Goldie warmed to his task and, in fact, progressively improved his speed throughout the ·run. His penultimate lap, the 13th, was covered at 146·5 m.p.h., thus fully justifying Enever's preliminary arithmetic.

And so to change engine, blower and axle, and prepare the car for its high-speed runs. But while this was going on a most interesting event occurred. Among the American journalists who had been assigned to cover the Gardner record attempts was Dick van Osten, Associate Editor of *Motor Trend*. He arranged with the A.A.A., at Wendover, to attempt to establish American Class F Stock Car Records, in the Open Car Division, using an MG TD. Mark II. The expression 'Stock Car' in this context does not mean a jalopy with angle-iron bolted all over it, such as is used for racing on dirt. It means, oddly enough, exactly what it says: that the records will be attempted with a car selected by the A.A.A. from a Dealer's stock and then simply run-in, under Three A's supervision, prior to crossing the start-line.

The car was drawn from the showroom of the Foreign Motor Car Company of Salt Lake City and run-in for 1000 miles. Van Osten collected as crew one of the *Motor Trend* Publishers, Pete Petersen, Swede Jensen and Bill Cramer. At 5.25 a.m. on Aug. 22 they started and circulated the 10-mile circular course for twelve hours, stopping only for refuel and change of driver. In a most astonishingly consistent run, they established 23 Stock Car records and broke five existing National ones. An indication of the consistency with which the car ran is given by the fact that, though the records varied in distance from 25 kilometres to 12 hours, the speeds recorded varied only between 74·62 and 75·36 m.p.h., reflecting the greatest possible credit on all concerned.

By the evening of this day, EX 135 was ready again, equipped with its sprint engine, and was taken for brief trials at 160 m.p.h. or so. Then early to bed in readiness for a 5 a.m. start on the morrow. These early starts are dictated by the weather and the need, where possible, to complete the job before the sun rises sufficiently to produce the sizzling heat and dazzling white of the salt desert. Wendover, where the *équipe* was housed, in the Motel there, is some distance from the course, and a 5 a.m. start involves a morning call at 2.30. The hotel boy was an Indian, and it was not discovered until too late that numbers meant less than nothing to him. An instruction to call Rooms No. 3, 7, 9, 23 and 46 left him completely bewildered, with the result that to make quite sure, he called the entire Motel at 2.30 a.m.!

For sprints, the circular course is forsaken and a dead straight stretch of salt, fourteen miles long with a black line down the middle, is brought into use. With a two-mile run-in at either end, photo electric timers are set up for one, five and ten miles, and one, five and ten kilometres. These were connected by bare copper wire on not very high poles, and therein lay the prescription for downfall. With everything set to go, a spectator drove his car through the wires and put the timing gear out of action. With this repaired, it was found that static, collected by the overhead wires, had damaged the apparatus itself. It remained out of action all day, all night and most of the following day, during which time nerves tautened, tempers became uncertain and the threat of storms added to the all-pervading gloom.

Timing equipment has already been commented upon and it is perhaps, unnecessary to labour the subject. But this was the third time, referred to earlier, that MG has been frustrated by failures, the apparatus being operated on the three occasions by three separate national authorities. Record-breaking is an expensive and worrying business and it is no laughing matter when all the effort is brought to naught in this way. The control of motor sport by a national body is a thankless and onerous task at the best of times, and can only be adequately discharged from a position of near-faultless strength. Those bodies would do well to endeavour to emulate Caesar's wife.

By the evening of the 24th, all was pronounced ready. Goldie put in a couple of runs estimated to be at 190 plus, but still the apparatus failed to record correctly. The weather broke, the storm came and the salt was flooded. It would be unusable again until the following year. The crew had no alternative but to fold its tents and steal silently —and dejectedly—away.

While men returned to England, car went on an exhibition tour of America until early January. It did not need second thoughts to decide that a return visit should be paid in the late summer to have another go at the Class F sprint figures. But what was the second string to be this time? Class E, up to 2 litres, was attractive, but the nearest available engine was the VC.22, of 2215 c.c., as fitted to the Wolseley 6/80. Certainly, nobody had made a really determined effort to blow this one to pieces yet. It might have possibilities. Enever would try.

Thus the pattern for 1952 took shape. The 1951 TD. blown would be used for the Class F sprints, target 210 m.p.h. A two-litre version of the VC.22 would go for Class E sprints on the straightaway and the Class E hour on the circular course. But let it be earlier in the month, this time, please.

With the Class F engine, the aim was 210 m.p.h. To make sense the two-litre engine would have to go at least as fast as that, even though the existing records stood at a considerably lower figure. Desirable horse-power was therefore of the order of 250, and it was immediately apparent that something quite out of the ordinary in size of supercharger would be necessary if it were not to be turned over too fast. Orders were placed for components to provide a blower to sweep 7 litres per rotor revolution!

To bring the total swept volume of the engine within 2 litres, a special crankshaft shortened the stroke from 87 mm. to 77·5 mm. and connecting rods to suit were machined from the solid. As on previous highly blown MG engines, water had to be kept from the cylinder head joint, so a block and head were cast with the water holes deleted. Water was conveyed from block to head by external pipes. The distributor, in its normal position on the top of the overhead camshaft vertical drive, would have come well through the engine cowling on EX 135 and therefore had to be moved. In the event, a magneto was substituted, driven from the rear end of the camshaft, and a surgical operation on the engine bulkhead was necessary to accommodate it.

At a very late hour—with but fifteen weeks to go to the date of the attempt—the blower manufacturers announced that they were unable to supply. This was the first of a long series of set-backs which were to reduce the 1952 venture almost to the point of failure. Existing smaller blowers now had to be considered, which would have to run much faster than was desirable.

The first test rig incorporated a vane-type, with aluminium casing and cast-iron end plates, running at engine speed. Power was disappointing, the exhaust stubs belched flame and, with very little running, things went from bad to worse. After rather less than an hour's total running time, the tests were stopped and the engine stripped. Havoc! The engine was worn out. The blower vanes had scoured the casing and the engine oil had the quality of a high-grade lapping fluid. Piston clearances exceeded twenty thou, and the journals of the one and only two-litre crankshaft had to be seen to be believed.

Search for the cause of the exhaust flames did little to bolster up flagging spirits. With a large-overlap camshaft there is a period when both inlet and exhaust valves are open at the same time. This is normal and, on supercharged engines, provides the cooling blow-through mentioned earlier. When, however, the exhaust of an adjacent cylinder is in full blast into a siamese port, burning gas may, indeed will, pass through backwards into the inlet manifold. With such a head construction, perfectly satisfactory on a touring engine with normal timing, such a course is inevitable until an engine speed and blower pressure is reached at which the gas flow is fast and strong enough to overcome it. There was no time in which to re-design a head, so the work had to continue, flames and all.

With a new block and pistons and the crankshaft reground, tests re-started, this time using a large Roots blower in direct drive. Quite early on, the engine "banged-off" in the inlet pipe with such vehemence that the blow-off valves were unable to cope. The back-pressure stopped the blower dead and sheered the drive off the front end of the by-now much abused crank. This time, the shaft had to be built up and reground, and all the while the clock was ticking away towards shipment date.

Eventually, some sort of order began to emerge, but the power absorbed in driving the blower rose so steeply in the upper range that high engine speeds were useless. With the sands of time running against him, Enever called it a day when he saw 249 h.p. at 5400 with 27 lb. boost (*Fig.* 17), at which he estimated that the blower was taking between 80 and 90 h.p. The power curve peaked sharply in contrast to the easy, flat curves of the earlier engines, and it was clear that gearing the car was going to be a tricky business.

The fuel specification was much as usual: 86 per cent Methanol, 10·5 per cent Acetone, 1 per cent Ether and 2·5 per cent water. To this was added 5 per cent of Nitro-benzine, and 300 gallons were shipped off to Utah. As if further indication were needed that the Abingdon star was not in the ascendant, news came that the U.S. Customs had decided to treat this mixture as "potable alcohol" for duty purposes. To rub it well in, this duty of one dollar per pound weight of fuel was to apply not only to the 300 gallons sent this trip, but retrospectively to the 200 gallons sent during the year preceding; in short, a little extra bill for $4000. The aid of almost everyone, from Anthony Eden downwards, was invoked to help sort this one out, and the arguments were finally settled, months later, by the 150 gallons left over being poured into New York harbour under customs supervision.

Aug. 12 was the date which had been fixed for the first record run. Profiting from the previous year's experience, transport went without hitch, the car being followed from point to point on its transit across America through the good offices of the American Express. But the main party arrived in Wendover on Aug. 7 in a thunderstorm and torrential rain, and there began the wearing process of sitting around waiting for the salt to dry.

By Saturday 16th, conditions were judged to be good enough to start, and Goldie took off round the circle. The salt was 'slick' and adhesion far from good. There was, of course, plenty of power— over 200 h.p. if he wanted it—but his instructions were to drive on the blower pressure gauge holding 8 lb. as nearly as possible. With the slippery nature of the salt, throttle operation was very delicate. After a couple of laps he came in, firmly under the impression that the hand on the oil thermometer was on its second lap of the dial, but this was disproved, and he finally started at 11.37 a.m. The first lap was slow but the second, at 155 m.p.h., set the pace for the run. But on lap 8, 74 miles from the start, Goldie spun out.

Now, on the flats, one can look in all directions and see nothing for miles except a timing box and a few marker posts stuck in the salt at quarter-mile intervals. One would think—and with justification— that if one was to have a slide here indeed was the one place in the world to have it. But Goldie, as he finished the waltz, slid up against one of these marker posts which broke off, smashed through the perspex bubble and cracked him over the head quite hard. It was a chance in a million.

He was somewhat dazed but quickly recovered and, after a judicious application of sticking plaster, was ready for more. Three International and eleven American National records had fallen, the fastest being at 155·7 m.p.h., but further work on the circle was abandoned. On the following day, Sunday, the straight course was used, and although a speed in excess of 190 m.p.h. was recorded, the top of a piston fell in before any records could be established. The mechanics accepted with some enthusiasm the decision to abandon Class E and convert the car to Class F.

This work took a couple of days, but it was clear from the first run on the Wednesday morning that the car was under-geared. Even so, the International and National Class F flying 5 miles and 10 kilos fell at 189·5 and 182·8 respectively. During the rest of the day the axle was changed from 2·9 to 2·8, and the car was out at first light next morning. But the gremlins were still at work. The car was visibly very fast, it ran without falter and showed a clear 7000 r.p.m. through the measured distances. On form that represented better than 220 m.p.h. But the recorded times were 202·14 for the kilo, 202·02 for the mile and 200·20 for the 5 kilos. These speeds established very attractive American National figures, but the old 1939 International still stood.

The answer was, of course, slip, and a good 10 per cent slip at that. Based on the previous year's experience, smooth unpatterned tyres with a mere 3 mm. of tread had been brought. With the prevailing conditions, peculiar to the salt, a patterned tread would have been advantageous, though it will be for ever in doubt whether even this would have produced 220 m.p.h.

Before Goldie was off the ship on the way home he was formulating plans for 1953. Though 1952 had brought some result, a chapter of accidents had been written, and the achievements were but a shadow of what had been intended. To put this right in the succeeding year was a clear challenge and arrangements went ahead: the old faithful XPAG, this time opened out to 1517 c.c., was brought in for Class E and developed to a high pitch; Jabbeke was to be the venue, transport arranged, and everything laid on. Then, late in July came the news that Goldie was ill and that the attempts must be postponed, later to be confirmed that his medical advisers had finally convinced him that further high-speed driving was not for him. As to the causes, nothing is quite clear. Stated originally to be sun-stroke, an opinion has latterly been expressed that the blow on the head which he received from the marker post at Utah was a good deal harder than his reactions at the time indicated. Whatever the truth, he was removed from active participation in the quick motoring scene immediately following one of the most frustrating and disappointing ventures of his career.

In the ordinary course, though, these were just the circumstances which would have spurred him on. He enjoyed his successes. He enjoyed the preparations for them. But as the time came near to start, he tightened up inside. To the casual observer—even to those with whom he spoke—he preserved an appearance of phlegmatic calm, but those who knew him well were aware that, as the minutes ticked away to the time when he must get into the car and move off, he suffered the tortures of the damned. "Careful, chaps. The Old Man's on edge" was a not uncommon comment in the *équipe* at these times. This, indeed, was the measure of his sheer guts. Had there been neither apprehension nor fear his performances would have merited but a tithe of the credit which was accorded to them. About every run there was an element of the unknown. Remember, for instance, that nobody else ever drove this car at 200 m.p.h. and, whereas every precaution was taken which calculation and wind-tunnel tests could devise, there could be no absolute guarantee that the car would not aviate or flip at some critical speed. With a distinguished military career behind him, a long history of suffering with a leg originally smashed in a war-time flying accident, and subsequently 'modified' a little by the crash in the T.T., he was, by any standards, a brave man.

As to the car, the MG Company bought it back from him. For it to appear in association with anyone else was unthinkable, and it was promptly turned into a show-piece by having perspex panels let into the whole of one side.

CHAPTER XII

EX 179

IF this were a radio script, it would probably begin "He was quite a guy, was George". The character referred to would be George Phillips, a rabid MG enthusiast, if ever there was one; bluff, genial, endowed with almost unlimited powers of invective and an entirely synthetic bad temper. From very shortly after World War II he had taken some sort of an MG to almost every race-meeting or hill climb within range, and driven it with mounting skill and immense verve to whatever success his stars protended. In both 1949 and 1950 he secured a private entry in the Le Mans 24-hour race, designed and built his own special bodies on a TC. chassis and—footing the entire bill from a far from bottomless bank account—put up very creditable performances. In the former year he ran fast and consistently until, in the nineteenth hour, he was disqualified for a technical infringement by his co-driver. In the latter, he finished 18th in general classification and 2nd in his class, well within his prescribed time-limit, thereby securing a qualification for 1951.

By way of some recompense for these efforts, the MG Company undertook to provide him with a fully prepared motor-car with which to take up this qualification. This was basically a standard TD. chassis but was surmounted by a long low body, designed by Sydney Enever, in which the influence of EX 135 was clearly discernible. The story of the appearance at Le Mans of this exciting-looking machine, though of no direct concern in the present chapter, must be told, albeit briefly, in fairness to Phillips.

In practice, the car behaved and performed beautifully and George was delighted with it. Clearly, he had a class win in his pocket. But two factors prevented this. Firstly, from a long experience of the use and abuse of the XPAG. engine, Phillips was definitely of the opinion that it was absolutely unbreakable. Secondly, with a lap speed up in the eighties and 116 m.p.h. through the kilometre trap down by Mulsanne, George gave more thought to the Index of Performance, indeed perhaps to the general classification, than to the Class, and saw himself in the big money if only he were to keep his foot down. This he accordingly did, his inspired drive causing quite a flurry while it lasted but, in the third hour, the exception proved the rule, a valve dropped in, and that was the end. Some high words ensued—not least from the co-driver who had no ride at all—but these were somewhat out of proportion to the event and stemmed largely from thoughts of what might have been.

But the appearance and behaviour of the car had inspired Enever. As it then stood, it was not a production proposition. Though the body was very low, the driver sat above the chassis frame and most of his torso stuck up above the scuttle. A windscreen some twenty inches deep would have been necessary to afford protection, so Enever set about putting it right. He designed a chassis frame in which the side members were swept outside the passenger space, and lowered the floor between them until it was but six inches from the ground. A new body with detailed refinements, windscreen, hood and sidescreens, followed and gave rise to a beautiful-looking motor-car still affectionately known as HMO6, though its official designation is EX175. The important point of this story is that, when Enever ordered the first experimental frame, he ordered two. HMO6 was put away for a rainy day.

During the latter half of 1953 George Eyston appeared again upon the Abingdon scene after an interval of some sixteen years. In the course of his work, he spent almost half his life in America where he kept his ear to the ground and was completely sold on the benefits, publicity-wise, of the annual pilgrimage to the land of the Mormons, Utah. With Goldie Gardner incapacitated he was keen that efforts in this direction should not be allowed to lapse, and urged that some project should be formulated for 1954.

From the time of the introduction of the MG TD. into America there had been a clamour for an increase in engine size and power. Some there were who had taken their courage in both hands and bored out the 1250-c.c. block, fitting liners to give some 1460 c.c. In the boring process, the tool had almost invariably gone through into the water jacket, and the liners were therefore a curious mixture of wet and dry, held in position more by luck than science. Though these engines worked, and pleased the venturesome souls who built them, the method was clearly not one which could commend itself to a firm in serious business as car manufacturers. Quite briefly, the casting and boring limits necessary to secure 1500 c.c. on the existing bore centres were for a time in advance of existing foundry technique. It was necessary to wait for this technique to develop before the new block could be introduced.

Meantime, a few blocks had been made by 'knife and fork' methods with bores of 72 mm. These had passed into the hands of drivers who consistently raced sports cars, and for some few seasons the overbored XPAG. powered the majority of the successful racing-sports cars in the U.K. It was decided to use such engines for the new record attempts. American National records up to 12 hours stood at such figures that it was thought that they could be broken unblown, and the 10-mile sprint, which had remained untouched by Goldie, was felt to be similarly vulnerable.

EX 175 was unwrapped again, fitted with wheel spats, undershield, an overall cockpit cover and a perspex bubble, and submitted to wind-tunnel tests. The results, when related to expected engine powers, were just not quite good enough. Further, it was considered to be bad policy to expose so early to public view a near-prototype of what it was hoped would one day become a production model. A new body was needed.

Experience had shown that EX 135 was as nearly aerodynamically perfect, for its size, as it was possible to be. Its chassis was, however, somewhat unorthodox in having oblique transmission, and it was very definitely 'monoposto'. It was felt that its successor should be more orthodox, certainly in the chassis, and that the car should be basically a 2-seater. The chassis frame, the spare one from HMO.6, stood ready made, and here was an ideal opportunity to test it. Wheelbase and track, however, together with the greater wheel movements permitted by the more modern suspension, precluded the use of a 'Chinese copy' of the EX 135 body shell, and so Enever set to work on a new outline, being prepared to sacrifice some efficiency by virtue of the foreshortening which the reduced wheelbase compelled. Books on airframes began to litter his office, and discussions ensued with long-haired gentlemen in charge of wind-tunnels in various aircraft factories. And in due time there emerged a new body, not so very different in appearance from EX 135 and which, in the wind-tunnel, proved to be slightly more than its equal. Thus EX 179 was born.

Eyston's two engines—one sprint, one endurance—were well advanced when a decision was taken to put the 1466-c.c. XPEG. engine into production. Improved foundry techniques and increased clamour from the U.S.A. for more power conspired to force the issue, and the introduction was decided upon in the face of an inevitably high proportion of foundry and machine shop scrap. A race then developed to get the TF.1500 into America in time to tie up with the record attempts, The race was won, but an accumulation of 1250-c.c. engined TF.'s delayed the announcement, so that much of the impact of the publicity arising from the records was lost.

Let us now digress once more and consider something of the history of this astonishing XPAG. engine. The basic design originated about 1934–5 when, with a high degree of commonality, side valve and push-rod overhead lay-outs were used in Morris and Wolseley cars respectively. The XPAG. as such appeared in late 1938 as the power unit of the MG TB., when it superseded the 1292-c.c. TPBG. as used in the TA. In its then standard form, which was to persist through the TC. and TD. Mark I until 1953, the compression ratio was 7·25 and the nominal power 54 h.p. at 5000 r.p.m.

From the earliest days, MG owners have fiddled with their engines in order to coax more power out of them. The amount of real knowledge behind such operations was distinctly variable—sometimes non-existent—and almost without exception the expenditure of time and money was out of proportion to the results ultimately obtained. The attitude of the factory to this enthusiasm was curiously detached and aloof: the cars are good as they stand; tune at your peril; any departure from standard will invalidate the guarantee. Such was the policy up to June 1949 when it was realised that, whatever the factory said, owners would continue to raise compression ratios, spend large sums of money on alternative carburetters and so on, and even then not secure the best results. Surely it was in the best interests of both factory and owner that those competitively inclined should get the best from their cars as cheaply as possible.

Thus, in June 1949, appeared the first of a series of MG 'Special Tuning' booklets. The foreword to the first edition read as follows:—

" The MG Midget, as delivered from the factory in its standard form, is tuned to give maximum performance with ' pump' petrol, consistent with complete reliability and reasonable freedom from pinking. There is, however, a more or less continuous demand from enthusiasts all over the world for information on methods of improving the performance for competitive purposes, and it is to meet this demand that this booklet has been prepared.

It must clearly be understood, however, that, whereas it is a simple matter to increase the power output of the engine, this cannot be achieved without the use of fuel having better anti-detonant qualities than ordinary 'pump' petrol. In addition, this increase in power must inevitably carry with it a tendency to reduced reliability.

It is for this reason that the terms of the guarantee on a new MG expressly exclude any super-tuning of the kind described in this booklet, but this does not mean that tuning in this way will necessarily make the car hopelessly unreliable. In fact, it may be assumed that it will be at least as reliable as other cars of similar performance.

This booklet is laid out so as to give details of progressively increasing power. With the above ideas firmly in mind, the owner should select the simplest tuning method which will give him the performance he requires, remembering all the time that here, as elsewhere, POWER COSTS MONEY. "

Appendix V, at the back of this book, contains extensive extracts from the 1954 edition of the tuning booklet. It will be seen to run through the whole gamut of higher compression ratios, special camshafts, larger valves, larger carburetters, leading the intending competitor, by easy stages, from a modest increase of a few horse power to a maximum of 82 h.p. at an extended speed range of 6300 r.p.m. An earlier edition had described the use of a low-pressure supercharger, to give 97·5 b.h.p. Typical power curves are shown in *Figs.* 18, 19.

K

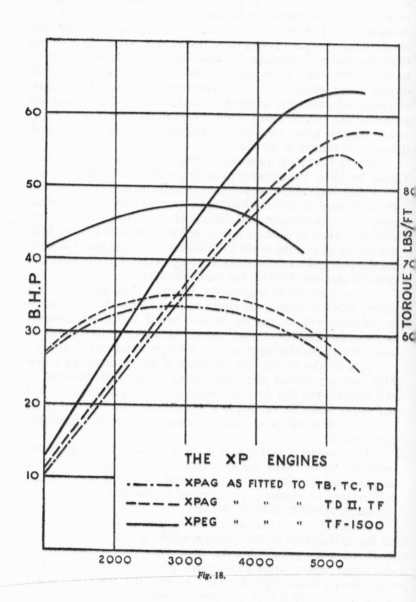

THE XP ENGINES

.... XPAG AS FITTED TO TB, TC, TD

------ XPAG " " " TD II, TF

——— XPEG " " " TF-1500

Fig. 18.

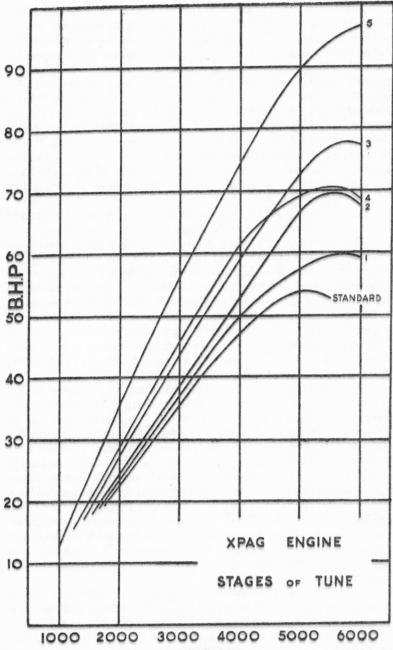

XPAG ENGINE

STAGES OF TUNE

R.P.M

Fig. 19.

These then were the stages of tune which any owner could apply. Reliability was high and when major disaster occurred it was usually traceable to excess of zeal or plain clottishness on the part of the driver or his mechanics. But in the course of the use of the engine for record breaking purposes, tuning was taken far higher. Eyston's sprint engine for 1954, as will shortly be seen, gave 97·5 h.p. at 6500, unblown (*Fig.* 20). Goldie's 1250 in 1951 gave 213 h.p. at 7000 r.p.m. with 30 lb. boost (*Fig.* 17). The XPEG., opened out still further to 1517 c.c., as prepared for 1953, but not used, gave 219 h.p. at 6900 with 27 lb. boost. And, to crown all, while this engine was being tested, an addition to the fuel of 15 per cent nitro-methane was tried and 231 h.p. appeared. But this frightened even the case-hardened habitués of the test bed and the experiment was not pursued. There was some vestige of feeling left for the willing horse.

But to return to EX 179, some data must be given of the state of tune of the two engines, and the construction of the car itself.

The 12-hour engine followed very closely the state of tune shown by Stage TF.4, Appendix V, and was, in fact, the prototype of this stage. Slight variations improved torque in the middle range at the expense of power at 5500 and above—which, for this run, would not be needed. As an insurance measure, lest No. 1 engine blew up or, at Enever's insistence, in case his calculations should be adrift, a second engine was taken, tuned to slightly higher standards. Events proved it to be unnecessary and it was never installed. Instead, it was handed over to Ken Miles, who used it to very good effect in his own MG special during the ensuing racing season in California.

For the sprint, in order to achieve 150 m.p.h., a sea-level 91 h.p. was needed. Nothing less was worth contemplating, and Enever would have to pull out all the stops to get it. The characteristics of the 85 per cent Methanol fuel were known, and experiments began in order to determine the highest compression ratio which could be used. This was determined not so much by the fuel itself as by mechanical considerations. High-crowned pistons machined to fit the combustion space, while allowing room for the valves and for flame development, finally settled the ratio at 11·8 to 1. The long overlap "blower" cam-shaft—as used on the XPAG. with supercharger in previous years—was thought to be the most suitable of the shafts readily available and, to take maximum advantage of it, two enormous S.U. carburetters of $2\frac{3}{16}$ in. throat diameter—also as used with the supercharger—were installed.

The only serious functional difficulty with the engine was that the limited induction manifold depression, at full throttle with the large carburetters, was insufficient to raise the pistons to their limit. In short, the pistons could not be made light enough. Various materials and methods were tried, but finally a rod, attached to each piston and

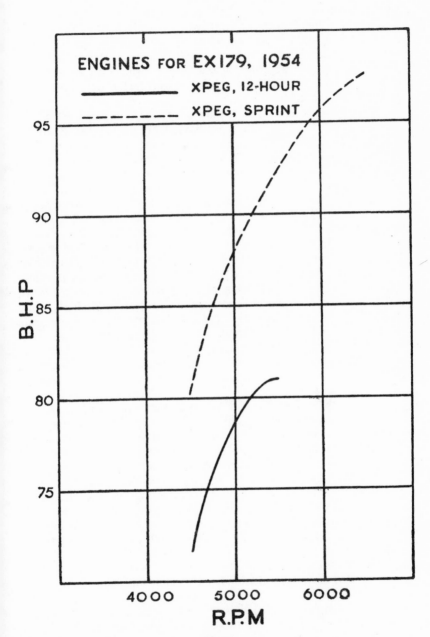

Fig. 20.

passing downwards through a hole in the body of the carburetter, was attached to a light spring so arranged as to tend to raise the piston. Here was another of those mechanical occasions which needed a paradoxical spring which became weaker the more it was deflected. The nearest simple approach was to use a spring long enough that its rate, over the required movement of two inches or so, was substantially constant.

The overall result was more than satisfactory, the engine delivering 97·5 h.p. at 6500 r.p.m. with a very reasonably shaped top end to the power curve (*see Fig.* 20) and quite astonishing sweetness of running.

With the exception of the limitations which the body imposed, the lay-out of the chassis was substantially orthodox. Indeed one of the objects of the exercise was to use as many standard components as possible. Front suspension, steering box and road wheels were standard TF., but front brakes were omitted, as on EX 135, in order to reduce unsprung weight to a minimum. The rear axle was a composite affair using a VA. nosepiece, but TF. brakes and wheels. The standard nosepiece would not accommodate gears of the high ratios intended—of the order of 3 to 1—and the opportunity was therefore taken to use a non-hypoid assembly, thus making a simple matter of the production of whatever gears might be necessary. Similarly, noise not being of much importance and strength paramount, these gears had straight teeth. Coil springs at the front and laminated semi-elliptics at the rear were of higher rate than normal in order that wheel movement could be more readily limited, standard hydraulic damping being supplemented by light friction, which would be more effective with small deflections.

The radiators, water and oil, and their associated plumbing, looked more complex than, in fact, they were. Aluminium units, mounted side by side on a tubular cantilever outrigger extending forward from the frame, were some three feet forward of the front axle centre-line and but eight inches from the ground at their lowest point. The water header-tank and the main oil storage tank were, however, mounted aft of the power unit, as high as possible. Water connections were by light alloy tubes terminating in hose connections and, as was now customary, no water passed through the cylinder head joint but transferred from block to head by an external pipe.

A rectangular slot situated at a pressure node at the front of the car admitted air to the radiators from which it was ducted to discharge at a low-pressure area just in front of the engine compartment. This latter was completely sealed off by the undershield, thereby necessitating not only the oil cooler, but also a ducted intake to the carburetters. A similar duct, on the opposite side of the car, supplied fresh air to the cockpit in a quantity under the control of the driver.

The body itself was made completely and quickly detachable. The alloy panelling was built up in one piece on a framework of $\frac{5}{8}$ in. square, 16-gauge, perforated steel tube and mounted on the frame at fourteen points. Facia and instruments, seats and flooring, were made integral with the chassis, which was therefore left complete—and, indeed, drivable—when the body was removed. Spats covering all four wheel arches and the engine cover were secured by quickly detachable coin-slot fasteners. The cockpit cover was in two pieces hinged on the centre line, one half, with perspex dome, covering the driver, the other giving access to a 30-gallon fuel tank which occupied the position of the passenger's seat.

The original intention had been to attack the American National Class F Records from 300 kilometres to 12 hours, which stood at speeds of 103 m.p.h. downwards. When the new body proved to be of such good shape and the engine power so satisfactory, sights were raised a little to aim at the International records which, for similar distances, stood between 105 and 114 m.p.h. With this decided upon it was felt that to go so fast and yet no faster was rather a pity when two miles a minute for the twelve hours had, as an achievement, a quality all its own. Out came the charts and slide-rules again. The car required only 51 h.p. to propel it at 125 m.p.h. at 4200 ft. The engine had a maximum of 70 h.p. at the same altitude. The more one looked at it, the more sure did it seem that 1440 miles in 12 hours was a part-throttle job.

With the disappointments of 1951 and 1952 still in their minds, the boys at Abingdon were more than ever keen that, whatever might go wrong this year, it would be no fault of theirs. With a completely new car, completely new engines, and adequate preparation time, they had everything in their favour. Engine performance was known and was, in the absence of a supercharger, directly correctable for altitude. Wind-tunnel figures for the body and two years' accumulation of data on the previous attempts enabled Enever to predict performance with greater accuracy than ever before.

The journey out was uneventful. The ground-work, laid on by Eyston who had gone out in advance, was faultless. The weather was perfect and the salt in excellent condition. Small wonder, then, that this venture was a model example of how the job should be done.

The car had been shipped with the 12-hour engine installed. Once uncrated, the wheels were changed, fuel, oil and water put in, the remaining fluid levels checked and grease applied to the inside of the wheel arches and other places where the salt was known to tend to stick. Nothing else was touched. The car push-started first time and, after a couple of warming-up laps of the ten mile circle, was ready to go. Driving three-hour shifts, George Eyston and Ken Miles lapped consistently at 124 m.p.h., plus or minus one m.p.h., capturing seven

International and twenty-five American National records, all at 120 m.p.h. or thereabouts. The National Standing Start figures, when arranged in order of time and distance, show the consistency of the running and the diminishing effect of the standing start and of the subsequent three-hourly stops:

250 K.	118·71
300 K.	119·17
400 K.	119·98
250 M.	120·00
500 K.	120·55
3 Hours	120·91
400 M.	119·63
500 M.	120·28
1000 K.	120·92
6 Hours	121·38
1000 M.	120·13
2000 K.	120·19
12 Hours	120·74

During the following day the sprint engine was installed and the axle ratio changed. A cable to Abingdon reported that George Eyston had most sportingly offered to stand down in favour of Ken Miles for the 10-mile run. Here, the car having been geared for optimum in accordance with Enever's calculations, the orders were "foot on the floor and see what happens". The result was a mean speed for the flying 10 miles of 153·69 m.p.h. with a push-rod 1½-litre engine, unsupercharged!

Before the *équipe* left England, Enever had prepared a most informative chart showing power at various r.p.m. for both engines, both at sea level and at 4200 ft.; ground speed against r.p.m. for various alternative axle ratios, and power required to propel the car, both at sea level and at 4200 ft. According to this, at 4200 ft. the car required 85 h.p. at 150 m.p.h. and 92 h.p. at 155. The sprint engine gave its maximum power, 84 h.p., at 6500 r.p.m. On the strength of this, the 3·125 axle was fitted which would give 154·7 m.p.h. at 6500. From this there was every justification to expect that 150 m.p.h. would not quite be achieved. That it was exceeded proved that the drag figures were just a little conservative. Sydney Enever is a realist. He will never be caught kidding himself.

What of the future of this car? Its shape approaches the ideal for speed (frontal area 11·8 sq. ft. K = ·00061). Its chassis is reasonably modern and by virtue of its method of construction, lends itself well to "chopping bits off and welding bits on". Inside its skin is an enormous amount of room for experimentation of all kinds with the added advantage that such things are better shielded from prying eyes than on more orthodox vehicles. It will undoubtedly play its part as a mobile test-bed for some time to come. Meanwhile, the records just spoken of have been pushed up some 7 m.p.h. by an Osca, but at that are still very vulnerable when it is realised that only about 70 per cent of the available engine power was used. Otherwise, all is conjecture, but EX 179 will certainly be seen about again.

Footnote: Goldie Gardner died in 1958, and both EX 135 and EX 179 have long since passed into honourable retirement.

CHAPTER XIII

THE DAWN OF A NEW ERA

IN point of fact, it was George Phillips who started things moving by providing Enever with an excuse and an opportunity of proving to his own satisfaction, and demonstrating to the sceptics, that a motor-car of modern line could be designed which was yet unmistakably MG. Now that it is all over, one wonders what the fuss was about, but at the time it took some courage, in the face of all sorts of forebodings, to throw away the old traditional shape. But all good things must come to an end and so departed the spartan line, with square radiator and slab tank, which had been in vogue from the J2 of 1932 right through to the TF. of 1955.

The application of the various stages of the tuning booklet did more than anything else to convince the doubters that something had to be done. Consider the total resistance curve of the TF. shown in *Fig*. 21, particularly in relation to EX 135. At 85 m.p.h. or so the TF. finds the atmosphere almost as impenetrable as a brick wall. One can go on piling on horse power, pouring petrol in the tank and money down the drain and getting practically nothing in return except improved acceleration. With a perfectly standard TF. engine, EX 135 or EX 179 would have a maximum speed of 130 m.p.h. or so. Clearly, in this age of increasing speeds and expensive petrol the Old Faithful shape had had its day.

Nevertheless, EX 179 has some pretty severe limitations as a road vehicle and one can do no more than tend towards it. The road vehicle needs headlamps—26 inches off the ground—bumpers, number plates, a windscreen and a hood, all of which detract from the ideal shape and increase the frontal area. Undershields are not entirely suitable for everyday wear and front wheel-spats restrict the steering lock to a few degrees. And lastly, an overall length approaching seventeen feet with the three feet, plus, of overhang fore and aft—necessary for ideal penetration—would make parking tricky, to say the least, apart from which the insurance companies would be up in arms.

The *modus operandi* for the designing of the body must be to lay out the four wheels, the seats and occupants, the pedals, the rest of the machinery and two headlamps at the statutory height, and then endeavour to wrap the whole lot up in the smoothest possible envelope. But give this job to half-a-dozen different designers, telling them that

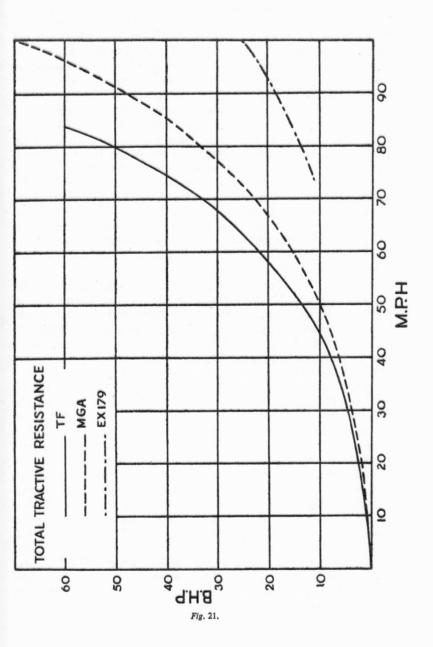

Fig. 21.

maximum penetration is the sole criterion and they will, if they know their job, all produce the same answer—because there is only one. At this point, the problem becomes intangible; the slide-rule is put away and the eye takes over; the engineer steps to one side and the artist steps in. It must be decided to what extent efficiency, or 'functionalism', may be sacrificed to aesthetic appeal, to give the car character, distinction and difference. On the success of this part of the operation depends the car's ultimate acceptance by the public.

In considering the replacement of a body such as that on the TF. by an all-enveloping style, grisly problems of cost arise. If the wings, fuel tank and bonnet are removed from any of the T. types, there is not much left, and that, as some unfortunate observed when wallowing in problems of cost comparison, is made of "two sheets of tin and a bundle of firewood"—an over-simplification which stresses the point very well. Not only is the all-enveloping body inevitably more complex, but the cost of tools, necessary for the production of every square inch of the outer skin and much of the internal structure as well, can be very high. It was such considerations as these which caused HMO.6 to be shelved in 1953.

In June, 1954, Enever was given the green light to design, for production, a new MG to replace the TF., on the general lines of HMO.6. The fact that HMO.6 existed meant that the back of the design work was already broken, and the performance and behaviour of the car known with reasonable accuracy. The car, however, looked large by comparison with the TF. and, in any event, had been built with lavish detail and equipment and with no very keen eye on cost.

The T. types, all of them, had earned for MG an enviable reputation for rugged reliability. They were not machines which had to be coddled; they were built to go anywhere, to keep going and to put up with more than the average measure of abuse. The new car had to be in no way inferior in these respects. For years, MGs had been built under the slogan 'Safety Fast' and this, at Abingdon, was regarded as no empty phrase but rather as a challenge. A car could easily be built which was too fast for its own inherent stability, as certain examples in the world-wide race for higher and higher speeds were tending to prove. The new car would have a maximum speed of the order of 100 m.p.h. and some of them would be bought, as MGs had been bought down the years, by tyro drivers. Above all, therefore, the new car had to be stable, to keep "its feet on the ground", to have stopping power commensurate with its performance and to be entirely free from any of those vicious unpredictable tricks which can so easily arise—and, unfortunately, not infrequently do—from careless or incompetent design.

The designers' brief, therefore, was to make a car which was, first and foremost, 'safe' as defined above; which, secondly, was at least as rugged, as well-appointed and well-finished as its predecessors; and, thirdly, was to sell as nearly as possible at the price of the TF.—certainly inside £600. Only then were speed and acceleration to be considered and they should, of course, be as good as could be contrived. The above sequence is important. It underlies the confidence in the future success of the car, and of its continued acceptance by a discriminating public. It is *not*, be it admitted, a prescription which wins races—the more is the pity—but for every owner who wishes to go racing, there are a hundred and more who do not. And they are entitled to—indeed, must be given—their motoring and their fun in the safest possible form.

The project was allotted the tag EX 182, and detailed finalisation of design, and the construction of prototypes, went forward under this number. It was estimated that production could begin in April, 1955, and that a world-wide announcement would be possible in the first days of June. The Le Mans 24-hour race of 1955 was fixed for June 11, and it was therefore decided to enter a team of three production cars in order to demonstrate their high-speed reliability and at the same time secure qualifications for the Biennial Cup Race in 1956. June was to be an important month in MG history.

The chassis frame of EX 182 followed closely that of EX 179, some small alterations being made to simplify quantity production and ease the tooling problem. The front cross-member and, with it, the front suspension, were almost pure TF. though set at a slightly different angle from that in the earlier model. Subject to a small reduction in track, the rear axle—and the brakes—came straight from the MG Magnette. Current American fashion dictated that wire-spoked centre-lock wheels should be provided, at least as an alternative, though the opinion is firmly held at Abingdon that this is but a passing phase. Speed of wheel changing is of importance only in long-distance racing and the greater strength of the wire wheel over the disc is doubtful, so the only merit left is one of appearance. And nowadays a larger proportion of owners have to clean their own cars! The centre-lock disc is the wheel of the future for sports cars, but was not, at this time, developed sufficiently for quantity production.

The question of engine for the car gave rise to a little soul-searching. The XPEG. was still a difficult and costly job to make. The new British Motor Corporation 'B' series engine, of 1489 c.c., as already fitted to the MG Magnette, was, on the other hand, being produced in large numbers at a satisfactory price and, in its Magnette application, was already giving almost as much horsepower as the XPEG. in the TF. Not an inconsiderable argument in its favour was that world-wide distribution of spares and replacements would be common between the two models. And so, despite the known longevity of the XPEG. and the facility with which it could be supertuned, the decision went against it. If one could be supertuned, so could the other; it only remained to discover how.

While the normal experiments with porting, valve timing and compression ratios were going on, Harry Weslake was toying with a new cylinder head in which he had arranged the inlet ports so that they passed right through the head and appeared on both sides of it. This was, potentially, an immensely flexible arrangement, as it would be possible to put carburetters on the exhaust side, if one wanted them to be heated; on the opposite side if one wanted them kept cool; or on both—operating either concurrently or consecutively— if one wanted the best of both worlds. Early trials showed that, with the carburetters on the 'hot' side and a substantial balance pipe between the two ports on the cold side, very good filling was obtained, and more than 80 b.h.p. was available, at 5500 r.p.m., with 9·4 compression. The one great practical disadvantage of the head was that, with machined faces on both sides, instead of only one, the design did not lend itself to production on the automatic machinery used for standard production, and the head would, therefore, be comparatively expensive. This led to the start of experiments to determine if similar results could be obtained without the ports emerging through the right-hand side of the head.

With the general design of the car in a fairly advanced state, the body shell and chassis frame having long since been cleared for production, it was learned that body tools could not be produced in accordance with the delivery promises already given and that, therefore, the announcement date of the new model would have to be deferred. This being so, it was clear that it would not be possible to run at Le Mans with Production Cars as, although the conditions of the Race Regulations had been satisfied—in that far more than the minimum required number of sets of material had been provided—it was obviously impolitic to expose the car to public view some months before its announcement. If it ran at all, it would have to run as a prototype and permission for this was, accordingly, obtained from the Automobile Club de l'Ouest. Meantime, the date of the début of the production car was deferred for at least three months.

Whilst this was a disappointing upset of the original coordinated plan, it had the one advantage of providing somewhat greater freedom in drawing up the specification of the race cars and of using the occasion as a first-class high-speed test. Whatever might be the ultimate fate of the 'dual-entry' head, it could certainly be used for the race; that an oil-cooler would now be permitted meant that the cars could have complete under-shielding. Bodies were constructed—to the exact contours decided for production—from light alloy, it being considered that these same bodies could subsequently be used for the Alpine Trial. For this reason, provision was made for the attachment of the standard windscreen and hood, and the near side door which, for Le Mans, would be permanently closed, could be made to open again. A 20-gallon fuel tank was installed in the tail with a large diameter quick-opening cap protruding through the boot lid. The cockpit was covered with a quickly-detachable sheet alloy cover embodying a sloping perspex half bubble. Externally, therefore, the car followed the intended production car very closely.

For the race, endurance was the prime necessity. With 82 horse-power available, maximum speed would exceed 110 m.p.h., and the race average required for a Biennial Cup qualification was a shade under 80. A consistent lap speed at around 85 m.p.h. was the aim, with the engine doing as little work as possible. A few weeks before the race, a car went to Le Mans with two alternative sets of gearbox ratios, several pairs of final drive gears and sundry tyres of assorted sizes. A complete lap was unobtainable as the tunnel at Tertre Rouge was in course of construction at the time, but sufficient data was secured to enable the gearing to be decided. Unless conditions during practice proved to be very different from those obtaining during this early test, a 3·7 to 1 axle, 6·00 × 15 rear tyres, and the close ratio gearbox would be almost ideal. The only doubt sprang from specula-tion upon the possibility of a car having to restart up the 1 in 30 slope at the pits, late in the race with a sick motor, the fierceish racing clutch and a 9 to 1 first gear!

Two firm entries had been secured for the race with a third in the position of 6th reserve. Past experience tended to show that in these circumstances it was almost certain that three cars would start. This had been assumed from the beginning and four cars had been laid down, three for the race and a fourth to bear the brunt of pre-race testing and provide a reserve in the event of damage. All were built with great care and prepared with tremendous thoroughness under the watchful eye of Alec Hounslow for whom the process was a return to his old love, he having built C types, J4s and K3s twenty-odd years before. It was interesting to watch how the hand had not lost its cunning, how the high standards of workmanship remained, and how there was no need for anyone to try to 'teach the old dog new tricks'. Best of all it was to see that the ability remained to infect a new generation of racing mechanics with the same thoroughness and enthusiasm. By the time the cars were ready to leave Abingdon they were as suitable for their purpose and as near perfection as the most fastidious could desire.

Of race week itself the story is best told by Russell Lowry. He and his wife accompanied the MG *équipe* as interpreters, with a specific duty to monitor the interminable outpourings of the French public address system, thereby not only keeping the team manager informed of interesting snippets of race news, but also enabling corrective measures to be taken in the event of mis-statements affecting MG. As it so happened, the commentaries virtually ceased after the first three hours and Lowry was able to divert his mind to other things. What follows was written immediately after the return to England, primarily for the record and for internal consumption at Abingdon. It captures so accurately the spirit of the occasion, its excitements and its depressions, its fun and its tragedy, that it is repeated here *in extenso*.

"The 'End of the Beginning' in MG's return to active competition was surely marked by the departure from Abingdon of the advance guard with the four new cars, the magnificent new transporter, and the mechanics, all under command of Marcus Chambers—destination, the Château Chêne de Cœur, Le Mans. Those with long memories must have recalled other departures of 20 years ago. . . .

"The main party converged on the Burlington Hotel, Folkestone, on Sunday evening, June 5th. Present were John and Joanne Thornley *in loco parentis*, Sammy Davis the Great and Wise, the drivers, Dick Jacobs, Joe Flynn, Johnny Lockett, with their wives, Ken Miles over from California for the purpose, and Ted Lund. Hans Waeffler would join us at Le Mans coming direct from Zürich. In support were Babe Learoyd as Transport Officer and assistant to Marcus Chambers, and Fred Crossley, resident assistant to Dick Jacobs. Also several B.M.C. 'boffins' who remained somewhat nebulous presences busy with their own secrets—except Sydney Enever, very boffiny, but far from nebulous in MG spheres! George Eyston's brief presence seemed a good augury, and we were encouraged by news of success in the Scottish Rally. The Lowrys with furthest to come, at least by road, were last to arrive. During the evening John Thornley briefed us on transport arrangements, and distributed tickets and travel funds.

"Monday, June 6th. All aboard the Lord Warden at Dover in good time and shape for a perfect crossing. Reports that certain seagulls following the ship were devoid of feet and even legs raised interesting aero-technical discussions, but could not be substantiated, and the sceptics claimed the argument though the original observers remained unrepentant! Boulogne was cleared at about 12.15, with rendezvous at Etaples for lunch, our 3 Magnettes, the Pathfinder full of boffins, and Sammy Davis in his Austin Healey proceeding independently. Owing to a mysterious affliction to one of Madame's legs at the Etaples restaurant, the meal took longer than expected, and an element of pressure became necessary if Le Mans was to be made by dinner time. On the road South we all ran into a quite fantastic storm. Solid water reduced visibility to absolute zero, lighting glared, trees and branches rolled in the road. But all emerged safely—Sammy Davis with a hole in a sidescreen.

"After a hasty luggage-drop and wash at the Château, all proceeded to the nearby restaurant, Les Rosiers, where M. Menard was to feed us all throughout the week. Convivial atmosphere. Cheers for

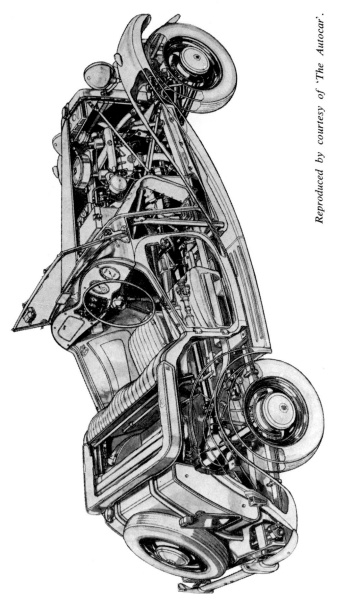

Reproduced by courtesy of 'The Autocar'.

The TD chassis, the starting-point for the development of the MGA.

(*a*)
George Phillips' 1951 Le Mans car.
An Enever-designed body shell on a TD chassis.

(*b*)
'UMG 400 put right'.   The first prototype, EX 175.

(*a*)

The baptism of the new chassis frame. EX 179 at M.I.R.A.

(*b*)

The second prototype—EX 182—in Le Mans trim.   Ken Wharton operates the
loud pedal at Silverstone.

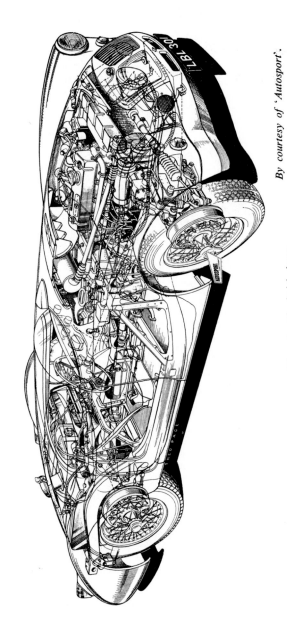

By courtesy of 'Autosport'.

The truth laid bare.

Mr JACOBS   Mr LOCKETT   Mr KEN MILES   Mr FLYNN   Mr WAEFLER   Mr LUND   Mr TORNLEY   Mr CHAMBERS

Le Mans — 1955.

The French cartoonist, 'Heljy', is cruel and kind.

The
ultimate
ordeal.

EX 182
prototypes
at
Le Mans
1955.

The finished article. The production MGA.

Enever's toys.
Wind-tunnel models used in the search for the shape of things to come.

all new arrivals. Reunion with the advance party. Everyone in good form. Early to bed—with queues for nocturnal sanitation. Wide variation of beds, from four-posters to truckles, and of rooms from Louis XIV state apartments to powder closets. The sanitation itself, even if vocal and scarce, was a vast improvement on rumour and report! The general impression of the Château was of former splendour in some decay—but it was obviously ideal for our purpose, taking the whole party of 36 under one roof, plus the racing cars and transporter in the stables. Bags of parking space on the gravel terrace. A large salon to serve as an office, where Marcus Chambers and his wife toiled all day and most of the night, and where conferences were held by the Upper House of Thornley/Davis/Chambers with drivers, lap scorers, etc. A chart in the hall showed the functions of all personnel and general information or instructions—with a crafty cardboard arrow to point at the latest item. The board also displayed various goodwill messages, including a particularly appreciated one from the Vice-Chairman of B.M.C.

"Tuesday, 7th. The main operation of the morning was attendance at the 'Pesage', commonly miscalled 'Pressage', but actually the weighing-in or scrutineering of cars and crews. This was sited in an enclosure off one of the town's main squares and, taking several days for the full entry, was a major social and technical occasion. The MGs, immaculate in British Racing Green and shining like the morning sun itself, in perfect formation, dead on time, and attended by smartly green-overalled mechanics, made a terrific impression. Word of this was reaching us directly and indirectly, officially and unofficially, for days afterwards. And everyone was most congratulatory about the new cars, as cars. Certainly we made a sharp contrast with some of the others, tatty, ill-painted, with extemporized fittings, and sometimes with bodies far from regulation requirements. We were passed from table to table, every detail being gone through, checked, noted and approved. The only modification ordered was that the tail pipes be cut off square, instead of diagonally, to comply with dust-raising provisions.

"The lighter side was not lacking—especially at the medical examination of drivers, where our cheerful Irishman, Joe Flynn, gave his religion as Republican, he having no French and his interlocutor no English. A sad afterthought of this examination is that if blood pressure had been taken, as formerly, it would have been a valuable guide in the case of Dick Jacobs. But on this morning Dick, under the tuition of Hans Waeffler, was making rapid, if violent, progress in French. A little cartoonist was found doing sketches of the team and was suitably encouraged. Names were proving difficult—Lockett was to emerge later in print as Sockett, and then as Kickett!

"In the afternoon Sammy Davis and Marcus Chambers directed intensive pit-stop drill in the Château yard. It was observable that the flippant approach of some members soon changed when they were

L

gently asked why, for instance, they'd left that chock under a wheel supposedly about to go racing again—or a raised eyebrow indicated a bonnet strap still undone. Sammy showed complete mastery of every detail—and infinite patience. Every man had to know not only what he was doing, but why, and when.

"Wednesday, 8th, produced a really filthy morning. Intensive shopping by the Thornleys and Lowrys for such items as electric torches, sheet aluminium, blocks of wood, brooms, cellophane, rivets, a frying pan, chewing gum for the drivers. This activity recurred daily throughout the week. Quite incredible how many and how diverse the articles needed.

"Stan Nicholls, our orientally imperturbable time-keeper, flew in from England, bringing further spares, these having been ordered after a protracted battle with the local telephone system—and the Château instrument which bears the inscription 'Modèle de 1910' and behaves accordingly.

"The King brothers and wives also arrived to complete the scoring staff. We jocularly deplored their transport—a pair of TR.2s.

"The drivers received individual initiation into the mysteries of the Le Mans circuit from Sammy Davis. In the evening all hands out to the circuit for practice. A bit chaotic, but very impressive. Too many cars for our pit space (one double pit for 3 MGs and the Macklin Austin-Healey). Also obvious that we had too many people in the pits. But the cars looked splendid, sounded good and according to the drivers, handled superbly. Lapping started in the 60-m.p.h. bracket, rising gradually to the 80's. After dark the lamps received attention from 'Mr. Lucas'.

"The feature of the evening was the airbrake on the Mercedes. Most disconcerting, flying open like a huge desk-lid, as the engines screeched down into third gear.

"We gained a place in the 'suppléant' or reserve list, when the unfortunate Behra was shunted by Moss' Mercedes—a fateful, but of course unperceived, indication of things to come.

"Depression spread in our pit when Johnnie Lockett (41) became overdue. The trouble proved to be no more than a thrown fan belt resulting in boiled-away water. The head was lifted next morning and all found undamaged. Car running again by mid-day under the ministrations of Dicky Green.

"Thursday, 9th. Improved pit signals being devised from sheet aluminium and tube, the transport of which incidentally had caused some despondency in the streets of Le Mans—but vive le sport! Also improved lighting of the signals. Drivers say they can't see them. Sammy Davis says sorry but they've got to see them.

"Many visitors from the outside world. All much impressed. Especially, we hope, the spiers-out-of-the-land. There would be far more but for our seclusion. And yet we are only a few minutes from Le Mans for shops or official business.

"The local press come out and give the cars and mechanics a first-rate write-up, with photographs. 'A welcome return . . . morale sky-high . . . perhaps only in Italy does one find such camaraderie . . . such enthusiasm.'

"George Eyston a visitor at lunch at Les Rosiers. Brings further word of the good impression made. Catering and general relations at Les Rosiers excellent, thanks mainly to cultivation by Meg Lowry. But artichokes are not universally popular and won't be tried again.

"Only car No. 41 out for practice to-night to make sure all well after last night's incident. Some other people's cars beginning to sound very rough already. We go up to 1st reserve following a spin-out by the Arnott. Car wrecked. Driver tended by our Dr. King. Incidentally, we take over Arnott pit which adjoins our own, and will be used for time-keeping and lap-scoring.

"Two Porsches bearing the same racing number are observed in front of their pit. The Commissaires descend . . .

"Lighter moment of the day provided by Ted Lund, an inveterate postcard writer who, noticing a letter-slot in an official looking wall, pops in his daily output—then finds it's the local taxation office. Next morning it is ascertained that the staff, after reading the cards with great enjoyment, have posted them properly. Toujours vive le sport!

"Friday, 10th. John Thornley learns at the Préfecture that our third car, No. 64, Lund and Waeffler, will certainly be 'in'. He also learns of much opposition to the Mercedes flaps, which everyone hates and regards as dangerous. They unsight following drivers, quite apart from slipstream disturbance, etc.

"At the Château great activity packing up for tomorrow. Tea nevertheless is dispensed from the Transporter, the milk problem having been put on a satisfactory basis. Secret milking, by agriculturally minded mechanics, of cows housed in the yard is not popular. And a very fierce (stuffed) Alsatian guards the kitchen.

"John Valentyn, of the Belgian M.G.C.C., arrives and being completely bi-lingual from birth is going to be more than useful. It should be recorded that in this Company endeavour we now have MG Car Club representation by at least the following, apart from those, who, like John Thornley, have dual capacity:—

"The Kings (S.W. Centre), the Jacobs (S.E. Centre), the Flynns (Irish), Ted Lund (N.W.), Ken Miles (Long Beach, California), Hans Waeffler (Switzerland), the Lowrys (Gen. Secretary). These are on the strength. We have Club supporters from far and wide.

"During this afternoon Sammy Davis and Marcus Chambers conduct practice of the 'Le Mans Start' in front of the Château.

"All cars being in complete readiness, drivers trained, pit personnel coached, and everything ship-shape, no cars were sent up to the circuit this evening and the company retired early to get what sleep it could.

"Saturday, 12th. Weather absolutely perfect. The cars and the transporter pause on Château terrace for photographs before leaving for circuit. Impressive sight, in a perfect setting. Towards 10 a.m. none of us had any finger nails left to bite, so a move was made. Huge crowds converging on the circuit, but wonderfully well handled. Eventually our camp is established, with two cars and the transporter behind our pits and the necessary gear and spares moved in or erected, though our tent-poles seem to have gone missing. Pit situation greatly relieved by take-over of the Arnott compartment. Still too many people though, and a white line has been painted, behind which everyone not vitally concerned must retire on the sounding of a whistle. Awful job buying the whistle for some reason!

"The Commissaires move in and the interminable business of checking off spares and equipment begins. One of the 'plombeurs' has no teeth at all, and a seemingly impossible degree of squint. He is not easy to talk to, even in French! The music blares, the sun shines, the loud-speakers plug their publicity. All the cars are lined up along the pits, and the nations of the world walk up and down inspecting and photographing. The MGs look good, even if some of the others look more exciting. 'Real little sports cars' seems to be the general opinion.

"Eventually 4 p.m. came. A patter of feet in the silence and the crash of engines heralded the wild congestion of the start. Fangio, jumping into his car, put his foot through the steering wheel and was stuck. Even the great make mistakes sometimes! Our boys went away neatly, Johnny Lockett in 41, Dick Jacobs in 42, and Ted Lund in 64. They were soon lapping in 5 min. 45 sec. well within the required limits. As they quickened to the 5·30 level, no doubt dragged on by the frenzy of those early stages, with lap records falling like ninepins, Sammy Davis had 'slower' signals flown and was obviously worried about the observation of rev. limits. The cars continued to pass smoothly, 64 (Lund) leading, with 41 (Lockett) and 42 (Jacobs) following in that order.

"No doubt the race and the performance of the cars will be subject to detailed analysis. The following is therefore a very general narrative. The writer's personal job was to listen to and report on the French commentary. This, during the early stages was entirely devoted to the continual breaking of records by Mercedes, Jaguar and Ferrari, making no mention of the smaller catagories, except, for instance, when the unconventional Nardi spun repeatedly and then retired. Unlike the usual British commentaries, this French one seemed to be based on indirect information from Control, rather than direct observation around the track. Nevertheless had it continued much information (some of immediate value to our own pits, in case of trouble) could have been gleaned. Unluckily the loud-speakers, directed mainly at the stands, could not be followed from within the pits, and it was necessary to take up a rather inconvenient stance within a narrow area. Later, of course, the commentary ceased altogether.

"However, as said, our cars were running beautifully, and everything in the garden was lovely. Then just as the first relief of drivers came due, tragedy struck. A bang, a gasping shriek from the crowd, the commentator's voice rising in a frenzy. A huge billow of black smoke. People running. From our pit calm instructions to mobilize fire extinguishers. And keep out of the way. Sammy Davis is not easily rattled. Although the crash was only 150 yards or so away, none of us knew the magnitude of the disaster. All we did know was that Macklin's car of our own group was involved, had been hit, and that he in all probability must be dead. Happily we were wrong in this one thing. Apart from that, the situation was worse than any of us dreamed. Frankly, we didn't believe all we heard as shocked onlookers came away, some seeking first aid duly rendered by Dr. King. For once, however, rumour under-estimated. More than enough has already been written about this affair, and present comment may well be limited to its effect on ourselves. The race went on, at slightly reduced speed, but as a great sporting occasion it died too, in the welter of flame, smoke and mangled bodies.

"Even before the black drift of smoke from the Mercedes had faded, I saw a much smaller, grey, curl of vapour rising from an undeterminable point further away. Soon it was gone and attracted no further attention. Then Dick Jacobs became overdue. Had not personal drama been smothered by general disaster, for the moment, and had the commentary still been operating, no doubt this grey smoke and the missing car would have been associated. As it was, the loud-speakers called only for calm, for blood donors, stretcher bearers, for priests. The continuing race had become detached from news outside the range of personal vision, which from the pits was very restricted.

"Meanwhile, Ken Miles and Hans Waeffler had relieved Lockett and Lund, the incoming drivers being in excellent spirits and reporting that the cars were going beautifully. Refuelling and check-over followed routine.

"Occasional race announcements filtered through from the P.A. system. Jacobs was said to be in the sand at Arnage. Then he was proceeding slowly. Then he had crashed at Maison Blanche and the car was burnt out. Not until nearly 8 p.m. was he reported as 'slightly hurt and in hospital'. Confusion followed as to the hospital he was in—the P.A. saying one thing, the Control office another. The suspense of his wife can be imagined, but she behaved magnificently.

"Eventually John Valentyn, firing volleys of French in a manner given only to the angry Gaul, broke through the information barrier, also through police cordons, car parks and traffic. Dick Jacobs was reached in hospital at Coulaines, and Fred Crossley brought rather alarming reports. Jacobs himself was only worried that he had crashed the car, and sent messages to John Thornley. An acute problem arose as to whether Janet Jacobs should be allowed to see her husband at the risk of additional strain on herself, and him. It was felt to be wiser to keep her away for the time being.

"The race—and the short but endless night—dragged on. At 71 laps Lockett and Lund took over again in Nos. 41 and 64. Lockett in particular drove with remarkable regularity, lapping time after time in 5 min. 37 sec., or a second either way, as the ' Maintain' signal hung from the pits. Actually, the fastest laps were put in by Miles and Lund at 5·22 and 5·23, or approximately 94 m.p.h. A speed of 117·39 m.p.h. was recorded over the flying kilo on the Mulsanne straight, the drivers reporting that they held their rev. limits on a whiff of throttle once speed had been built up.

"Just before 2 a.m. Stirling Moss' father told us Mercedes had withdrawn after consultation with Stuttgart, and shortly afterwards the public announcement was made in tones strangely reminiscent of Neville Chamberlain's broadcast of 3rd September, 1939. Nobody had either heart or stomach left for racing, but the job went on. The P.A. was calling for magistrates and for the Procureur de la République. It looked as if the race might be stopped. The dead and wounded had been evacuated. Blood donors were no longer needed. Communication with the outside world seemed impossible. Calls were made for all telephone and telegraph operators to report for urgent security duty in the town. John Thornley drew up a message for transmission to England, which the Castrol people promised to put through when possible.

"Miles and Waeffler had taken over at 2 a.m. still in good fettle. They didn't know the identity of the burnt out car at Maison Blanche and we thought best not to tell them. Lund, however, knew and had seen Jacobs receiving attention at the roadside. So it went. Drivers and mechanics were relieved, fed, and sent to sleep on the transporter's bunks. Other staff and the Commissaires and plombeurs were fed— and slept, if, when and where they could. The indefatigable wives merely changed one duty for another, resting their eyes from lap-scoring by using their hands to help with meals. Joanne Thornley and Meg Lowry scarcely left the galley during the 36 hours we spent at the track, maintaining a steady stream of tea and soup in between meals. The mechanics, under Alec Hounslow and Dicky Green, kept their vigil in the comfortless concrete pits, ready to jump into action at any moment. John Thornley shared the worries of all, but could off-load none of his own. Sammy Davis looked more and more like a moulting eagle, but was always firm, kindly, and several mental jumps ahead of the situation. Marcus Chambers incessantly on watch. Babe Learoyd, huge, nimble and cheerful. Of the backroom boys in the Arnott compartment, we saw little, but Stan Nicholl's fingertips were blistered by his watch-buttons in the morning. Deprived of the ordinary stimuli of sport, and weighted with lead, this was indeed a Grand Prix d'Endurance for humans as well as machines.

"With dawn it rained. At first absent-mindedly and then with increasing, vicious, intensity. Oddly enough, and this is confirmed by others, one had little impression that daylight did return. The aftertaste of that Sunday is of a dismal half-light.

"We had to move our pitch, the toilets adjoining the transporter having overflowed and turned the ground into a malodorous bog. We got a sort of laugh, however, when a pumping waggon dedicated to 'National Salubrity' came to empty the tanks, and the harpy who farmed that noisome retreat for the offerings of an interminable queue of both sexes found she would be charged for the service.

"At 5 a.m. Lockett and Lund took over the wheel. The latter, perhaps trying to pull back some of Waeffler's deficit, overdid things at Arnage and struck the protruding tail of Beauman's Jaguar stranded there during the night. Damage was only superficial, and the mechanics quickly bashed away the crumpled metal from the near front wheel, checked everything and sent the car away in six minutes, with Waeffler driving.

"Only 26 of the original 60 cars were now left running. We were lying 15th and 19th. Determination began to sweeten itself with excitement. Maybe it stopped raining. Anyhow the menfolk shaved at the tailboard of the transporter, and felt better.

"The race swept on, trailing dirty spray behind it. The girls changed menus again, but went on cooking and serving.

"Retirements increased and pit stops lengthened. The MGs sounded as sweet as ever, and only needed their brakes taking up a shade. Drivers in good spirits. Lockett and Miles exchanging take-over news, agreed that 'there was very little traffic about this morning!' Waeffler reported a phenomenal avoidance of a spinning Porsche.

"The lap scorers rubbed eyes and sharpened pencils. The mechanics squatted, waiting. Alec Hounslow sucked the debris of a French cigar. Our senior officers became a bit less communicative. Dr. King left his scoring and went to see Dick Jacobs, Valentyn once more sweeping through barriers. His report was reassuring, but still pretty grim. Dick himself still worried only about crashing the car.

"The idlers, the curious, and the hung-over revellers from the night, became a pest. With so many pits out of activity all seemed to have become ports of call. Strenuous methods of exclusion had to be enacted, particularly with the French. Valentyn was again invaluable, but needed a filter to assist him. 'Vous êtres des notres—eh bien, en dehors!" does not go down well with Race Officials. Nor is 'And who are you?' the best form of address to MG's Chief Engineer! But it worked, and peace was maintained in the vital control areas.

"At 11 a.m. 200 laps was marked up against No. 41 on the big scoreboard behind the pits. It looked good among so many smaller figures obliterated by the red diagonals of retirement. The French commentator during one of his short breaks in the silence even referred to us as a 'remarkable little car'. Unfortunately the mind was too tired to grasp and record the condensed figures of distance and time in hours, minutes, seconds and hundredths, embodied in these bald announcements. The English announcer, who gave a half-hourly résumé, seemed to work on the basis that only the first two places mattered. Infuriating, as we were by now lying 12th.

"At 2 p.m. with only two hours to go, Lund came in to report that his steering seemed queer. All was checked calmly and pronounced safe. Off again, with nine laps to go for qualification.

"Then, in succession the magic signals were shown that the necessary laps were complete, and it was just a matter of keeping going.

"No. 41 must have a final stop and check-over before the finish. Alec Hounslow is called from rest and asked who he'll have with him. Alec looks at Dicky Green and says 'You and me'. The car comes in, the jobs are smoothly completed, and Lockett goes back to his battle. 'So near and yet so far' never seemed a truer saying. The rain lashes down. The clock creeps round towards 4 p.m.

"The police bring down their barricades. The eminences begin to assemble. The pit counters fill with our own people. Even the galley is deserted. The chequered flag comes out, and Ted Lund in No. 64 is actually the first car to receive it. After an interval comes 41. Cheers, flowers, champagne, claps on the back. A mad scramble between photographers and the French police. Carefully phrased speeches— for this is a tragedy as well as a celebration. We cling to 248 laps at 86·17 m.p.h. and 230 laps at 81·97 m.p.h.

"The rest is, I suppose, anti-climax and the letting down of tension. But a spring unwound does not always, or at once, return to its original state, and we did not. The objective had been achieved, and dinner at Les Rosiers started off gaily with all the tables pushed into a single long line. But we fell asleep over our plates—and there was one position unclaimed—Dick Jacobs.

"Dr. King spent the night at the hospital, but language difficulties were acute now Valentyn had gone, and the hospital staff was just about out on its feet. In the morning Meg Lowry went down to interpret—fortunately the medical technicalities are similar in French and English. John Thornley was able to visit Dick, but he was much too ill for other visitors. As this account is written, he lies still critically ill.

"During Monday the unwinding process continued in its various departments. And there were flowers to order for the Cathedral service, and transport to arrange for the wrecked Healey and for No. 42, in which M. Hallard, the local Austin agent, was most helpful.

"Nobody slept much on Monday night in spite of weariness. Bruce Bairnsfather described a Flemish farm as a building with a rectangular smell in the middle. By the same standards a French château is an ornamental structure full of self-multiplying noises. By 5 a.m. most of us had given it up, and breakfast was in full session by 6. Thereafter we separated to our various destinations, and a diminished party had a final cup of tea—as far as this report is concerned—at Folkestone, with the Chambers, Babe Learoyd, Ken Miles and Ted Lund. The two MGs, even the slightly battered No. 64, still looked little thoroughbreds—and sounded quite fit to start the race all over again. Machines—good ones—are evidently more durable than human beings."

That, then, was the début of EX 182, a technical success for MG, but a disaster for the world of motor sport in general, and no red-letter day for Dick Jacobs in particular. His condition, during the ensuing week, deteriorated, with the result that the British Motor Corporation flew a thoracic specialist and medical team to France and brought him home. It was to be four months before he was on his feet again.

Meantime, the lessons learned in the high-pressure school of racing were analysed and the finishing touches put to the specification of the production car. But what was it to be called? Midget had been apt for the M type and the J2, but the MG open 2-seater had grown up since those days. In any case, such an appellation was unacceptable in America and certain other countries where it conjured up visions of little freak vehicles and things of the 'Dodgems' variety. TB to TF had all been successive evolutions from the TA; the new car was a radical departure; TG was out. Furthermore, such tags are open to the very real objection that their use encourages the omission of the name of the marque, thereby losing the advantage of the history, reputation and pride which that marque embodies.

The custom and practice of the Company had, for years, been to take a new letter for each new model—as the frontispiece shows. But at this stage they had truly 'run out of alphabet', because was not the Magnette the ZA? And so a new start was made and the car dubbed the MGA. At one hit, here is a title which signifies a new beginning and which also compels the use of the name MG whenever reference is made to it. What is more, there can be twenty-five more models before the problem recurs!

TAILPIECE

THE inspiration for this book is indicated by its dedication; its intention is given in the Nosepiece. How far it has succeeded is for others to judge, but it is certain that it has recorded much of the history and achievement and no little of the excitement and interest of the years during which the MG has grown from its modest beginnings to its present stature. And if that stature is measured by the numbers of people throughout the world who know and enjoy the MG, then it is considerable and ever growing at a faster rate.

No pains have been spared to make the story as factual as possible. The great proportion of the time in the preparation of the typescript has gone into the checking of the material with old records and with the memories of those who were directly concerned in the events of the time. In that portion of the book which deals with more recent years, years in which I have been closely associated with the events themselves, an attempt has been made not only to recount what was done and was not done, but to give some indication of the thought behind the actions.

Every community has its extremists and the MG world is no exception, but whereas, in most cases, extremists are regarded as a nuisance, if not a menace, the MG variety are a positive Good, even if they seem to be crying for the moon. Their view is that their MG should have a twin-cam engine giving 150 h.p., independent suspension all round, disc brakes, and an all-up weight of 1000 lb., and that the Company is all sorts of a fool if it does anything less. What they seldom stop to consider is what the manufacturer must never stop considering —price! The days when one is able to sell two-thousand pounds worth of motor-car—particularly of 'more-fun-than practical-value' motor-car—are fast evaporating, and the first need of survival is a saleable product.

But the carrot hangs before the donkey's nose and these voluble gentlemen continually prod him from behind. Although the hill of costs is steep and the sun of commerce hot, perhaps one day he may even catch his carrot.

APPENDICES

PRODUCTION LIFE OF MG CARS

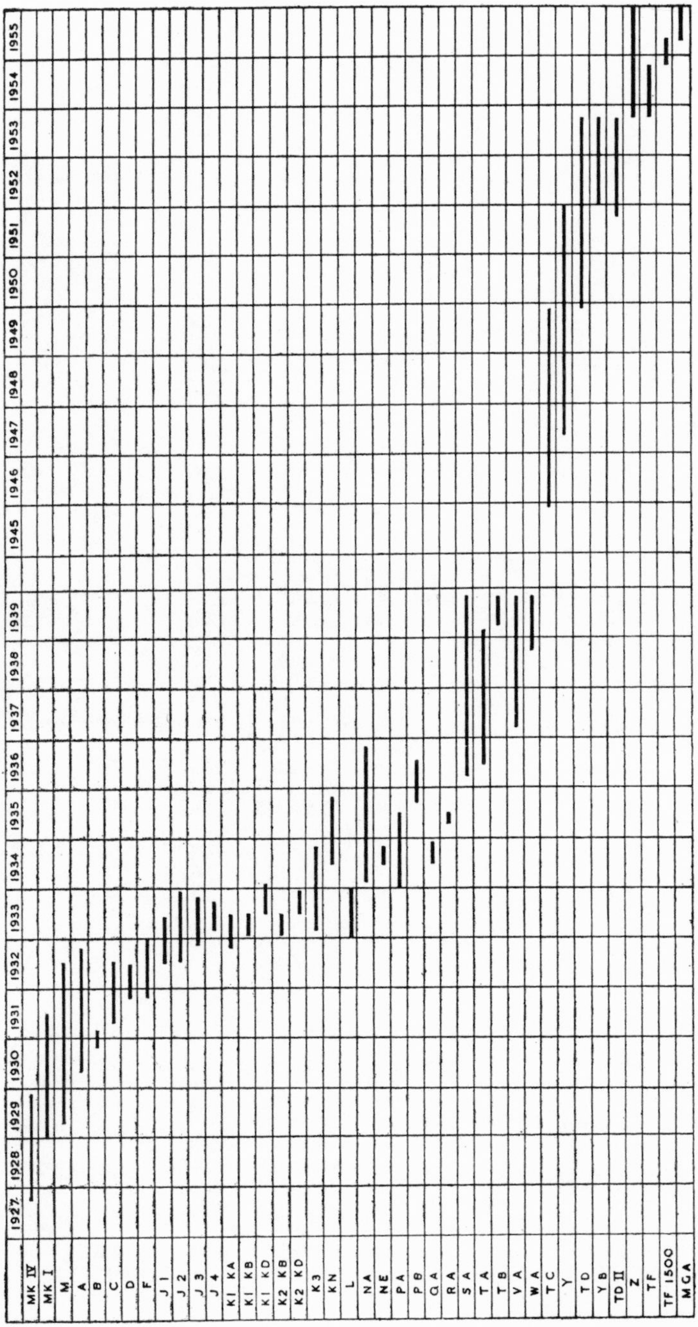

| | 1927 | 1928 | 1929 | 1930 | 1931 | 1932 | 1933 | 1934 | 1935 | 1936 | 1937 | 1938 | 1939 | 1945 | 1946 | 1947 | 1948 | 1949 | 1950 | 1951 | 1952 | 1953 | 1954 | 1955 |

MK IV
MK I
M
A
B
C
D
F
J 1
J 2
J 3
J 4
K1 KA
K1 KB
K1 KD
K2 KB
K2 KD
K 3
K N
L
N A
N E
P A
P B
Q A
R A
S A
T A
T B
V A
T C
Y
T D
Y B
TD II
Z
TF
TF 1500
MGA

Type Letter	Name	Spts. or Racing	No. of Cyls.	Bore and Stroke	Swept Volume	If Superch'ged	Max B.H.P. at	Gearbox (1)
—	MARK IV	S.	4	75×102	1802		35@4,000	3
—	MARK I	S.	6	69×110	2468			3
A	MARK II	S.	6	69×110	2468			4
B	MARK III	R.	6	69×110	2468			4
C	MONTLHERY MIDGET	R.	4	57×73	746		37·4@6,000	4
							44·1@6,400	
						S.	52·5@6,500	4
D	MIDGET	S.	4	57×83	847		27@4,500	3
F	MAGNA	S.	6	57×83	1271		37·2@4,100	4
J1	MIDGET	S.	4	57×83	847		36@5,500	4
J2	MIDGET	S.	4	57×83	847		36@5,500	4
J3	MIDGET	S.	4	57×73	746	S.		4
J4	MIDGET	R.	4	57×73	746	S.	72·3@6,000	4
K1(KA)	MAGNETTE	S.	6	57×71	1087		39@5,500	4P.
(KB)	MAGNETTE	S.	6	57×71	1087		41@5,500	4
(KD)	MAGNETTE	S.	6	57×83	1271		48·5@5,500	4P.
K2(KB)	MAGNETTE	S.	6	57×71	1087		41@5,500	4
(KD)	MAGNETTE	S.	6	57×83	1271		48·5@5,500	4P.
K3	MAGNETTE	R.	6	57×71	1087	S.	120@6,500	4P.
KN	MAGNETTE	S.	6	57×83	1271		56@5,500	4
L	MAGNA	S.	6	57×71	1087		41@5,500	4
M	MIDGET	S.	4	57×83	847		20@4,000	3
M12/12	DOUBLE TWELVE MIDGET	R.	4	57×83	847		27@4,500	3
NA	MAGNETTE	S.	6	57×83	1271		56@5,500	4
NE	MAGNETTE	R.	6	57×83	1271		74·3@6,500	4
PA	MIDGET	S.	4	57×83	847		36@5,500	4
PB	MIDGET	S.	4	60×83	939		43@5,500	4
QA	MIDGET	R.	4	57×73	746	S.	113@7,200	4P.
RA	MIDGET	R.	4	57×73	746	S.	113@7,200	4P.
SA	2-LITRE	S.	6	69×102	2288		78·5@4,200	4S.
				69·5×102	2322			
TA	MIDGET	S.	4	63·5×102	1292		50@4,500	4S.
TB	MIDGET	S.	4	66·5×90	1250		54·4@5,200	4S.
TC	MIDGET	S.	4	66·5×90	1250		54·4@5,200	4S.
TD	MIDGET	S.	4	66·5×90	1250		54·4@5,200	4S.
TD2	TD MARK II	S.	4	66·5×90	1250		57@5,500	4S.
TF	TF	S.	4	66·5×90	1250		57@5,500	4S.
TF	TF. 1500	S.	4	72×90	1466		63@5,500	4S.
VA	1½-LITRE	S.	4	69·5×102	1548		55@4,400	4S.
WA	2·6-LITRE	S.	6	73×102	2561		95·5@4,400	4S.
Y	1¼-LITRE	S.	4	66·5×90	1250		46@4,800	4S.
YB	1¼ SALOON	S.	4	66·5×90	1250		48@4,800	4S.
Z	MAGNETTE	S.	4	73×89	1489		60@4,600	4S.
MGA	MGA	S.	4	73×89	1489		68@5,500	4S.

Gear Ratios	Final Drive Ratios (2)	Tyre Size	Track	Wheelbase	Body Types (3)
1, 1·72, 3·2	12/53	28×4·95	4′ 0″	8′ 10½″	2·4.S.
1, 1·55, 3·1	12/51	19×5	4′ 0″	9′ 6″	2·4.S.
1, 1·306, 2·0, 3·42	11/47	19×5	4′ 4″	9′ 6″	2·4.S.
1, 1·306, 1·84, 3·42	11/47	19×5	4′ 4″	9′ 6″	4
1, 1·36, 1·86, 2·69	8/43, 8/44	27×4	3′ 6″	6′ 9″	2
1, 1·83, 3·5	8/43	19×4	3′ 6″	7′ 2″	4.S.
1, 1·36, 2·0, 4·02	9/43	19×4	3′ 6″	7′ 10″	2·4.S.
1, 1·36, 2·14, 3·58	8/43, 8/47	19×4	3′ 6″	7′ 2″	4.S.
1, 1·36, 2·14, 3·58	8/43, 8/47	19×4	3′ 6″	7′ 2″	2
1, 1·36, 2·14, 3·58	9/43	19×4	3′ 6″	7′ 2″	2
1, 1·36, 1·86, 2·69	8/43	19×4·5	3′ 6″	7′ 2″	2
1, 1·36, 2·0, 3·4	9/52	19×4·75	4′ 0″	9′ 0″	S.
1, 1·36, 2·14, 3·58	9/52	19×4·75	4′ 0″	9′ 0″	4
1, 1·36, 2·0, 3·4	9/52	19×4·75	4′ 0″	9′ 0″	S.
1, 1·36, 2·14, 3·58	9/52	19×4·75	4′ 0″	7′ $10\frac{3}{16}$″	2
1, 1·36, 2·0, 3·4	9/52	19×4·75	4′ 0″	7′ $10\frac{3}{16}$″	2
1, 1·36, 2·0, 3·4	9/44, 9/39, 9/52	19×4·75	4′ 0″	7′ $10\frac{3}{16}$″	2
1, 1·36, 2·32, 4·18	9/52	19×4·75	4′ 0″	9′ 0″	4.S.
1, 1·36, 2·14, 3·58	8/43, 8/47	19×4·5	3′ 6″	7′ $10\frac{3}{16}$″	2·4.S.
1, 1·83, 3·5	9/44	19×4	3′ 6″	6′ 6″	2.S.
1, 1·83, 3·5	9/44	19×4	3′ 6″	6′ 6″	2
1, 1·36, 2·32, 4·18	8/41, 8/43, 8/47	18×4·75	3′ 9″	8′ 0″	2·4
1, 1·36, 2·14, 3·58	8/39, 8/36, 8/33	18×4·75	3′ 9″	8′ 0″	2
1, 1·36, 2·32, 4·18	8/43, 8/47, 8/41	19×4	3′ 6″	7′ $3\frac{5}{16}$″	2·4
1, 1·36, 2·14, 3·58	8/43, 8/47, 8/41	19×4	3′ 6″	7′ $3\frac{5}{16}$″	2·4
1, 1·36, 2·0, 3·4 or 1, 1·31, 1·84, 3·097	8/36, 8/39, 8/33	18×4·75	3′ 9″	7′ $10\frac{3}{16}$″	2
1, 1·31, 1·84, 3·097	8/33, 8/36, 8/39	18×4·75	Ft. 3′ $10\frac{3}{8}$″ Rr. 3′ 9½″	7′ 6½″	1
1, 1·38, 2·13, 3·76	12/57	18×5·5	4′ $5\frac{3}{8}$″	10′ 3″	4.S.C.
1, 1·42, 2·2, 3·715 or 1, 1·32, 2·04, 3·454	8/39	19×4·5	3′ 9″	7′ 10″	2
1, 1·35, 1·95, 3·38	8/41	19×4·5	3′ 9″	7′ 10″	2.C.
1, 1·35, 1·95, 3·38	8/41, 7/38, 8/39	19×4·5	3′ 9″	7′ 10″	2
1, 1·355, 2·07, 3·5	8/41, 8/39, 9/41	15×5·5	Ft. 3′ $11\frac{3}{8}$″ Rr. 4′ 2″	7′ 10″	2
1·385, 2·07, 3·5	5·125,4·875,4·55	15×5·50	Wire Wheels Ft. 4′ $\frac{3}{16}$″ Rr. 4′ $2\frac{11}{13}$″ Disc Wheels Ft. 3′ $11\frac{3}{8}$″ Rr. 4′ 2″	7′ 10″	2
as TD.	4·875,5·125,4·55	15×5·50	As TD. II	7′ 10″	2
as TD.	as TF	15×5·50	As TD. II	7′ 10″	2
1, 1·35, 1·95, 3·38	9/47	19×5	4′ 2″	9′ 0″	4.S.C.
1, 1·418, 2·155, 3·646	9/43	18×5·5	Ft. 4′ $5\frac{3}{8}$″ Rr. 4′ $8\frac{3}{4}$″	10′ 3″	S.
1, 1·385, 2·07, 3·5	7/36	16×5·25	Ft. 3′ $11\frac{3}{8}$″ Rr. 4′ 2″	8′ 3″	4.S.
as TD.	5·143	15×5·50	Ft. 3′ $11\frac{3}{8}$″ Rr. 4′ 2″	8′ 3″	4.S.
1, 374, 2·214, 3·64	4·875	15×5·50	4′3″	8′ 6″	S.
as Z.	4·3	15×5·60	Ft. 3′ $11\frac{3}{8}$″ Rr. 4′ 1″	7′ 10″	2

NOTES:—(1) P=Pre-Selector; S=Synchro-Mesh. (2) First Figures=Standard Ratio; Others=Alternatives. (3) 2=2 Seat Open; 4=4 Seat Open; S=Saloon; C=Drop-Head.

APPENDIX III

SUMMARY OF THE MORE IMPORTANT
MG RACING SUCCESSES UP TO 1935

1930 Team Prize, J.C.C. Double Twelve-Hour Race.

1931 First six places and Team Prize, J.C.C. Double-Twelve.
First, Irish Grand Prix and Team Prize.
First, R.A.C. Ulster Tourist Trophy.
Team Prize, B.R.D.C. 500-mile Race.
First, German Grand Prix, 750-c.c. Race.
First 750-c.c. car to achieve 100 m.p.h.

1932 First, Phœnix Park Junior Race.
First, B.R.D.C. 500-mile Race.
First 750-c.c. car to achieve 120 m.p.h.

1933 First and Second, 1100-c.c. Class and Team Prize, Mille Miglia.
First, 750-c.c. Class, Avusrennen.
First, 800-c.c. Class, Eifelrennen.
First, R.A.C. Ulster Tourist Trophy.
First, B.R.D.C. India Trophy.
First, L.C.C. Relay Race.
First, Southport 100-mile Race.
First, Junior Coppa Acerbo.
Holder of all Class 'H' International Records.

1934 First, I.O.M. Mannin Beg Race.
First, B.R.D.C. Empire Trophy Race.
First, R.A.C. Ulster Tourist Trophy Race.
First, American A.C. Grand Prix.
First, 'Winter 100', Australia.
First, Coppa Acerbo Junior Race.
First, Swiss Coupe des Voiturettes.
First, 750-c.c. Class, Avrusrennen.
First, 800-c.c. Class, Eifelrennen.
First, Bol d'Or 24-hour Race.
First, Phœnix Park Junior Race.
First, Circuit of Modena.
First, Grand Prix de France, 1100-c.c. Race.
Holder of all Class 'H' International Records.
Holder of all Class 'G' International Records, from Flying Mile to
1 Hour.

1935 First, Grand Prix de France, 1100-c.c. Race.
First, Australian Grand Prix.
First, 'Southport Fifty'.
First, 800-c.c. Race, Eifelrennen.
First, Grand Prix des Frontières.
First, County Down Trophy Race.
First, Grand Prix de France, 1100-c.c. Race.
First, Bol d'Or 24-hour Race.
Holder of all Class 'H' International Records.

EX 135—RECORDS

Complete list of all International Class Records taken by EX 135 in the course of its useful life, 1934–52. No note is taken of Local (American or Belgian National) Records.

Date	Venue	Driver	Class	Record	Speed
27.10.34	Montlhery	Eyston	G	1 M	128·7
				1 K	128·7
				5 K	128·69
				5 M	128·62
				10 K	128·58
				10 M	128·53
28.10.34	,,	,,	,,	50 K	119·84
				50 M	120·72
				100 K	121·65
				100 M	121·13
				200 K	120·82
				1 Hour	120·88
9.11.38	Frankfort	Gardner	G	1 K	186·567
				1 M	186·582
31. 5.39	Dessau	,,	G	1 K	203·5
				1 M	203·2
				5 K	197·5
2. 6.39	,,	,,	F	1 K	204·2
				1 M	203·9
				5 K	200·6
30.10.46	Jabbeke	,,	H	1 K	159·09
				1 M	159·15
				5 K	150·46
24. 7.47	,,	,,	I	1 K	118·016
				1 M	117·493
				5 M	110·544
14. 9.48	,,	,,	E	1 K	176·694*
				1 M	173·678*
				5 K	170·523*
15. 9.49	,,	,,	I	1 K	154·91
				1 M	154·23
				5 K	150·51
24. 7.50	,,	,,	J	1 K	120·394
				1 M	121·048
				5 K	117·510
20. 8.51	Utah	,,	F	50 K	127·8
				50 M	130·6
				100 K	132·0
				100 M	135·1
				200 K	136·6
				1 Hour	137·4
18. 8.52	,,	,,	E	50 K	143·23
				50 M	147·39
				100 K	148·72
20. 8.52	,,	,,	F	5 M	189·5
				10 K	182·8

In the course of breaking these records, EX 135 became:

The first car with an 1100 c.c. engine to exceed 120 m.p.h.

,,	,,	,,	,,	,,	1100	,,	,,	,,	,,	150	,,
,,	,,	,,	,,	,,	1100	,,	,,	,,	,,	200	,,
,,	,,	,,	,,	,,	1500	,,	,,	,,	,,	200	,,
,,	,,	,,	,,	,,	750	,,	,,	,,	,,	150	,,
,,	,,	,,	,,	,,	500	,,	,,	,,	,,	150	,,
,,	,,	,,	,,	,,	2000	,,	,,	,,	,,	150*	,,
,,	,,	,,	,,	,,	350	,,	,,	,,	,,	120	,,

* Records marked thus were made when the car was fitted with a Jaguar engine. All other records were made with MG engines.

APPENDIX V

TUNING THE XPAG AND XPEG ENGINES

STAGE T.F.1 (1250)

Higher Compression Ratio Tuning (8·6 *to* 1)

THE engine is raised to 8·6 to 1 compression ratio by removing $\frac{1}{32}$ in. from the cylinder head face.

The standard head is 75·16 mm. thick; the finished thickness after machining should be 74·37 mm.

Remove any frazes left, and polish, but do not grind out the combustion chambers as these are already quite clean and are machined nearly all over.

Make sure the gasket edges do not overlap the combustion spaces.

The ports may be lightly ground and polished, but should not be ground out so heavily that the shape or valve choke diameter is impaired.

The inlet port outer separating stud boss may be ground away slightly—about $\frac{1}{16}$ in. off each side (still maintaining its streamline shape)—so that oblong ports are obtained $1\frac{3}{16}$ in. high, $\frac{11}{16}$ in. wide (minimum).

Do not remove this boss completely or it will affect mixture distribution.

Match up, by grinding, all the exhaust and inlet manifold ports with the cylinder head ports.

Grind out and polish the inlet manifold, also matching the carburetter bore.

(a) Use standard cylinder head gasket.
(b) Use $\frac{3}{32}$ in. thick × $\frac{3}{4}$ in. O.D. washers under cylinder head nuts (to correct for reduced head thickness).
(c) Use fuel 80 octane.
(d) Plugs: Use Champion N.A.8 for ordinary road work. For sustained power use N.A.10.
(e) Use carburetter needles G.J.—Jet 0·090 in.
(f) Tappet setting: 0·012 in.
(g) Ignition setting: T.D.C.
(h) Use standard $1\frac{1}{4}$ in. carburetters.

The engine should then give approximately 61 brake horse-power at 5000 r.p.m.

STAGE T.F.2 (1250)

High Compression Ratio Tuning (9·3 *to* 1)

The standard engine is raised to 9·3 to 1 compression ratio by removing $\frac{1}{16}$ in. from the cylinder head face.

The finished thickness after machining should be 73·575 mm. This is the absolute maximum to remove.

Polish head, ports and manifolds as in Stage 1.

It will be noticed that a sharp edge is left on the combustion space profile at the end of the sparking plug hole.

File this sharp edge back vertically until it is a minimum of $\frac{1}{32}$ in. thick at the centre.

File this only locally at the plug hole (approximately $\frac{3}{4}$ in. wide scoop) and blend into the combustion chamber shape with a radius each side. Do not file back too far. Check that the combustion space edge still extends safely over the gasket edge.

(a) Use standard cylinder head gasket.

(b) Use $\frac{1}{8}$ in. thick × $\frac{3}{4}$ in. O.D. washers under cylinder head nuts (to correct reduced thickness).

(c) To allow for the cylinder head machining it is better to shorten the push rods $\frac{1}{16}$ in., by drawing off one end in an extractor jig, machining $\frac{1}{16}$ in. off the tube end, counterboring the tube $\frac{1}{16}$ in. deeper for the push-rod end to enter, refitting the push-rod end and spot welding through to retain end.

Alternatively, use four rocker-shaft bracket packing pieces to correct rocker adjustment. These are $\frac{1}{16}$ in. mild steel with three holes to match base of bracket.

(d) Plugs: Use Champion N.A.8, or for sustained power use Champion N.A.10 or Lodge RL.49.

(e) Tappet setting 0·012 in.

(f) Ignition setting: T.D.C.

(g) Use standard 1½ in. carburetters.

Using fuel 90 octane, with carburetter needles G.J., Jet 0·090 in., the engine should then give approximately 64 brake horse-power between 5500 and 6000 r.p.m.

If your car is not fitted with the high pressure "S.U." fuel pump fitted at the rear of the car, it would be advantageous to fit one.

Stage T.F.3 (1250)

*High Compression (9·3 to 1) Semi-Racing Tune
using Special Camshaft*

Carry out the procedure of raising the compression ratio as Stage T.F.2.

Fit new Camshaft (AEG.122).

This camshaft gives the following timing:—

Inlet opens 13° B.T.D.C. Inlet closes 59° A.B.D.C.

Exhaust opens 50° B.B.D.C. Exhaust closes 22° A.T.D.C.

The tappet setting is 0·019 in. hot, inlet and exhaust, but they may be set down to minimum 0·015 in. for quietness.

The valves should not flutter until 6300 to 6400 r.p.m.

This camshaft may be described as semi-racing and some feeling of lost power at the lower revs. may be felt, but the free-running of the engine at the higher revs. in top and the intermediate gears should compensate for this. But be reasonable when using the revs. available, as, due to the design of the camshaft, the valve crash-point is not loudly audible, and the maximum revs. could be considerably exceeded. A good driver is aware of this point of uselessly over-revving his engine (with resulting expensive noises) and drives on the rev. counter with due respect.

The oil pressure should be raised to approximately 80 lb. maximum by fitting a spigoted steel washer (SK.1039) on the lower end of the oil pump release valve spring. Or turn one up yourself to the following dimensions: 0·490 in. O.D. × 0·075 in. thick with spigot 0·368 in. O.D., making total thickness ⅛ in.

Insert the spigot into the lower end of the spring and this should hold the washer in position during assembly.

The standard distributor will be reasonably satisfactory, but a special distributor to suit the characteristics of this tuning is available.

Static ignition setting is T.D.C.

Use 80 octane fuel, or 90 octane may be used.

The engine should give approximately 66 brake horse-power between 5800 and 6300 r.p.m.

Use carburetter needles G.J., or richer L.S.1.

STAGE T.F.1 (1500)

Higher Compression Ratio Tuning (8·6 *to* 1)

The engine is raised to 8·6 to 1 compression ratio by removing 0·020 in. from the cylinder head face.

The standard head is 76·75 mm. thick; the finished thickness after machining should be 76·25 mm.

Remove any frazes left, and polish, but do not grind out the combustion chambers as these are already quite clean and are machined nearly all over.

Make sure the gasket edges do not overlap the combustion spaces.

The ports may be lightly ground and polished, but should not be ground out so heavily that the shape or valve choke diameter is impaired.

The inlet port outer separating stud boss may be ground away slightly—about $\frac{1}{16}$ in. off each side (still maintaining its streamline shape)—so that oblong ports are obtained $1\frac{3}{16}$ in. high, $\frac{11}{16}$ in. wide (minimum).

Do not remove this boss completely or it will affect mixture distribution.

Match-up, by grinding, all the exhaust and inlet manifold ports with the cylinder head ports.

Grind out and polish the inlet manifold, also matching the carburetter bore.

(*a*) Use standard cylinder head gasket.
(*b*) Use fuel 90 octane.
(*c*) Plugs: Use Champion N.A.8.
(*d*) Use carburetter needles G.J.—Jet 0·090 in.
(*e*) Tappet setting: 0·012 in.
(*f*) Ignition setting: T.D.C.
(*g*) Use standard $1\frac{1}{2}$ in. carburetters.

The engine should then give approximately 65 brake horse-power between 5000 and 5500 r.p.m.

Stage T.F.2 (1500)

High Compression Ratio Tuning (9·3 *to* 1)

The standard engine is raised to 9·3 to 1 compression ratio by removing 0·050 in. from the cylinder head face.

The finished thickness after machining should be 75·50 mm.

Polish head, ports and manifolds as in Stage 1.

It will be noticed that a sharp edge is left on the combustion space profile at the end of the sparking plug hole.

File this sharp edge back vertically until it is a minimum of $\frac{1}{32}$ in. thick at the centre.

File this only locally at the plug hole (approximately $\frac{3}{4}$ in. wide scoop) and blend into the combustion chamber shape with a radius each side. Do not file back too far. Check that the combustion space edge still extends safely over the gasket edge.

(*a*) Use standard cylinder head gasket.

(*b*) Plugs: Use Champion N.A.8, or for sustained power use Champion N.A.10 or Lodge RL.49.

(*c*) Tappet setting : 0·012 in.

(*d*) Ignition setting: T.D.C.

(*e*) Use standard $1\frac{1}{2}$ in. carburetters.

Using fuel 90 octane, with carburetter needles G.J.—Jet 0·090 in., the engine should then give approximately 67 brake horse-power between 5500 and 6000 r.p.m.

STAGE T.F.3 (1500)

*High Compression (9·45 to 1) Semi-Racing Tune
using Special Camshaft*

The standard engine is raised to 9·45 to 1 compression ratio by removing 0·068 in. from the cylinder head face.

The finished thickness after machining should be 75·16 mm.

Polish head, ports and manifold as in Stage 1.

Fit new Camshaft (AEG.122).

This camshaft gives the following timing:—

Inlet opens 13° B.T.D.C. Inlet closes 59° A.B.D.C.

Exhaust opens 50° B.B.D.C. Exhaust closes 22° A.T.D.C.

The tappet setting is 0·019 in. hot, inlet and exhaust, but they may be set down to minimum 0·015 in. for quietness.

The valves should not flutter until 6300 to 6400 r.p.m.

This camshaft may be described as semi-racing and some feeling of lost power at the lower revs. may be felt, but the free-running of the engine at the higher revs. in top and the intermediate gears should compensate for this. But be reasonable when using the revs. available, as, due to the design of the camshaft, the valve crash-point is not loudly audible, and the maximum revs. could be considerably exceeded. A good driver is aware of this point of uselessly over-revving his engine (with resulting expensive noises) and drives on the rev. counter with due respect.

The oil pressure should be raised to approximately 80 lb. maximum by fitting a spigoted steel washer (SK.1039) on the lower end of the oil pump release valve spring. Or turn one up yourself to the following dimensions: 0·490 in. O.D. × 0·075 in. thick with spigot 0·368 in. O.D. making total thickness ⅛ in.

Insert the spigot into the lower end of the spring and this should hold the washer in position during assembly.

The standard distributor will be reasonably satisfactory, but a special distributor to suit the characteristics of this tuning is available.

Static ignition setting is T.D.C.

Use 90 octane fuel.

The engine should give approximately 70 brake horse-power between 5800 and 6300 r.p.m.

Use carburetter needles L.S.1.

STAGE T.F.4

Hints on Extra Tuning for Specials

A. Special Exhaust System for use with Semi-racing Camshaft

Carry out procedure as for tuning to Stage T.F.3 (1250 or 1500).

Make up and fit a 4-pipe extractor exhaust system similar to illustration below.

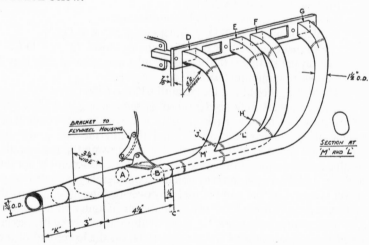

This will increase the power 2 or 3 b.h.p. all the way up the range, or alternatively, a twin exhaust system, with a branch from cylinders 1 and 4 and another branch from cylinders 2 and 3 running into separate pipes is partly effective.

B. Racing Tune for 1500 Engines

For racing purposes, the best way of improving performance is to use a high compression ratio, in conjunction with a special camshaft.

If run on 90-octane fuel the compression ratio can be put as high as 10·7 to 1.

The cylinder head depth should be 73·575 mm. for this compression ratio. This is the absolute maximum to remove. When raising the compression ratio from the standard engine, shorten the push-rods by the same amount as is removed from the cylinder head face. This can be done by drawing the push-rod end in a small jig, machining the tube and pressing back the push-rod end. Check that the undercutting inside the push-rod tube is deep enough to allow the push-rod end to go right home.

Fit high overlap camshaft (168551).

The timing of this camshaft is:—

Inlet opens 32° B.T.D.C. Inlet closes 58° A.B.D.C.

   Exhaust opens 60° B.B.D.C. Exhaust closes 30° A.T.D.C.

Tappet setting 0·012 in. inlet, 0·019 in. exhaust.

Make up an exhaust system similar to that illustrated on page 184.

It is most important this extractor-type system is fitted, otherwise the camshaft will not be at all effective.

Some erratic running may occur below 2000 r.p.m. The standard exhaust manifold is of no use. Variations to the system illustrated are no doubt possible, but this one has been proved successful, and it would be wise to follow it closely, unless you can prove your engine and its system on a test bed.

The camshaft will operate with the standard flat followers on this 1500 engine.

On the $1\frac{1}{2}$ in. carburetters the engine should give:—

R.P.M.			B.H.P.
6300	..	..	78
6000	..	..	79
5500	..	..	78
5000	..	..	76

A further slight increase on these figures can be made:—

Fit two $1\frac{3}{4}$ in. carburetters (S.U. Specification 723).

They are fitted with needles C.V. (If richer required use G.K., or weaker required use B.C. or K.T.A.)

For maximum performance, blue springs are fitted to the carburetter pistons, but where acceleration only matters it may prove better to fit heavier springs (red), with a slight loss of maximum power.

The "TF" inlet manifold (168434) can be bored $\frac{25}{32}$ in. diameter and an adaptor plate fitted to accept the $1\frac{3}{4}$ in. carburetters.

Taper grind the $\frac{25}{32}$ in. diameter into the inlet manifold, making the passage through the manifold as large as possible.

The "TF" inlet manifold (168434) used as suggested above with the adaptor plate for the $1\frac{3}{4}$ in. carburetters is rather heavy, and for the sake of lightness could be replaced with a sheet-metal one, built directly into the exhaust manifold, following a similar design, with boxes up from main branch and $\frac{5}{8}$ in. I.D. steel balance tube across with a balance restrictor in the centre of this pipe having a 11-mm. hole.

When fitting the large 1¾-in. diameter carburetters it is advantageous to increase the width of the inlet ports in the cylinder head and the inlet manifold. It is just possible to remove a further $\frac{1}{16}$ in. down each outer side of the inlet port by grinding the wall and tapering into the port for approximately ⅝ in. Do the same with the inlet manifold port, tapering out as far as possible. Grind the leading edge of inlet port separating boss to a rather sharp edge and taper back as steeply as possible around the stud boss, do not thin down the walls of the stud boss excessively or the strength to clamp down the cylinder head will be impaired. Cut away the inlet manifold gasket to the shape of the enlarged port opening.

To prevent vibration of the carburetters, it is advisable to use a Neoprene gasket ⅛ in. thick and double coil spring washers under bolt heads, so that the carburetters may be left not quite tightened solid. Wire bolts in pairs to prevent them becoming slack.

The engine should give the following:—

R.P.M.			B.H.P.
6300	..	..	82
6000	..	..	81·5
5500	..	..	81
5000	..	..	78·5
4500	..	..	73
4000	..	..	66
3500	..	..	57
3000	..	..	49
2500	..	..	41

Use plugs KLG.FE.280/4 or softer KLG.FE.250/4, or harder KLGF.E.290/4, or alternative Champion N.A.10 or N.A.12, or Lodge RL.47 or Lodge RL.49.

As the carburetter float-chamber will come close to the exhaust pipes, it will be necessary to fit a large asbestos-lined black steel sheet heat-deflector plate between pipes and carburetters. Also if cold air can be arranged to blow on the float-chambers this will prevent any chance of fuel boiling.

As the exhaust manifold (shown on page 184) has a large area of hot pipes under the carburetters, hot air rises and enters the carburetter chokes and seriously impairs the efficiency. The carburetter chokes must be in or fed with a cold air stream.

If the engine is fully enclosed, especially when in a streamlined body it may be necessary to fit an air-box feed to the carburetters with an extension pipe to a cool air position such as at the nose of the car, although not essentially head on into the main air stream. A quiet spot behind the body nose adjacent to the grille will do. If the pipe is put head on into the main air stream, it may be necessary to connect (by unions in the air box) the float-chamber top air vent pipes to the air box to balance the pressures, or alternatively, drill three ⅜ in. holes in the centre bottom of the air box to prevent any pressure variation building up.

Such an air box is depicted below:—

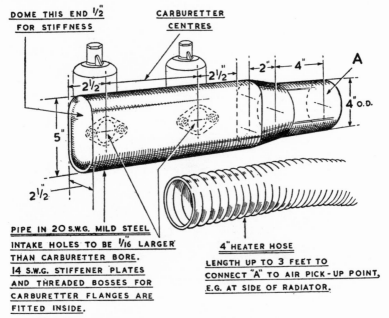

DOME THIS END ½" FOR STIFFNESS

CARBURETTER CENTRES

2½"

2½"

2"   4"   A

4" O.D.

5"

2½"

PIPE IN 20 S.W.G. MILD STEEL INTAKE HOLES TO BE 1/16" LARGER THAN CARBURETTER BORE. 14 S.W.G. STIFFENER PLATES AND THREADED BOSSES FOR CARBURETTER FLANGES ARE FITTED INSIDE.

4" HEATER HOSE LENGTH UP TO 3 FEET TO CONNECT "A" TO AIR PICK-UP POINT, E.G. AT SIDE OF RADIATOR.

A satisfactory alternative method to the above is to use a length of 4-in. car heater hose, fitted with the front open end in the main air stream at the body nose and the end supported 3 or 4 in. ahead of the front carburetter, with the direction of the air stream crossing the carburetter intakes.

If maximum overall car performance is required, do not overgear these engines. Let them attain 6300 r.p.m. in top gear.

Valve crash is 6500 r.p.m. to 6800 r.p.m.